Insurmountable Faith

A Novel

L.J. BERNARD

This book is a work of fiction, names, characters, places, and incidents are either products of the authors imagination or are used fictitiously, any resemblance to

actual events or locales or persons, living or dead, are entirely coincidental.

Originally published in 2024.

ISBN 978-0-473-69547-7

Cover Design by 'Get Covers'

Dedicated..

To my beloved children

Meghan and Christopher forever in my heart.

Matthew 6:34

Take no thought for the morrow: for the morrow shall take thought for the things of itself. Sufficient unto the day is the evil thereof.

Sermon on the Mount.

ACKNOWLEDGEMENTS

This is the page I love to include. It shows the book is finished and finally

on its way to publication, there have been so many people who have helped me

along the way perhaps without even realizing it.

They have unwavering belief in my ability to produce this outcome and I thank

them for their patience as I embarked on this massive challenge.

A few of those people are of course my work colleagues who knew of my life challenges and supported me with a listening ear, in particular my friend Teresa Barlow who never doubted I would overcome and was always ready with a shoulder to share my burden.

The church has provided me with knowledge, and I couldn't have done any of this without the Lord's strength to keep going, I'm so grateful to

Jim Foster for giving of his time, thank-you.

Of course my fantastic kids and family who have put up with me writing madly and discussing various electronic issues along the way. I'm grateful to have my younger generation around to sort the technical problems.

Writing a novel has been challenging with Covid getting in the way of publishing and

I understand the economic challenges putting pressure on resources, you have all been so supportive through that process, I pray that you experience the passion in my writing.

So thank you everyone and this is for you.

L J Bernard

INSURMOUNTABLE FAITH

A love story of faith, determination, and courage.

CHAPTER 1

Reminiscing about their lives, Gemma sat in quiet solitude beside the glistening pond situated at the bottom of a New Zealand lifestyle property she and Mason Brownlie had bought together. Snuggled into her leg is Ombre' their ageing Labrador whom she is so grateful to have during many times of desperation and loneliness, he brings her smiles with his furry companionship as Gemma's personal situation continues to worsen and she prays for her husband.

Mason is of Pacific Island heritage, he's fit and slim, olive skin with masses of straight black hair in contrast to his lovely prickly white beard and she loves him very much. Although he endures significant hearing loss, at 60 years old it does not deter his bright vivaciousness for life. Gemma adores his lovely blue/grey eyes, a stunning contrast to the usual brown that would be customary. Early in Mason's life he married Rose and raised two healthy strong lads and a beautiful young daughter who tragically passed away as a teenager.

Gemma's mirror image reflected in the calmness of transparent water kept beautifully clear by numerous goldfish, shows her youth compared to Mason. Her weary mind contemplates as she seizes private time on the moist grassy edge of the pond, soaking in the warmth of the early morning sun, relaxing and welcoming as it penetrates the depths of her pale skin, her life, and the trauma she suffers as she confronts Mason's ever changing cognitive difficulties and absurd behaviors, her personal struggle to tolerate the contemptible cruelty and wrestle with her heart, soul and duty as his wife, her faith is what keeps her going. Gemma welcomes this retreat as countless days she *'takes one day at a time'* in total numbness.

In her attempt to stay well she tries to clear her mind and diminish upset emotions; she makes do with a walk down the property to this special place.

Gemma moved to Northland with her mum and brothers when only six years old to enjoy the warm climate. Her siblings grew up and they went their separate ways, with her marrying and having two children Bridget and Carl (to her earlier husband). Mason has two grown up sons from his earlier marriage, the eldest 42 yr. old Dwayne strongly objects to his dad forming any relationship as he continues to hope his dad will one day return to Rose who has not formed any meaningful relationship since the divorce. Since Gemma and Mason married, this perpetual rift prevents Mason from finding true peace as he felt the pressure from his sons and the lack of their acceptance of his new wife.

Mason and Gemma met during five wonderful years of working at a residential home for the elderly, he was a very compassionate driver who took the older residents out for a ride in the wheelchair accessible van, and started working there before Gemma, leaving when he found a position that provided more hours driving buses at the Mt Aspire suburban bus depot.

One Wednesday outing she organized for ten residents to have lunch and take part in games with another rest home. The extended trip involved a lovely country ride and would fill in the morning with socializing and stimulating armchair exercises, plus intellectual crossword games before enjoying a delicious lunch together. Reminiscing about the return trip when the residents were tired and restless Gemma supplied friendly smiles, she amused them by commenting that she had not seen any sheep.

"Where are all these New Zealand sheep, I've only seen cows?" She called out through the van.

A loud chorus of, "We do have sheep, there will be plenty on our way home."

"Let's find sheep then." Gemma called out to Mason as he drove.

It wasn't long before "There's one." Came a weak elderly voice from somewhere, followed by an enthusiastic,

"I see some in that paddock over there."

Secretly smiling she again faced the front of the van and left them to it.

Mason smiled from the driver's seat, calling out, "I thought there weren't any." As he continued with the ruse.

Chatting alongside him as he drove, they found a common interest, a love of the countryside and every time he saw Gemma after that inspiring outing his face lit up and they became friends.

Kelly looked on, (a caregiver) she commented, "He likes you; you should go out with him."

"No, it's too complicated, we work together. If we fell out it would be too miserable to work here, best to keep a distance." Gemma replied.

It was just the usual goodbye to a great work colleague when he left and they thought no more of it, people come and go as she continued to fill weekdays making the lonely lives of the elderly worthwhile and fulfilling in the residential environment, creating crafts, and arranging outings and entertainment for them. Life rattled along and Gemma got a lot of enjoyment and self-satisfaction making people happy. Years later, what an unexpected pleasure it was to meet Mason by chance at the shopping mall, and with loads of smiles he invited her for a cup of hot chocolate at the local café. They had a long catch-up chat and compared how their personal lives had changed since working together.

They both swapped phone numbers and arranged to catch up again, and after numerous outings together she invited him to leave his small flat in Kaitaia, which was a miserable affair anyway, and live in the bedsit situated on the property at her Chelsea Street home, pulling together their resources and sharing Gemma's property with Mason the friendship grew. But sitting by the tranquil pond she recalls how life was not all fun and games as family members began to see and realize how much they meant to each other, so began their crusade. Dwayne the eldest, continually strove to cause friction providing his mum with Gemma's home phone number as Mason did not have a phone, along with the many calls to Mason she began to harass him whenever she could, even jumping onto his bus while he was working and talking in the stairwell holding up passengers.

While spending a lot of time talking together about the things they both enjoyed, they became inseparable despite any interference from others. Their happy times passed quickly and the burning desire to live together ignited, but with Gemma's age and faith she believed in marriage! Mason understood her strong beliefs as he came to know her really well and the suggestion of living together never arose!

A little smile spreads across her face as she fondly recalls that special evening, they were just strolling through the local mall on a Friday night after work and as they passed a jewelry store he paused, squeezing her petite hand he held tightly in his, it caused her to stop walking, puzzled she turned to query it. Looking lovingly into Gemma's eyes he asked unexpectedly.

"Will you marry me?"

"Yes, of course I will." She exclaimed absolutely thrilled and without hesitation, just like he had asked if she wanted a cup of tea. So much for romantic dinners or being proposed to during the heat of intimate contact, it was unexpected and so beautifully memorable. Feeling both surprised at hearing her instantaneous response and elated all at once, time stood still it was so wonderful. Completely oblivious to the myriad of shoppers around them, it felt right to get married, like it was the next step to take in their progression through life.

After that, shopping was quite impossible though with her head up in the fuzzy clouds, so floating down the escalator holding hands they flew back to the carpark in a quiet state of euphoria, the warmth of his hand on her back imprinted in her memory as he guided her into the car seat. She could not wait for his arms to embrace her, cuddles in the car couldn't come soon enough, and the next payday they rushed back to the jewelry store to choose a diamond engagement ring together and then set about informing everyone that they were engaged.

After a lot of deliberation Mason and Gemma agreed to secretly marry in a registry office in Auckland which was witnessed by strangers they asked in off the street.

With no familiar faces present, after all the conflict they had both endured from family members, they were adults and capable of making that decision for themselves. There was no desire for a fancy wedding, it really was not about the party or wedding dress, it was all about being in love, at peace together in the eyes of God and making a legal commitment. With Mason by her side it was perfect bliss being there in their best clothes, tidy hairstyle, and no angst from anyone, it was especially close, just them! plus a fancy wedding would have been a huge unnecessary expense. Being prepared to compromise and blessed in the warmth of happiness, knowing that it did not matter where the marriage took place, God was everywhere. Not to say that Gemma did not feel a little devoid of family right then when saying her vows, but like an oasis in a desert, this felt an essential part of their lives.

Mason moved from the bedsit accommodation outside to live with Gemma in the house and no-one commented on it, the young ones live together these days.

Gemma's daughter Bridget accepted Mason as part of her mother's life, she's a highly motivated and hugely independent girl and Gemma is proud to admit that she must have done something right rearing her to be so happy and self-assured. At 33 years old with dark burgundy hair she inherited from her dad, her pale ivory skin similar to Gemma's, height somewhere between both parents, she is a lovely combination of both parents. Unfortunately for Gemma, after graduating from university Bridget never returned to Kaitaia because she found the love of her life, married, and set up home in Christchurch.

Her husband John is of short stature with thick glasses

exactly like one would expect from such an intelligent individual, at 45 years old he's 12 years older than Bridget. Most mums would find that concerning but she didn't because she had watched them together. Gemma saw that John is aware of her every move and dotes on her, he is quietly confident and shows love for Bridget.

When she tires and becomes impatient with the stresses of life he just continues on silently sorting all that came their way in support of a genuine relationship. They complement each other in many ways and Gemma believes that Bridget is really fortunate to have met him, it is a mystery how some people get these phenomenal partners while she and Mason are both on their second marriage enduring family interference, life is so unfair.

CHAPTER 2

Mason's eldest son Dwayne is living with a young lady from South Africa, somewhere in Morrins Bay near Kaitaia, Mason is aware of where the unit is, but no-one informed Dwayne's stepmother 'Gemma.' Dwayne is a stocky devout bodybuilder, spending all of his spare time at the gym increasing his gorilla-like muscle size and Mason wondered why anyone would want to do that! Saying it looked unnatural. While he felt it was a wonderful idea to stay fit and Gemma was a strong advocate of that also, but Dwayne had succumbed into over kill, it became an obsession! It also hindered him when climbing and doing physical things where huge thighs didn't work well. Dwayne's character was to always be in control of everything and everyone.

Mason's youngest son Peter is 40yrs old, is of slight build and average height, similar appearance to Mason but he is clean shaven and has unfortunately lost most of his hair at an early age. There's no real resemblance between the two boys, not in appearance or personality as Peter has a happy go lucky attitude to life and couldn't really care less, he cocoons himself like a caterpillar does and nothing else exists in his world except his wife and children. He and his wife Norma and their four children continued to reside in Mason's family home after he walked out of his marriage to live in Kaitaia, and Gemma remembers how Mason struggled financially as he continued to pay the mortgage on that house for them all, while also renting the little flat he had lived in before she invited him to stay at her home.

After three years of struggling to cover the bills on the family home and no help forthcoming from his family, Mason had no choice but to sell it. He suggested the family buy him out as his ex-wife Rose had a decent job. With three adult wages coming into the house between them it would be easy enough to do and they wouldn't have to uproot the grandchildren,

Mason was happy to let them have it for a fair price and with interest rates great for getting a mortgage he was hopeful, but no-one wanted to take responsibility of paying a mortgage to buy Mason out. Unfortunately, a forced sale was imminent.

Their marriage had since fallen apart and now Peter had returned home to live with his mother, in the house she bought with the help of an inheritance and her half share following the house sale. Gemma can accept that maybe Peter felt resentment towards her and Mason in the face of the house sale and upset because of his own separation. Meanwhile back in suburbia Gemma owned her Chelsea St home that Mason and she lived in together, it was built by herself and her ex-husband Paul, and was the only home they had during their long marriage where they raised their two lovely children, so it was a home packed with memories from a previous life for Gemma.

Not feeling ungrateful to own her own home, with the knowledge it provided them with a roof over their heads while neither of them earned very much money at the time, still the awkward reality was haunting, this was not their place! (Mason and hers) but the home from a past marriage with all of its ghosts.

Ombre' looks up from the soft grass that he is sprawled out on beside the pond, checking whether they are going back up to the house yet, he decides to lie down again as she strokes his thick coat of fur and is still lost in thought.

Patting softness and thinking back on her life with all of the good memories at the forefront and wondering why this has happened to them, how did they get to where they are now? The grey sky above full of fluffy white clouds warning that winter is just around the corner, with small spaces to allow the sun to peep through, endeavoring to spray warmth down on her for a little bit longer.

Gemma remembers how they struggled to make do, saved

money and as time passed so grew a longing for a fresh start in a home of their own, their place! There were times when his sons caused friction and Mason would put his arms around her and tell her he's happy with just the two of them, those memories will always stay in her mind no matter what happens, reminiscing over the moments that she could almost feel his caresses when he would reassure her that he didn't want anything to do with his past, and had walked away from it several times prior to meeting her, he quietly confided in her.

Twice before, his commitment to his boys had made him return to Rose for the sake of keeping the family together. He vowed that he was never going back a third time and was certain that he wanted his life with her. These constant reassurances were for her benefit, but they did not ease Mason's pain and frustration that he felt as Dwayne continued to add stress to his life.

Constantly under duress, her poor husband understood that his boys were old enough to manage, and that he should not feel responsible for them anymore. Mason often said that if he had not met her when he did, then he would have met someone else! He would have sold up the family home eventually and the result would have been the same! So it didn't matter to Gemma when Dwayne often repeated those cruel words.

"If you leave my dad alone, he will go back to my mum!"

He sounded so pathetically childish it didn't warrant a reply. She knew in her heart that that would never happen, and that Dwayne was dreaming, in Gemma's opinion Dwayne was not in the real world and certainly not acting his age, a control freak. His dad's choice of partner was none of his business anyway.

Gemma continually looked for opportunities to create fun family gatherings, trying to become accepted while Dwayne usually refused to take part. Fortunately for Mason, Peter and the grandchildren would turn up quite happily. Sadly for Gemma, it was near impossible to have her family come as her son Carl was roaming around New Zealand with a girl he had just met, at only 19 years old and hormones running riot he was all but consumed and infatuated with Sue so was not in need of catching up with his family. While Bridget and John had a home and mortgage they couldn't afford to travel from Christchurch too often.

So they had a series of noisy and spectacular bonfires for Guy Fawkes night, Easter egg hunts and Christmas gatherings at the Chelsea Street house. At times leaving Gemma feeling left out, she pulled together some justification for fun times when she looked into Mason's beautiful eyes, as he proudly watched his four animated grandchildren, and she silently dealt with the gut-wrenching emptiness gnawing away at her insides, sometimes feeling lonely and sick when Dwayne and Peter would have a sulk and avoid eye contact with her.

They were in Gemma's home accepting her hospitality and yet they looked straight through her, as though she was not even there! Gemma knew that was what they really wanted, for her not to be there! Could they be any ruder or merciless displaying their ignorance, to not realize that their behaviors affected not only her but dangerously affected their dad's emotional wellbeing?

Looking back at those times she was patient and accepting as she contemplated and reminded herself of the intense love they shared, and that overrode and healed any hurt his sons inflicted. She knew that the intense wounding that was searing her inside would fade into oblivion when relatives all went home. They would be alone together again with Mason feeling content and all was right with his world. Gemma couldn't take that away from him by letting him know how much she hurt. The intensity of being together would spill over as they embraced, exploding with joy. They were so lucky to have found each other.

They had an immense unconditional love, voluminous as they drank it in and thrived, Mason's happiness was Gemma's pleasure. One of the joys they shared together in those first years was to escape into their reliable van they purchased, they bought a cheap little two ring gas stove which was magical, running on a small tin of gas resembling a can of fly spray, this really appealed to them both as they didn't want to carry a huge cylinder of explosive gas in the van while they were driving or sleeping, and had heard of cases where people just go to sleep oblivious of a gas leak never to wake up again!

They planned out the inside, putting a good quality mattress down on the cold hard floor of the van and made up the bed so it was really comfortable, as they both felt strongly that to have a good night's sleep was probably one of the most important preparation steps for creating the perfect trip, it was a basic primal instinct if they were to drive around exploring the breath-taking New Zealand countryside with a smile on their faces, an absolute must to avoid getting overtired and grumpy. They spent every night locked in each other's arms away from everyone and everything, together in the wild, being comfortable and searching out fresh nutritious food was a blissful experience and privilege.

Wasting no time they drove down the North Island of New Zealand as they had both seen the many beautiful cities on short trips before, but driving onto the ferry to enter the wilderness of the South Island of New Zealand was an adventurous goal, praying that they didn't have to cope with flat tyres or breakdowns. They stopped at everything that appealed and they thought they wanted to see, oblivious of time and of things tourists are expected to see, they decided to eat crayfish at Kaikoura because they enjoyed the taste of the fresh crayfish straight out of the water and into the pot, explored lush native forests and inhaled smelly seals sunbathing in their natural habitat all of their senses were filled, they tasted, saw, smelled, and touched, creating memories unaware of impending tragedy to come. During their time exploring the South Island of New Zealand they were both happy, at peace, in love. It was on one of those trips that they decided to buy a piece of land and be at one with earth, life, and death.

For generations, people at some stage of their life think that they crave self- sufficiency! But Gemma and Mason didn't want to go quite that far, they still needed to earn a living. They deciding it sounded too much like arduous work and not much fun to be completely self-sufficient, but to grow as much nutritious food for themselves to live on, and know that it was chemical free, have a few pet chickens to get fresh eggs from, so that Gemma could bake and never have to buy biscuits again. That would be enough for them to start on their dream for tomorrow, thinking that they would do it together unaware of the need to prepare for future eventualities.

After banking the majority of Mason's wages every week for a year, while Gemma worked and financed all of the bills, they had saved a lump sum, and they were excited to be able to use that money as a deposit on a property for them to begin their dream. While working at the rest home Gemma had also been attending classes at the local university and had become a qualified fulltime real-estate salesperson, she left the rest home to sell houses so she could bring in better money. As coincidence would have it, she was then right in the center of the hive, like bees making honey, although she didn't find selling houses particularly emotionally rewarding like at the rest home, she found that it was alive with activity and unbeknown to them contributed enormously towards their journey and shared endeavor to find a new place in the sun.

Finding the right home was a daunting task, maybe it was wishful thinking, continuing on with hope in their hearts until one day everything seemed to fall into place. On Wednesday while at work in the office, staff were talking about a property that no-one wanted to buy, all the real-estate agents got into a couple of cars and set off on a road trip to view this Panguru 10-acre lifestyle property, it had an old farmhouse on it and gossip had precluded it as being a haunted house.

Discussion among the agents had estimated the derelict farmhouse to be at least 40 years old, and as soon as she stepped out of the car, beside the broken wire gate and overgrown wilderness of yesteryear gardens with ugly long grass Gemma agreed that it was definitely old and in need of repairs. The amount of deterioration and neglect caused her to wonder what kind of history this house has had with its flaking paint, leaky roof, and unloved appearance. It had an airy feel about it and didn't really appeal to her, but later on that evening when she discussed it with Mason he was insistent on seeing it. He fell in love with it and wanted to make an offer. Gemma was taken aback and more than a little apprehensive by the amount of work that needed to be done to make it livable, but then in the back of her mind was that childhood lesson *'that the best things in life don't come easy, you must work for them'*, and of course the fact that no-one wanted to buy into this mess also made it affordable for them to buy, but what was the strange foreboding she had about it?

There was a warning inside her that she now wished she had listened to, her fate might have been different if she had.

After the first excitement had dissipated and she was calmly weighing things up, she started to feel concerned about buying the property, is it the right thing to do? The points in favor; It was only a stone's throw away from both of their places of work and close to Kaitaia shops, schools, and the highway, it also had incredible rural countryside vista stretching out in front of an old moss-covered deck, in need of replacement, but the structure was sound. The points against; It was an eyesore and what would they do with so much land when they're not used to having that much to maintain, after summing it all up, talking it over they could not believe that they could afford this beautiful property. Yes! It was full of gorse, noxious weeds, no decent fencing, with a house that had a bath sitting through the floor!

Then, on the other hand, it was silly to be afraid when an opportunity presents itself and it was close to suburbia and life as they were both used to, so it's not like they would be going bush or anything, a big plus was that it also had a hidden treasure. A huge manmade pond resembling a small lake, which they came across quite by chance when nosily pushing their way through the gorse, wanting to get to the end of the property, a really beautiful, serene lake surrounded by rich green paddocks which all sloped down to it. The entire area was silent except for the sound of the few ducks swishing on the clear blue water and the peaceful tweet of the birds in the surrounding Manuka trees, the whole place looked like an overgrown forgotten world, yet it held a hidden beauty for them that no one else seemed to appreciate. In their minds eye they could unmask the mess and ignore the work, to appreciate the breathe-taking beauty that they both saw beneath, it was a world apart from what either of them had ever had in their lives, they were seriously considering making it Mason and Gemma's world!

Looking past all that she remembered thinking that at the time and wondering why they had found it. Was this meant to be, should they buy it? It seemed incredible, sure it had two-metre-high gorse everywhere and unbeknown to either of them it would bring her tears of exhaustion and frustration many a time in years to come, as the gorse would get in her hair, and they would both battle with prickles in their fingers and get it down the top of their gumboots, causing them to hop helplessly on one foot while shaking the other boot out. Through the excitement she continued to feel an uneasiness about the place, it just didn't feel right and maybe she should heed her first impression.

The house was Gemma's immediate concern, so she set her mind on that and shut out any doubts. She was not familiar with living in a mess, and she had been called a super tidier in the past, so could she stand to live there? Or would it overwhelm her and be too much? They would definitely need plenty of patience and tolerance to knock it into shape.

But they were a couple in love and assured each other that one room at a time was manageable, they would conquer the disgusting puppy urine-stained carpet that a previous owner had left and after some serious thought they were determined to buy it!

Bravely setting about working on it together, completely redoing one room at a time, while trying not to be swayed to branch out all over the house, which did take great self-control. Challenging was an understatement as they set aside every weekend to rip up stinky carpet, the first priority with its many carpet tacks and edging that had multiple nails in it, the whole place smelt like a toilet. Then replacing the kitchen was the next priority as Gemma needed to prepare delicious meals in hygienic conditions. They planned to completely remove all cupboards and bring in new modern design cabinetry, but logic dictated they had to wait for finances to improve, the bathroom had to come first so they could move in.

Fortunately, they were okay financially and able to stay at Gemma's house for a little while, and not have to sell it as long as they were careful with money, worked hard and went without. Both being older and mature enough to know that you had to work for what you want in life. They went without holidays to achieve their dream and being so much in love with each other definitely motivated them, when exhausted from decorating they still summoned that last push of energy from the excitement and adrenaline rushing through them to gain the strength to keep going, working hard to show devotion to the other partner. It was the two of them against the world and a year passed very quickly before they even got to live in their would-be dream home.

All the determination and hard work at their age in life you'd think would have shown Mason's boys to back off, that it was love and they deserved to be happy, but in actual fact the animosity was heightened. The sons became more determined and jealous as they continually invited Mason to their homes for parties in their garages and made it quite clear that the invitations were for him alone, invites to celebrate New Year's Eve, birthday parties etc. without Gemma, and all the time keeping their addresses a secret from her. She is reminded about the lonely times she endured when they did that.

Not only because she was seeing in a new year alone but

because she felt betrayed by Mason and also knew that he was socializing with his ex-wife as the family contrived to drive a wedge between him and Gemma, every year she hoped they would stop the harassment and see that she trusted Mason, surely they would see the strain they were putting their father under.

'I can't understand why they don't accept me?' Was something she started to ask Mason as time went by. Many a time hoping and praying that Mason would stick up for his wife and tell Dwayne that it was both of them or he wouldn't go, but he never did. If only he had put his foot down with them right from the start, then maybe life would have been so much easier, especially later on in the years that followed. Gemma understood that it wasn't a normal situation and at the same time she knew that it was emotionally torturing Mason, and she didn't want to add to the pressure.

Dwayne constantly tried to upset Gemma which made her more determined to put on a brave face and pretend not to be hurt by the ongoing rejection that she felt.

It was about that time that Mason decided to get her a puppy for company (he felt guilty). Looking down at the affectionate little golden treasure glowing in the remaining bit of sun that is close to disappearing behind the hills, she constantly confides in her furry friend, she smiles and continues to reminisce with him nuzzled into her side as they sit on the grassy bank of the ponds edge.

"I love you Ombre' you are such a good little friend." Lifting his head up he looks intelligently at her and listens wisely to everything she says while he patiently waits to return to the present.

CHAPTER 3

Soon after moving to Panguru Mason had the idea of getting goats to help destroy the gorse and save some work, Gemma was never keen on this idea as she didn't know the first thing about goats and whether they were dangerous to manage, she knew enough to know that they would be stronger than her, and this caused enough concern as she didn't want any accidents happening. Although she made her worries known to Mason he was undaunted and unfortunately was so mesmerized by the thought that he had found the grand solution to the gorse dilemma that Gemma's concerns didn't matter. Of course, to add to the danger it meant that they would be individually tied, because the paddock fencing was sub-standard and non-existent in some places and goats would definitely go next door if they could, guess who got that job!

Even though she didn't need any more work, it actually became Gemma's job to move the goats around the property on chains and various lengths of rope that she could find cheaply or preferably free, keeping them fed and giving them access to more new gorse to destroy, consuming not only the gorse but Gemma's days as well. They loved to eat gorse, especially the yellow flowers that constantly bloomed on top. Devouring the flowers prevented it from forming seed heads that the wind would eventually blow, scattering the seed to start multiplying around the paddock.

While moving goats to fresh trunks of gorse they would wander in every direction and quickly wrap their ropes around her legs, this painful and continuous danger she endured morning and night every day before and after work, she became agile and good at quickly turning faster than they could, but always fearful of getting tangled and falling in the gorse she endured painful skin burns and grazes on her legs, that happened all too often, she looked down at the scars left on her right leg from the bad rope burns received one time.

Gemma was often driven to tears and began to resent Mason for getting the goats before the necessary fences. All of her spare time spent on moving goats as they ate continually, and her heart pained her that there did not seem to be any concern for her welfare coming from Mason. The last thing needed was for Gemma to be injured and be out of action, she was needed to keep everyone fed and well looked after.

Progress was slow with the house as they tried to do as much as possible themselves to save money, Gemma decided that her house that she had rented out to help pay the mortgage would be better off sold and the lump sum used to lower the mortgage on their lifestyle block. The old kitchen was replaced with a lovely new one, along with many big expenses incurred while renovating, they were all paid off. All debts were reduced significantly which made their lives less stressful financially.

Then on one miserable chilly day in June, something happened that she would remember for the rest of her life, Mason decided to repair the house roof, and thinking back she's still angry today. Of all the days to choose, why did he choose then? It was wet and stormy, and the old roof was in serious need of repair, they had been tolerating it for a year because of the huge cost, it kept getting put down the list of things to do. Mason must have felt that he could just do a makeshift patch over the leak. Gemma was at work, and he was tired of emptying the two plastic buckets sitting on the lounge floor under where the ceiling had turned to mush from constant dripping, it had suddenly collapsed into the room the week prior, and they had been living with ugly plastic buckets catching small drips since moving in.

He had refused to bother with fixing the rusty roof during the beautiful week-end weather when she had suggested it to him and she would have helped, so she just lived with his poor judgement and as usual said nothing. Unfortunately, he ventured up onto the old roof and bravely patched up the hole in the corrugated iron, he was satisfied the temporary repair would hold until a later date when the weather was better, and they had time and money to replace some of the old rusty iron with their dream of lovely shiny new stuff. When leaving the roof, as he felt for the top rung of the ladder with his foot, he only had one foot on when a strong gust of wind took the light aluminum ladder and flung it backwards onto the wet and weathered deck, Mason crashed onto the landing!

His back taking the full force as his head was flung back to hit the deck, he has explained to Gemma since the accident that he lay stunned in the heavy rain unaware of how long for, because he was probably knocked out. When he came around the rain was dripping onto his face and the deck had rivers of blood running across it, trickling off the edge and onto the ground, Gemma is sure that at that moment he must have asked himself why he hadn't waited for better weather.

When Gemma drove up to the house an anxious neighbor rushed over to tell her Mason was on his way to Kaitaia Hospital. Black fear and dizziness swamped her, but running on adrenalin she found strength, sliding onto the car seat and in a dazed state proceeded to drive 81 Km to the hospital. Terrified of what damage he had done to himself she drove frantically with her mind thinking the worst, but also reassuring herself that he was capable of getting himself help, that had to be a good sign. The drive to the hospital was a blur, it's amazing how people get to their destinations sometimes when their minds are not on the road, she had no idea how she arrived safely at the accident and emergency department as she couldn't remember any of the drive there, her mind and body fraught with concern for her husband and all she remembers is her whispered prayers on the way, that he be okay.

He'd had x-rays of his back taken before she arrived and then when she tracked him down through the A & E department she found him strapped onto a bed, as she stretched her shaking arms across the bed to bend down to hug and kiss him, she felt so relieved to see him looking and talking, she also remembers being aware of doctors eyes piercing through her as one of them called out authoritively.

"Don't move him, we're just looking at the x-rays and will talk to you shortly, he mustn't move!" He shouted from across the emergency room.

Professionally clad in white, doctors and nurses are everywhere, and the unemotional efficiency hung heavy in the air like a newly washed blanket along with the sickly sanitized smell. They waited anxiously to find out what the outcome would be and there was an unspoken aura of fear between her and Mason because they both silently knew that he could be paralyzed! A group of doctors were diagnosing whether or not his spinal cord had been compromised.

They looked at the glaringly bright screen. When approached by a single doctor; he pulled the curtain around the bed as he looked down at the x-rays grasped firmly in his hands.

"The x-rays show three fractures to your spine Mr. Brownlie, but with time they should heal!" He spoke quickly and to the point. "You will be transferred to Auckland Hospital to have a special brace fitted that you must wear whenever you are standing. It's very important that you do wear it until the bones have knitted back together." And continued to add that he was incredibly lucky that the spinal cord wasn't damaged. Hearing those words in her head *'Wasn't damaged'* wasn't damaged was all she could hear amidst her heart pounding.

Standing silently beside the cold and sterile looking bed covered in its starched, white hospital sheets, just being together was a weight lifted off her shoulders, just then she heard a rush of air and a huge sigh of relief escape from within, she must have been holding her breathe. Mason was transferred to Auckland hospital by a hasty ambulance for special treatment as Gemma followed in her little Fiat car, it was a very strange scary thing to be following an ambulance and they both knew that he would be in the best place for treating that kind of injury, even though it meant they would be apart with quite some distance between them it was inevitable, there was nothing else they could do. The long trek to visit him began.

On arriving home later in the evening exhausted, she phoned the boys about their dad, and they visited him once during his stay in hospital, much like duty called them to do so which was very disappointing. The more visitors an ill person gets the more positive they are likely to be during this hiccup in their lives, and it all serves to help in a quick recovery. They had received a huge shock and were very grateful that he would walk again. Gemma often found herself silently fighting back the tears in the days and weeks that followed coping on her own, it was hard for her to be without her husband, thank goodness she had Ombre' every night snuggling up against her legs, sensing that something was wrong because Mason wasn't home and there was a sad silence in her world.

During the downward slide from the roof Mason had been reaching out grabbing at anything to slow his speed on the way, no doubt optimistic of preventing the terrifying outcome of a painful landing. He had latched onto the plastic spouting which gave way under his weight, leaving it hanging down from the roof and rainwater was now pouring in under the front door. With her husband in hospital, she didn't have anyone to help, and she couldn't ask his sons.

It was too high for her to climb up the ladder as she has a fear of heights and tears of helplessness threatened to flow yet again as she watched the water coming in under the door, threatening to do more damage to the home they were making together. Searching for strength she firmly reprimanded herself, she was home alone now, and she had to be strong for Mason to recover, everything would be okay, she had to be independent and grateful that it wasn't worse.

After moving there and doing everything themselves neither of them had gotten to know the neighbors well enough for her to ask for help, so she felt completely alone, she remembers that was a desolate lonely time. She attempted to prop up lengths of timber to push the broken spouting away from the door, but the strong wind kept blowing it down and rain continued to flow under the door soaking their beautiful tongue and groove wooden flooring, not unlike the tears that continued to flow down her face. The only thing she could do was push towels against the door and hope the rain would soon stop. She felt lost, lonely, and exhausted with everything that had happened. Where were his precious sons now? Why hadn't they phoned to see if she was okay after the shock of it all? Nowhere to be seen, a sign of things to come!

She had the responsibility of managing the goats, working part-time, and traveling many hours to visit Mason, her days were long and tiring. After a month Mason came home and went on accident compensation, it was another setback to their already strained financial situation, thank goodness she had sold her Chelsea Street house. Mason got around with a molded plastic brace strapped around his waist for support so they were grateful as it could have been worse! Together they managed to glue a joiner up into the tired old spouting and she continued to work as much as she could. They pulled together again and slowly got back with their very ordinary lives and he went back to work after a few months, all his sick pay and savings were used up with no chance of any holiday for an exceedingly long time.

His back had healed but he was short tempered and more irritable than before the accident. She tried to understand by putting herself in his position, convincing herself the huge upset in their plans and perhaps the shock of what had happened would take time to wear off. Irritability turned into temper tantrums, and he would sometimes forget things. Gemma became more concerned as Mason started to physically lash out at her, it was out of character, but he refused to see the doctor, so she promised herself that next time she went the doctor for any reason she made a subconscious note to ask if something could still be wrong with Mason following the accident.

At the time she remembers noting that Dr Carter didn't appear to be listening to her! But not wanting to appear pushy, she politely asked him to check his notes to see if Mason's head had been scanned after the fall, but he looked down at the prescription pad and continued to write out a three month repeat for her arthritis medication, it felt like he was brushing her off! If he wasn't concerned, then she reasoned it must be post-traumatic shock or something, and it would come right with time. Looking back now she wishes she had insisted on information, been more assertive, but at the time when it was all new to her she told herself that she should stop worrying, move on and forget it happened, everything would come right.

While awaiting the first kid to be born from their pair of goats, they were a mixture of excitement and nerves, after reading all the books and ready to deliver it, if necessary, but of course very apprehensive and hoped Ginger would give birth without help. On tenterhooks waiting to see what would happen, as soon as Gemma arrived home from work each day she would rush down to the paddock to check everything was okay, hoping for a surprise, checking Ginger had water and patting her. She was certain the pregnant goat enjoyed all the special luscious garden weeds or a few new spring leaves bursting out from the apple tree that she was spoiled with. Mason and Gemma both focused on this big event and had been watching Ginger's udder increasing in size like a balloon about to burst, they knew a kid would soon be born, so Gemma prayed that this first baby goat would be straightforward.

How wonderful that they were both at home as a pair of little feet appeared, they watched and waited, it wasn't long before the kid dive bombed onto the ground. Mum turned to look at the little wet creature moving and even though she was the first one to have a baby in that paddock and she hadn't witnessed others being born she instinctively knew to start licking the yellow stuff off the tiny creatures face, causing it to cry out to her, Ginger looking up as if to say,

"Look what I have!" She was very proud and kept checking on her new-born as if she couldn't quite believe her eyes, tiny teardrops pooled in the corner of Gemma's eyes as they looked on, she couldn't explain why, except to say that new life was awesome and completely overwhelmed her with happy tears. Lifestyle blocks are all about life and being at one with nature. Sometimes she needed to assist goats with the birth, just by watching them over the years she soon understood when to lend a hand and possibly save a struggling life.

Many times she reached out and gripped the tiny slimy feet sticking out and helped to pull the soft, warm body, breaking the suction that held it fast, it would drop onto the grassy paddock when the prospective mum had become too tired. A look of relief radiated as she looked up at Gemma, hearing her new-born first sound. What a great privilege to be part of it all. Gemma placed the warm wet new life on the ground in front of the doe to clean and bond with. Perhaps it's a women's thing though, as Gemma never understood why over the years Mason would never lend a hand he always maintained.

"It's nature's way if the kid doesn't make it."

Gemma couldn't be that hard and believes everything and everyone needs help at some time in their life. She wondered if he didn't feel the special something that happens inside when a new life is created, remembering how awesome and awe-inspiring it was. During those special times if either of them saw a doe about to give birth they ran and told the other and stopped whatever they were doing, just to sit on a log or lean against the fence post with Ombre' lying in wait.

Being in the countryside witnessing life happening in their place in the world was absolutely amazing, how fortunate to be given those special times together. Every soft new-born gave them endless joy, it didn't seem to matter how many. Each one brought tears to Gemma's eyes, just to see the new life and to watch the love happening between mum and kid as they talked and bonded together, she warmed with fuzzes inside, and it was the sort of stuff that made other issues pale in significance.

Goats are very much family orientated and the other goats came around to have a look, the mum really does look proud as she licks and grooms her tiny new one, the adoration is so apparent and a privilege to be part of.

The years passed in the Northland country environment, their little patch of heaven, where stock numbers grew to 20 woolly sheep, with a dozen brown shaver hens scratching around the newly fenced paddocks, with reduced numbers of goats to six, even the pond glistened brilliantly in the sunshine like a fresh raindrop on a new rose-petal on this their ordinary little piece of nature.

Gemma understands that it's not for the faint hearted, she's experienced visitors that don't appreciate the blood, sweat and tears that the tough country life brings, it's not for the suburbanite that feels happiest in bright night clubs and high heels, and sometimes animals die. She lives in gumboots and jeans when she's at home and walks amongst the animal poo when collecting the kindling and pinecones for the fire. The farmhouse is not flash but to her they have the equivalent of the wealthy living in a mansion as they enjoy nature, at night the sparkle of stars clearly visible in the reflection less sky is a far cry from city nightlife and streetlights. If only everything was right with Mason.

CHAPTER 4

Their much-loved dog Ombre' has spent his whole life ruling over his empire sniffing and licking any little orphan that Gemma brought up to the house to be bottle fed. He's a pretty ordinary looking Labrador, lively and affectionate with a soft golden coat of deep warm fur, the depth of superior intelligence portrayed in his ebony eyes as he greets everyone and sizes them up! Friend or foe?

With avid hearing ability from the one ear pointing up and the other one slightly bent, he looks friendly, almost comical, he warns strangers off with ferocious ear-piercing barking until he's ordered to cease and allow them onto the property. He's a loyal companion and protector taking his job seriously and offering security even with his lack luster eyesight in his advancing years. Gemma settled at night without fear of unannounced intruders. She thinks back with fondness to that glorious day Mason took her to choose a puppy from a large litter of seven, he was the fattest and also the only one to run up to them for a pat, Gemma adored his friendly boisterous puppy ways which he continues even now at seven years old. He's undoubtedly the best present Mason ever gave her.

They had their ups and downs after Mason's fall off the roof, but they remained strong through everything as couples do. Life continued on at a fast pace with work around the lifestyle block, nevertheless Gemma was constantly alerted to a cantankerous, impatient, and changing Mason. As soon as they could afford to, a contractor was employed to pound the many fence posts into the ground with a tractor and then the two of them managed to attach sheep netting, creating well-planned six fenced paddocks which definitely made rounding up stock a lot easier.

During the early days on the land, Peter and Norma came around to visit, Norma was overheard to say.

"This house will be good to have eh!" Looking startled and embarrassed when she looked up to see Gemma approaching and undoubtedly hoping she wasn't overheard she quickly enquired. "Hi, how's Mason these days since his fall?"

"He's still not well, and his memory is worse, he often gets very grumpy." Gemma gave an honest reply.

This information didn't warrant an answer, she apparently didn't have anything to say, perhaps she was just speaking out of formality because people ask how you are but don't expect the truth as a response or she was wondering how long it would be before they both died, and she could inherit.

Gemma found it difficult to forget her comment, knowing that someone is after your home, however their marriage failed after she had an affair and the wife turned up on their doorstep, demanding that Norma leave the husband alone. Norma continues to hang around Peter even though he's disillusioned and returned home to live with his mum. The memory of what she heard would always remain with Gemma as it showed intent!

They hadn't had any goats for a couple of years as the smelly and sometimes unmanageable buck passed away and they decided not to replace him, no-one was getting any younger and something wasn't right with Mason.

Then one Sunday morning unexpectedly, Mason said, "Let's have another kid, I know you always enjoyed their frolicking in the paddock!" He had his lovely smile back that day.

Quite stunned and taken back for a minute because it was so unexpected, she queried. "Are you sure? I'll have to think about it."

Mason knew how much she loved having the baby goats before getting the sheep and she was mesmerized and stood in awe of their evening antics. To her, kids were cuter than lambs they definitely had more character and intelligence, but it was a revelation out of the blue and she didn't understand why! Perhaps he wanted to feel what she felt, or maybe he had a guilty conscience.

She was hopeful that he was healing and one day be that quiet caring man that he used to be before the fall from the roof.

The good and the bad memories are forever there, like the time waking to another beautiful summer's morning, wanting to rush out and move the goats quickly so they could enjoy the day together. Mason was already outside doing some clearing because it was a very calm, still day he could light a fire. It was blazing away safely in the middle of the paddock burning the many lengths of dead gorse bushes.

"Morning darling, do you want a cuppa?" She recalls yelling out from the top of the sloping grass bank, which formed part of the orchard when the small mandarin trees grew.

"Yes please." Came the reply from a red faced and sweaty looking husband.

"I'll bring it down to you." Gemma turned to make her way to the kitchen returning with two mugs of refreshing tea.

Smiling up at him, "I love it when we can just sit and talk in the middle of nowhere, sitting in the long grass pondering over how lucky we are, how lovely it is to be out of the city and in the breeze of the country with our dog and forever hungry goats." He smiled.

Well, after putting their empty cups down it was time to help tidy up, she recalls a lot of old bottles and rubbish was hidden under the gorse bushes and thrown down the bank from the road above. She paused to watch him collecting things and throwing them on the fire after carefully putting any glass into a separate pile for the recycling back up at the house, so she enthusiastically started joining in with her rubber gloves on. After collecting up some old bits of broken electrical tape that must have been discarded many moons before when horses roamed the property, she threw them onto the fire.

"Aarrr!" She let out a cry of pain as her face stung and she was nearly knocked over, Mason had forcefully hit her across one side of her head. "What happened?" She gasped. Automatically staggering backwards from the force, she reached her hand to her right ear and face, seeing a hand but not really knowing if it was hers or not, but she seemed to be in control of it, although it appeared to be disconnected.

She was aware of Mason yelling that she had burnt a piece of string that he wanted.

"I didn't know you wanted that old broken stuff." She replied with the tears flowing uncontrollably down her cheeks and the lump in her throat making her want to be sick. "I was just trying to help you tidy the paddock."

Words were coming out, but she wasn't sure if she was making any sense, just sounds that she had heard before. Very aware that although he had never hit her before, he started to approach her again. She instinctively dropped the mugs she had just collected and put one foot in front of the other running to the best of her ability, she knew that she had to get away, the look of utter anger on his face, fury that she'd never seen before, *what's wrong with him*? *Did he get too hot by the fire*?

Somehow, she scrambled up the bank on all fours with her head pounding and staggering into the house she headed to the phone for help, as she watched fingers push the buttons to contact Mason's son Peter who only lived a short distance away.

Thank God that she was able to get away from Mason! Fearful and disbelieving what he did she was scared of his look. "Can you come around; your dad hit me?" She pleaded to Peter when he answered the phone.

"Okay." Was the haphazard reply before he hung up, he didn't seem concerned or questioning when she failed to explain anything because her head hurt, feeling sick and confused as to what had just happened?

Gemma's stomach was wanting to hurl its contents and her head was wanting to fall off its stem, it felt too heavy to support. Telling herself to stay calm and everything would be okay wasn't working, her headache got worse. No-one turned up and she knew she needed to seek medical help as something was not right, so she reluctantly found her car keys as she dare not go near Mason, not even to tell him she was going to the accident and emergency department, she was too scared to go near him.

Driving was probably not a safe option but there wasn't any other, she was confused and in shock so decided to just go slowly.

Gemma remembers that horrific drive, no sooner had she driven out of the street before half her vision went black. In between the nausea and only being able to see the black tar-sealed road and some wheels traveling on it, the body of the cars and anything above the wheels were gone, empty darkness! Tears continued to roll down her face unabated as loud sounds were heard crying out frantically.

"Please help me, don't let me hurt anyone while I'm driving, I need help, oh please Lord let me be okay."

She drove herself straight to White Cross carefully parked between the yellow markings on the ground, closest to the door and wondered if she could stand. Everything was difficult to make out with half vision as the headless receptionist asked her what was wrong? She could hear her jumbled sounds, only understanding she was holding out paperwork for Gemma to take.

"Have you been in an accident?" She inquired from a waiting room full of legs dangling from seats all around the room, she wished she wasn't distraught and crying as she blurted out it was a result of domestic violence.

Everyone must have been able to hear her words, with no privacy she felt like the patients would all be wondering what she had done to cause it, fully aware and self- conscience that she wore old clothes from outside in the yard, she wondered what she looked like and what impression did that give people, a lesson for her that it's important not to judge what people wear or look like because circumstances dictate that you will not be looking your best during an emergency.

She knew that she didn't deserve to be hit but she still felt demoralized and embarrassed.

Sometime later after being diagnosed with concussion, holding ice packs on her head, her sight returned and she listened to the failed attempts from concerned staff pleading with her to press assault charges against her husband, all she wanted was for it to all go away and for her to be home again like nothing had happened. She carefully tucked the written warning letter into her handbag, (not to be hit in the head again or it could be a major emergency) and as she walked into the house, hesitant as to what she might find.

"Where have you been?" He snapped angrily at her with no sign of remorse.

She quietly answered, "I went to the White Cross emergency doctors."

"Ha!" He scoffed, a very noncommittal reply leaving her stunned and questioning whether he even remembered what he'd done. She was in no state to ask right then, so slamming the receipt and warning letter down on the dining table for him to read as proof of what she said, and being ever hopeful that he may by some miracle become a caring human being, like the one she used to know. She went to the bedroom and collapsed into the soft duvet, burying her face into the pillow, the tears started to flow again but this time it wasn't from pain, but the realization of what Mason had done to her, and the tears unabatedly took hold as her body shook for relief and answers, that was the only comfort afforded to her for the concussion and humiliation she had gone through.

After falling asleep exhausted with Ombre' lying beside the bed she awakened the next day remembering that she had to report to her GP for a check-up, she's feeling determined to bring up Mason's behavior yet again.

"There's something wrong with him?" She pleaded with her doctor, who didn't reply. "He hasn't been the same since he fell off the roof and fractured his back, should we get a scan of his head or something?"

She pressed on, anxiety mounting in her body and shrieking voice as she felt frantic about getting her husband some help. Still no reply, but she kept on trying to get answers without knowing how to explain Mason's actions.

"Because he's very forgetful now, which he wasn't before." She blurted out as the tears of embarrassment filled her eyes and she again felt like a nuisance, trying to blink them away so they would go unnoticed but concern for Mason made her voice sound squeaky and frantic and her effort to stay strong failed.

He looked down at his paper in a strange deliberate kind of way and said.

"Scans are expensive, he might have post-traumatic stress, he'll come right! I can talk to him about it next time I see him."

Looking back now, she remembers feeling uneasy about his dismissive behavior, she didn't feel right but she trusted their doctor, she should have gone with her instincts.

Mason continued to work as a Northland bus driver, but the last ten years together had seen Gemma make some career changes. She gave up real-estate work and was fortunate enough to have secured part-time work in a local Panguru school during the day helping students that had learning difficulties. She also had a second job on late night Thursdays and all-day Saturday as shop assistant at the local ladies clothing shop, this all helped with finances while she studied extramurally at the local university to become fully qualified in her Teacher Aide work at the school.

Sometimes they were close just like old times, but she experienced times when love and hate seemed extreme, the intensity of moments being hard to distinguish exactly how she felt when Mason was very cruel, and she found him difficult to understand.

One day he separated a mother goat from her baby, tying it up on one side of the six-foot-high deer fencing. He laughed when the doe was calling and straining to get to her hungry baby, who was on the other side of the fence letting out painful continuous crying of baby sounds. The noise and desperation of them both was heart- breaking to listen to, but he watched on laughing and enjoying it.

The torturous sound went on until Gemma couldn't stand it anymore, risking her life she rushed over to open the gate and untie the baby to run away to its mum. She managed to quickly do it before Mason grabbed her arm and as she clung tightly to the wire mesh fence in fear of what he would do to her and to prevent being knocked to the ground, he continually hit her around the head. Appearing to enjoy cruelty and hurting her, she asked herself what's happened to the man she married? Should she reach out to him with love because he can't help what he does, or should she despise him for the despicable things he now gets pleasure from?

Days turned into weeks, and months went as usual with his unpredictable mood changes until one Sunday she couldn't believe his planning, he opened the aviary door to let her pet canaries fly free from the safety of their home, because he saw a Harrier eagle souring overhead looking to attack any rabbit or smaller prey that would end up being shredded to death. He sat on the deck laughing and watching her knowing that he was inflicting the most terrible fear into Gemma, as she couldn't close the door because he was sitting in wait.

She knew that she would be beaten if he caught her. Her recollection of her panic, distraught for the safety of her pet canaries, she fell to the ground with her hands over her ears unable to stand the sound of the screaming birds, their cries of pain and calls for help would forever haunt her along with the knowledge that she didn't save her pets. Her days became full of hidden fears of what he might do next, and she treaded carefully not to say anything to upset him.

What had become of their lives? Gemma spent a lot of time wondering why he did those things and living in hope that he would get better if it's post-traumatic stress. No one saw what he was like in private, and she hid it because of embarrassment and feeling protective for Mason. Constantly making excuses for his behavior and not wanting people to know what he did. She's in love with who he once was and understood that he maybe can't help what he has become, she struggled to know what to do and how to get him help.

The pond at the bottom of the property became a private retreat to finally be able to let the tears flow freely, no-one could see her as she felt ashamed, she didn't know why she felt that way when she hadn't done anything wrong but sitting in that beautiful place with her companion she talked freely to him, cleared her thoughts, and tried to understand Mason's behavior.

Looking up at the huge native trees that border the still water's edge and listening to the happy singing of the beautiful fantails sometimes drew her attention to 'happy' being a strange word she no longer understood. Often at these times she became aware of her physical pain from the grabbing and bruises he inflicted on her body but at the same time being grateful to be able to feel anything at all after her mind and body had become numb from many sleepless nights, full of hidden fears and anxiety brought on by sometimes being awoken with a thud as her body hit the floor. The sound of his laughter ringing in her ears through the darkness after he had pushed her off the side of the bed while she was asleep. Now her sleep pattern had changed, she's afraid to sleep.

Gemma has learnt to just click off by pretending to put all her concerns up on a shelf at night and take one day at a time, trying not to worry about what will become of her husband, she holds onto her belief that he will slowly get better.

CHAPTER 5

Mostly life became very routine for them, he worked shifts on the buses, and she worked part-time with children, plus salesperson in a clothing store. Until one horrible cold night in June 2008 a terrible life changing thing happened, Mason came home late from work while she was looking out the kitchen window, longing for him to be home. Dark nightshifts were lonely, and it was lucky that she had Ombre', Mason opened the kitchen door.

"Hi, do you want a cuppa?" she asked cheerfully. Aware that he'd be tired from work.

There was no reply, just wild fiery eyes staring blankly, he went for her! With his left arm stiffly out in front of him and his fist closed he rushed at her, pushing hard into her chest with his piercing knuckles, pain! But mostly she was afraid of falling and was instantly aware of all the obstacles that she could hit her head on, aware of what a head injury can do. Startled and unable to get away from his pushing she veered off backwards to the right, away from the corner of the kitchen bench, all the time unsuccessfully trying to release the hold he had on her, she pulled as hard as she could on his fingers and wrists, it was all so unexpected and she couldn't think, he continued to push with fury force. Gemma's slipper slid backwards into the dining room, in the panic and sudden shock of it all she lost her footing, which is what she'd feared. Mason had become exceptionally strong like a crazy person running on adrenalin, and as she fell onto the bare floor, her back took the full force of the hard, polished timber.

Neither of them spoke, it happened so fast! He hadn't said a word since entering the house and she was stunned, speechless; it was another one of his episodes where he had either lost his mind or was enjoying the control he had over her. She was on the floor, his weight bearing down on top of her as he straddled her smaller frame and panic gripped her, Gemma knew she was in trouble. His strong hands were around her throat squeezing the life out of her.

She grabbed at his fingers trying to release them, but it was hopeless he was too strong, and she couldn't breathe. Suddenly aware that she was going to die!

No longer having any air left with his grip squeezing so hard it was impossible to snatch even short breathes, she couldn't fight against his strength, so she stopped struggling and with her last bit of faith and hope in her heart she gradually let her arms and body go limp, staying completely still. This might be her only chance of survival and she just hopes that she can make it, her air is gone but she no longer struggles to breath, not moving or blinking she stared into space indefinitely. Feeling his hands around her throat release and his weight lift off her, he stood looking down. Don't blink, pretend you're dead, don't blink! She wills herself to hold on, she must. This is her only chance to survive.

Mason moved away to the kitchen, thinking the job was done! Can she do this? With his back turned she quickly snatched a tiny breathe of air and somehow scrambled to her feet, adrenaline pumping through her she made a run for it, the ranch-slider the closest way out. Mason had been working on the deck and had left half of it missing, so unsure if she would make it out without him grabbing her, all thoughts whirling in panic, head for the toilet, a locked door!

She needed to get past him, and he must have heard her gasp for air as he turned to face her. His evil fiery eyes held emptiness as he flew at her again, in that instant she grabbed for the kitchen sink desperately feeling around in it, her hand touched a small vegetable knife, grabbing it, thank goodness it was there, gripping its handle so tightly her knuckles hurt as she showed him, gasping for a breathe of air she cried out in the clearest husky voice she could manage.

"Don't come near me!" Shaking and scared. He seemed oblivious of everything, with a vacant look in his eyes like no one was home in his head. Mason wasn't listening or speaking, this was a wild looking, crazed stranger with one thing on his mind (to kill her) and as he again lunged at her throat with both hands, it caused the knife still held in her frozen fingers to pierce through the arm of his white work shirt, shocked as she never intended to hurt him, it seemed to bring him back to reality. He paused to look at the red liquid spreading into the cotton shirt sleeve and those few seconds gave her the opportunity to flee as fast as she could to the safety of the toilet, all the time acutely aware he could grab her from behind at any moment and her life would be over.

Her heart pounded and the blood thumped so loudly in her ears she was sure it would be audible to others. She made it, quickly turning the lock on the door she paused in disbelief, the knife still tightly gripped, throwing it onto the windowsill she hated the sight of it and began shaking uncontrollably, how could she have hurt Mason? She couldn't hurt anything. It's okay! she focused herself to breathe and remember that she's still alive, she fought for her life and now she must calm everything down. Her survival depended on her controlling the shaking and preventing herself from having a heart attack after her body had gone through unbelievable shock and her throat felt raw.

All of her senses enhanced, she listened to see if he would break the door down while she was trapped in a small space, think! She instantly searched for a way out but there was only a tiny window too high up for her to reach. Sounds of heavy breathing and footsteps coming. He's just outside the door!

"You're in trouble now you stupid cow, you're going to prison for that." He swore outside the door; and through the fear and shock she stayed prayerful that he'll leave her to breath; Mason is now only interested in himself. His injury had brought him back from wherever he was. Listening intently to heavy footsteps continuing down the hallway and hearing the back door slam, her ears strained to hear his car start up. Afraid, has he really gone?

She collapsed on top of the toilet seat with total fatigue setting in while she tried to get her mind around what just happened, wondering what she should do next, she couldn't even cry which is what she always does in a crisis, but this was different, she'd never gone through anything like this before. Her husband had strangled her, and she was in shock, unable to cry or even think, she just sat on the plastic toilet seat oblivious of time and contemplated, the sight of the blood on his shirt haunted her and she couldn't stop thinking and visualizing it, wondering if she should go to the police station and tell them what happened. Her heartbeat slowly calmed, and she'd be able to drive the car to the local police station even though it's now after midnight.

Finding Ombre' lying down outside the toilet door waiting for her, only now was she aware of his whimpering, he had seen what went on, praise the Lord that he wasn't hurt, bending over to hug him tightly.

"I'm okay." She whispered reassuringly as she bundled him into the car to keep him safe. After arriving at the police station, the constable looked relieved to see her, and she thought *that's odd*.

"We were coming up to see if you were okay, your husband is here making a complaint." He said.

Feeling shocked, her slow response was. "So even with an arm wound, instead of wanting to have it seen to his first thought is to get me in trouble." She blurted out.

A light bulb appeared to light up the constable's face reflecting that he too understood that wasn't normal behavior. The first reaction should be self-preservation and to get the bleeding stopped and cover the wound.

"Come around the counter, first door on the left and we'll

get a report from you as to what happened." He said authoritively.

He made her a cup of tea and although acting professionally he also appeared sympathetic as she watched his face taking in her appearance, her neck was red and her throat would only let out a squeaky voice, it was late, and she probably looked a mess. He offered to get her medical attention, but she declined and after making a statement as to what happened he said,

"That's self-defense if it happened the way you say. I'll now go and have a chat with your husband, and you can just wait here."

It's very late and she's beyond tired, exhaustion is creeping over her after the evening's events, it tasted like the best cup of tea she had ever had as it soothed her throat.

The constable came rushing through the door with a smile on his face. "You're okay, your husband has made a signed confession to strangling you and you're free to go. We strongly recommend that you have him charged with attempted manslaughter!"

"Oh no! He would lose his job; he drives the public buses." She was horrified at the suggestion.

"You need to make a complaint because this was a serious offence and the next time we see you; you could be in the morgue." He warned, sounding concerned.

She said nothing, shocked, tired, and unable to think.

"Please think about it! The police may decide to prosecute him anyway even without you as he has confessed."

"No, please don't, he's not well." She pleaded for her husband. "I've been trying to tell everyone that he hasn't been right since he fell off the roof. No one takes any notice of me as he appears to be normal, but you need to live with him to see he's not." She shrieked. Looking down at her watch, it's 2.30 in the morning she just wanted to go home.

"Okay, but if you charge him you could ask the judge to get a psychiatric report done. Think about it. You're free to go and we will have a stern word with your husband and give him a warning if you won't help us." He said apprehensively. The police's hands were tied because without her to co-operate the story, the police could do little in court.

She left the police station stunned, sleep deprived and unable to think about anything except getting back to her dog waiting in the car who will also be scared as to what's happening. When she got home Ombre' leapt out of the car, he wanted to go for a lie down, she stretched both arms around his neck and leaned into him for strength.

"Good boy, everything's okay, thank you for being my best friend." She said affectionately, unable to speak anymore she took him into the bedroom with her, not the laundry where he usually slept, putting a chair under the bedroom door handle so Mason couldn't open it. She didn't hear him come home and suspected he slept in the spare room, the next day as they passed in the hallway they didn't speak or have eye contact, they just avoided each other.

This event is now just another one of the domestic violence memories that invade Gemma's thoughts and will always stay with her. As morning light shines through the thin curtains, she dressed in a high neck skivvy and jeans, it's only 8.00am but she already felt ill, fatigued, and hungry. Thankfully, it was Saturday and not her turn to work in the shop. With a head thumping from little sleep and her neck now starting to show purple fingerprints, it was going to be a stressful day. She's relieved to hear Mason's car start up as she's unsure how to act around him, the police have warned Mason, but should she still be afraid? The phone rings, unusual for this time of the day, it's Bridget!

"Hi mum, I'm in Auckland, can I come visit? It won't take me long to drive up to see you."

"How come you're in Auckland?" Gemma queried, feeling so incredibly grateful to hear her voice. An intense *I'm not alone in the world* relief washed over her, unstoppable like a wave. She couldn't believe that her daughter could possibly be here now! Just when she needed her. She always believes that things happens for a reason. While speaking her eyes water, and she's welling up for the first time since it all happened. Needing to let it all out but being brave on the phone trying not to let on to Bridget that anything's wrong, listening to her happy bubbly voice.

"My friend wants me to take her back to Christchurch in my car as she has a little dog to take along with her belongings, so I thought we could catch up at the same time." She was babbling away being her usual cheerful self.

"I would love to see you, can't wait darling, and drive carefully." Hoping she managed to get off the phone quickly without Bridget noticing her voice cracking up.

"Okay, see you this afternoon." She replied.

Later that day Bridget arrived unsuspecting as to the events that had gone on, she planned to spend a night with her mum before driving the long five-hour drive to help her friend to pack up and move to Christchurch.

Her warm greeting hug was the final straw that broke Gemma's resolve to appear like everything was normal, as she reached her arms around her mum Bridget's caring embrace was too much and Gemma's sobs started involuntarily and unable to stop she blurted out the whole terror of the night before, Bridget looked at her horrified as she enquired,

"Are you all right? I have to take you back with me mum!"

"No, I can't leave Mason; he needs me plus the animals and Ombre' do too. I know he won't be able to look after everything. I don't know what to do." She sobbed frantically while trying to pull herself together for Bridget's sake, she continued,

"I'll be okay, don't worry I'll see the doctor and try to get some help for him." She cried while trying to reassure her daughter, being strong and trying not to show the fear and desperation that she was struggling to hide, she didn't want to burden her daughter with problems. Luckily, she has always believed that there is a reason why things happen and now more than ever she questions how she is still alive and wonders at how she got away, only to believe that she's still meant to be on this earth.

The following week she went to the doctor, he took photos of her bruises and said he would talk with Mason next time he came into the surgery, adding that he thought they shouldn't be together. Why would he think that? That's a strange thing for a doctor to say to his patient when he knows that she has stood by Mason through all of his back problems, his comments left her confused as she had always loved and protected Mason.

Bridget kept in touch more often and Gemma tried to put the abuse behind her. Sitting down at the pond, supplying thinking time she pondered on what to do next, and she decided that it came down to forgive and forget or leave him. She always felt that he wasn't well and in her wedding vows she promised in *sickness and in health* so she would battle on, deciding that leaving her husband wasn't the right thing to do. At the same time realizing that she had to stay safe and be prepared to leave if necessary. She hid a sleeping bag in the boot of her car along with a bag of dog biscuits! Convincing herself that the only way to move on with their marriage was to put those memories out of her mind and never ever mention the strangling! Surprisingly, he never did either. Gemma thinks he doesn't remember that he tried to kill her!

It doesn't pay to dwell on the past but the mystery of why he did it and why it happened will always exist for her, and all she can do is make excuses for him.

All the time knowing that the whole experience brought her a very real awareness and empathy for anyone who knows that feeling, *they are going to die at the hands of another*.

CHAPTER 6

"Well, Ombre, the sun is going down behind the hills so it must be time to make our way back up to the house and get some tea." Gemma's furry companion rises from his sleep as soon as he hears her voice and is probably feeling hungry as well after reminiscing and contemplation time.

Reading the local paper she discovered that just down the road they sell goats milk, so she made inquiries and yes, they can take a doe to be serviced on the farm for a small fee. Driving the van down the road in anticipation they found the farm and dropped Gracie off feeling a little apprehensive leaving her, but it was only overnight, she's very docile, a beautiful silver-grey doe that won't cause them any problems. The agreement is for her to honeymoon over night with Wilma's buck, and hopefully she will be pregnant when they collect her tomorrow.

To this day Gemma doesn't know why Mason wanted to have another kid, it was kind of weird and out of the blue that he suggested it, but goats are always so adorable and in past years they did enjoy them together. Sometimes sitting on a clean patch of soft grass and letting the kids climb all over them, their little noses would nuzzle in, and they were always very inquisitive, down in the paddock, it had to have looked pretty crazy sometimes the way they would cuddle and climb over them both.

Maybe Mason missed those times, or he was trying to relive the happy times they once shared before his fall off the roof, but whatever it was they both agreed sheep breeding is just not the same, they don't interact with the sheep, just look after and breed lambs for a bit of pocket money, during the spring lambs frolic around in amongst the trees. Life is fairly good, and everything has settled down, she doesn't fret the small stuff and accepts that Mason is different. Gemma's looking forward to a new kid. The others have long since grown, leaving only six ageing does and Gracie.

Mason finished work before she finished on Friday, and when she arrived home she found him waiting to get into the van to help collect Gracie. It's always Gemma that the animals respond favorable to, probably because she shows caring towards them and would coax them with branches and treats to go wherever she wants, treat them kindly and they follow. Whereas Mason would yell and biff them around the head if he can't get them to behave, he's always a hard man with the animals, other people don't see that side of him, but he's not what he appeared to be. The last few years Gemma had increasingly noticed that mean side of him, she has mostly learnt to accept it because she can't change it, on one occasion the cruelty reducing her to tears, he seemed to enjoy teasing and being able to create fear. There was the time she threatened to phone the animal welfare if he did not stop harassing the animals. These were episodes that the animals remember, and now he had trouble managing them. Mason is not the same since the fall from the roof, or is she just looking for an excuse for his cruelty and controlling ways because she still loves him?

They both climb into the massive van which is so much bigger than the old one that they still hold fond memories of. Gemma is suddenly keen to get Gracie home, she is around three years old and is just as intelligent as a dog would be. Gemma knows she will be anxious to get home to her paddock and re-join the others. It's only a short drive down the road and as she climbs out of the van, Gracie sees her, probable recognized the sound of the van and ran towards the gate, she may have been watching and longing to go home to the paddock she had spent her whole life in.

Mason starts up a conversation with Wilma while Gemma thanks her.

"Let's get her into the van it's time for our tea and we don't want to keep Wilma and her husband from their evening meal together."

After thanking them again they were left wondering if Gracie will be pregnant or not, she jumps into the van and Mason ties her rope to the metal rail at the back of the driver's seat, suddenly he starts to stumble,

"Oh, are you okay?" Gemma cries out, he starts to fall, she grabs his arm and helps lower him to the floor, finding the dead weight impossible to support.

"I can't stand up!" He said.

"Why, what's wrong?" She asked, it's reassuring that he's talking, and she instantly thought it must be to do with his back issues from the past, talking quietly from the floor of the van he tells her he has the worst headache you could possibly imagine, and he cannot stand up! But he doesn't sound panicked, actually surprisingly calm.

Becoming more concerned Gemma shouts out to Wilma, "Get an ambulance!"

As they waited for it to arrive Mason lay on the floor of the van in the recovery position and she began to feel a little stunned, bewildered as to what's actually happening! She has never phoned for an ambulance before. Mason asked her to remove his gumboots.

"Why?" she asked. Not really understanding that he's going in the ambulance and still thinking that everything will be okay, because they are just ordinary people going about every day.

"Because they will be dirty in the ambulance after walking across the paddock." Came the reply that jolted her back to reality.

Needless to say, the ambulance seemed to take an eternity but in actual fact arrived, and Mason settled in around 20 minutes before setting off for Kaitaia Hospital. It all seemed confusing because he was coherent and thinking more clearly than she was, although he seemed too calm, did he know something she didn't?

Snapping back to the present she's aware that she needed to focus and deal with the situation whatever that may be. Driving the van home wasn't an option as it was too big and she couldn't reach the pedals, it needed to be taken home so she could fetch her little car to go to the hospital. Wilma's very kind husband steps forward to drive the van, Gracie and her home, Gemma is dazed as to what's happening and struggling to comprehend the events of the evening, arriving home she put Gracie safely in her paddock, while in panic she rushed around in a frenzy.

Forcing herself to think what Mason would need in hospital and what she should be doing. Cellphone, money, phone numbers, feed Ombre' before she goes as no one has eaten, it's a cold June evening and she has no idea what's happened, it's crazy out of control.

Oh, I hope Mason's okay, why is this happening to us. Hums over in her mind like a lawn mower constantly rotating.

Driving the car out of the garage she dropped Wilma's husband, (whose name has flown out of her head), back to his house before starting to drive to Kaitaia hospital. She was so appreciative of her familiar car, she knew the vehicle off by heart and didn't have to think, trying to focus on the road amidst desperate feelings of uncontrollable panic (breath) she reminded herself as she drove through streets she never usually traveled on. Then a detour to take, while work is being done on a bridge, she didn't need that right now while in a hurry to get to Mason, can she find parking? She didn't want to pay for parking as their funds will again be low with him getting sick, yes! This space will be okay as the cancer clinic is closed at night; she won't get towed away. She couldn't cope with that as she just needed to be at her husband's side. The ambulance should already be there, she desperately longs to be with him.

Hurrying into the A&E department, quite disheveled, frantic, the nurse quietly and efficiently leads her to another room and tells her to ring family.

"What!" She shrieked, "Let me see my husband." She pleaded with her.

The tears haven't had time to appear because she's running

on adrenalin, but they are now glassing over her eyes as she takes in all the white walls and sterile look everywhere around her forcing this to be a reality as the antiseptic smells burn her nostrils.

The close bond their souls have she senses that he needs her to hold his hand as she battles to convince the staff to let her. Wilma arrives, that's so good! And she helps Gemma to ring Peter as now she's too frantic to function and he will contact Dwayne as the boys have never given her a contact number for Dwayne, too close to his mum and always following her wishes might mean he misses the chance to say goodbye to his father if they can't contact him.

Inconsolable waves of emotion wash over her as she demands to see Mason and pushes her way through to catch a quick glimpse of his stretcher and the back of his head as the power drill makes an awful screeching noise and a small hole is drilled into her husband's skull, a tube is pushed in, blood spurts out, stunned speechless unable to make any sound at all and feeling like she must sit down. People are pulling her away, but Wilma Is there, Gemma is aware of her gently gripping her arm, quietly leading her into a small room.

She's talking kindly to her; Gemma has no understanding of what she is saying at this time, it's just kind words. In a small room with chairs someone hands her a brown paper bag and she recollects hearing a voice somewhere in the fog saying,

"These are your husband's belongings!"

What? She is dumb founded and lost all presence, frantic and fast losing grip on her composure, this is not real it can't be! Two ordinary people and things like this don't happen to them! This man's wife felt panic as her hand reached automatically to take hold of a brown paper bag offered to her, she fought back the thought that her husband has died! All the time knowing inside her that it can't be true she still feels him in her heart.

Turning to Wilma for help, she could hear her familiar sounding voice, but without knowing it was her speaking she looked into Wilma's eyes and asked her.

"How can they give me Mason's belongings like that?"

Looking down at a brown paper bag which reads 'Patients Belongings', a terrible thought flooded though her head that this is all there is! Just a brown paper bag full of a few belongings! Wilma is quick to reassure her that it's just routine to keep his things safe and that Mason is being looked after, the shock recedes a little, she supposed being in new territory and quite shocked, it's all new to her. They were shown to a family room to await the sons' arrival.

Sitting at a long wooden table surrounded by many polished chairs, Gemma couldn't take anything in, not wanting to, it all became a blur as she wanted to deny it was really happening, just as Mason's sons arrive with two of his grandchildren. They are seated and Peter and Dwayne say the obligatory "Hi" to Wilma and Gemma, no hugs, or signs of affection for their stepmother even though she is obviously distraught.

Gemma's face tear stained she is only just managing to hold it together for the grandchildren's sake, they continue to be very indifferent toward her, anyone watching would think that she was a complete stranger to them. It was beyond her understanding how people can be so cold, so cruel. Mason and Gemma had a wonderful life on the land, but she was struggling with the fact that they have only been together for ten years, it's not enough, *'it's not long enough'* keeps running through her head over and over. Getting married out of love for each other and it wasn't up to his sons to tell him who he could spend his life with. She was full of mixed emotions, she wanted him back home with her, fear, and anger that they hadn't had enough time together without his son's interference. It's not fair!

While everyone is waiting to hear from a doctor, a nurse guides her to be beside Mason in intensive care. He had a nurse with him continually watching every vital sign, she was warned before going in there about him having a lot of tubes and she nodded acceptance, but she wasn't prepared. Confronted with the mind-boggling sight of tubes and apparatus, drains etc. it is more difficult to see when it's someone you love. She tried to be strong for her husband and bent down to whisper in his ear.

"I love you and I'll look after you no matter what, please get better, you can beat this." One at a time they each visit with him alone as there are so many machines keeping him alive that he has little room around his bed, with a nurse constantly monitoring him. Then they return to the family room to wait for the neurosurgeon to explain what has happened.

Her soul mate, her darling Mason has had a subarachnoid hemorrhage, which is a bleed caused by a brain aneurysm, (like a massive stroke) that is what the headache was when they were collecting Gracie, a brain bleed when he collapsed and another one on arrival at the hospital, (two brain hemorrhages) a second stroke, Gemma's tears wouldn't stop and her heart was breaking as the neurosurgeon carefully and slowly explained and she spluttered in an attempt to get out questions, her chest hurt as it heaved with uncontrollable sobs and she gasped for air, desperately gripping the edge of the hard table in an attempt to gain some strength from the solid wood, nothing could stem the flow of tears but it was comforting to know at least he was happy as they collected Gracie.

The internal pain was something she had never felt before and hoped she never would again. It's an actual physical and emotional struggle as she attempted to reassure his sons their dad was enjoying life when this devastating thing happened, she understood the severity of what was being said, and wondered how anyone could survive this? She wanted to set their minds at ease that she would always stand by Mason to help in his recovery!

The family all sat staring accusingly at her, listening without speaking and without compassion and she was grateful to Wilma as she took over and supported her, she tried to reassure them.

"Your dad was happy, chatting and everything was fine when

it happened." She said and explained they got help at once.

Dwayne was quick to snap back at her. "Who are you?" He snarled.

Wilma explained that they were at her house when Mason got sick. There is a long silence and Gemma is so grateful for Wilma's support and comfort as she struggles to cope, not needing family taking their frustrations out on her. They took turns to visit Mason once more after the doctor left, and when Andrew (the eldest grandson) returned from seeing his granddad in the intensive care unit at only 20 years old he couldn't contain his emotions, he began to cry in the corridor. It's an upsetting and shocking sight for anyone to deal with and Gemma rushed to him, reached out and put her arms around him, grateful that he obviously loved Mason as much as she did, she'll always be fond of Andrew for that moment they shared over his granddad, love for Mason gave them an unspoken bond that they probably both felt. While hugging him she whispered into his ear that she would look after his granddad and get him well again.

"It'll take time, but he will get better, you'll see!" She said to him quietly so the others couldn't hear her, Gemma wasn't in the mood for their snide remarks but her determination to help Mason was empowering her. They picked up their cell phones and coats prepared to go home then the surgeon arrived to carefully explain what happens next.

"If Mr. Brownlie makes it through the night and we can get him stabilized, tomorrow morning we will operate to clip the aneurysm and stop the bleeding in his brain." Nothing more is said, so they said goodbye and left.

Before Wilma got ready to go she took Gemma aside and quietly spoke with her, she expressed how dislikeable she found the sons to be and that the only person she thought anything of was Andrew. She explained how she believed Mason could still hear Gemma in his inner self and she nodded in agreement, Gemma felt him in her heart, and she knew he was still alive somewhere in that body, trapped by a brain that wasn't working.

Even when not in the same room with Mason, and he has no obvious consciousness she somehow felt his presence, she was experiencing another sense now that people must have when you love each other but one of you is unable to contact the other, a strange new level of understanding and togetherness that she'd not experienced before. Is this what is meant when people talk about two souls being connected? She couldn't bring herself to leave the hospital and stayed watchful vigil for Mason all night! It was a life changing event how could she go home and forget Mason's struggle.

It felt so important that they are still in close proximity to each other to give each other strength and so she stretched out on the waiting room seats in anticipation that he might wakeup and need her, she wished he'd just wake up and talk to her again. The staff knew to call her if there was any change, convincing herself that somehow being nearby will help him is all she can do for him now! She couldn't leave not even for a comfy bed or food, it felt like her insides were melting and running away onto the floor like an ice cube placed on a hot element as she clung to hope and everything was out of control, a totally unbearable pain engulfed her along with the thought that this could be his last night, she was going nowhere.

CHAPTER 7

The frantic desire to be closer to him was totally absorbing her mind and body, nurses told her that she must stay in the waiting room. Surely holding his hand and giving him some comfort would help, not hinder. Her only comfort in that lonely waiting room was in her thoughts, prayers, and positive attitude unsure what she could hope for. Was it selfish of her to want him to survive when he could be a vegetable, she didn't want that for him, but how would she stand the pain of losing him? Her best friend, yearning to talk to him she quietly whispered to him and to our Lord with all her heart and soul.

'Thank you for the happy times we have had together, I know that there's a plan for us and it's not for us to understand or decide our path, I trust that whatever is right for him will happen, but please also know that I'll look after Mason and help get him well again, please I plead, at 62yrs old he still needs to retire, if only he can come back to me and have another ten years? I will take on all the problems of everyday life, bills etc. for him to have a few years of no work, no worries before he dies.' The tears rolled down her cheeks as she spluttered on the words and wondered at how unsurprised he was when he fell, did he know he was sick?

She made her promise, an unselfish act of kindness and love in the hope that he would know and fight to survive. Will he still be alive in the morning? She felt lost and completely alone without him and wished she had Ombre' to cuddle, trying to think of what she needed to do. She worried in case her car got towed away during the night and about Ombre', he would wonder where they were. Sleeping would be impossible.

The gnawing ache and rumbling in her stomach reminded her that she hasn't eaten anything since lunch time at work, (which seems a million years ago) so much has happened, looking down at her watch it reads 10.00pm. Oh, what she would give to be back at school instead of here in the hospital. People are going about their business having tea with their families and here the two of them are, just ordinary people going through extraordinary trauma, nothing will ever be the same as it was for Mason and Gemma.

Visitors have gone and the hospital has locked the doors that surround the I.C.U. (Intensive Care Unit). This is unknown territory, and she doesn't know her way around, she finds a confectionary vending machine in the corner of the room, frantically searching in her handbag she felt some lose coins rolling around in the bottom of the torn lining it's only enough money for a muesli bar out of the machine.

Mason and she had their last cup of tea together about six hours ago so she would love to have another one right now, she munched slowly on the muesli bar to make it last as long as possible and although it may be healthy it only serves to make her thirst worse. Mason's discomfort had little relevance as her mind kept replaying the devastating events of the evening and she struggled to make some sense of it.

How could her husband be facing brain surgery? they both left for work that morning just like any other Friday, and yet here she sat alone in the dimly lit hospital waiting room, a caring nurse had brought her a pillow and she's thankful that the room is quite warm, but lying on an unforgiving leather sofa without a blanket for comfort of course sleep alludes her, Gemma's mind is about to explode with too many negative thoughts of dread, the fear of what tomorrow might bring and she battled with her subconscious not to think any more because it's all fearful, she needed to have a blank mind! She must be strong and not get sick, or else what use will she be to Mason when he comes home?

The night is spent nervously clutching her handbag in a clinical hospital environment, she's grateful that at least it is a warm night, thank goodness!

Without a blanket to cover her, strange hospital creaks and

unfamiliar noises, swing doors banging closed after some stranger has entered it's too frightening and she felt insecure, a lonely sick feeling in her stomach won't subside but she convinces herself that it's hunger and thirst, telling her subconscious to get a grip it won't kill her to go without! This must have been the longest night ever, she kept straining her eyes to look at her watch through a dimly lit room, but only an hour has passed. Hour by hour, bit by bit the dawn starts to fill the waiting room, as she continues to worry.

She anxiously waits to see people unlock the doors with the clicks and clangs increasing, he must have made it through the night! My darling husband, we're so used to it being the two of us, always just the two of us, can she dare to believe it will continue to be that way? It's morning and they're not together, she longs to feel his arms around her and to snuggle into his chest like every other morning, but today all she can do is reassure him that she is here, don't worry everything will be alright.

Looking out of the window with sore reddened eyes it's a relief to see her small reliable car still parked outside, but she knows it will need to be moved soon, before the cancer clinic opens and patients want to use the parking space that she parked in. Finding it difficult to leave the waiting room, there is that irrational fear holding her back that if she dashed out to the car it might be the wrong moment to go. Everything can change in a moment or a last breath. Fear and hope both have a hold over her right now!

Eventually after what seems an eternity a doctor appears (his name went through one ear and out the other as she grappled to focus on what he had to tell her, she cannot compute any information now, all she heard was a garbled noise as her health suffered and her heart pounds. She was able to pick out the things she wanted to hear as the neurosurgeon informed her that Mason had made it through the night and all his vital signs are good enough for surgery, they will attempt to put a small titanium clip (similar to a paperclip) around the leaking aneurysm this cruel June morning 2007, this is hoped to stop anymore bleeding into his already damaged brain.

A day that will be remembered for the rest of her life. Everything is going to be okay, she felt elated even while reminding herself that he's going through brain surgery, the risks are very high!

Walking along the silent sterile corridor grateful that her rubber soled sneakers don't make any obvious noise as she visited him before he went into have major brain surgery, looking at him lying in the hospital bed he didn't appear to be alive, his skin was too pale and he was unaware of her presence, but he's still here on this earth with machines doing everything for him, he made it through the first step he will get past this terrible thing that has happened, he is alive! After giving him a kiss and holding his hand she murmured into his ear that everything would be okay before she soberly returned to the waiting room where she had spent the most terrible night of her life. Dwayne & Peter had arrived, and she gave them the update and reassurance that their dad is okay.

Gemma is physically and emotionally exhausted, hungry, alone, and distraught, still in her clothes from 24 hours ago when she had left for work Friday morning, what seems a long time ago now, was only yesterday. She was desperately hoping that they may have brought some coffee or food with them, they knew she intended spending last night at the hospital on a sofa while they were at home with loved ones enjoying family dinner, but of course it's too much to expect of them! That would require some kindness and recognition of how devoted she was to their dad.

So much has happened. Feeling a little lightheaded she is aware that she needs to do something for herself as the stress has all been too much. Her mind hadn't stopped going over and over the events of the day before and what if's, just like a merry go round.

Mason is wheeled into the operating theatre and will be in there for some time.

So, Gemma reasons it would be the best time for her to go home, possibly the only chance for a while to have a shower and eat before he needs her to be back in the unit. She tried to convince herself that he's not going to have any ill effects from the hemorrhages because it doesn't bear thinking about, she continued to be positive that he will make it through the surgery when she's back clean and well to help him with his recovery. Reluctantly saying farewells to the boys, sullen and standing in the corner of the room, she checked with them that they would stay there in case anything happened.

"Please ring my mobile if anything changes!" She begged them and got a begrudging grunt in reply. Seconds pass as she refused to move until she received a proper assurance.

"Okay!" Peter loudly snapped back.

As they stared down their noses at her disheveled state, she exchanged cell phone numbers before getting into the lift, she felt anxious that they won't phone her, she didn't have any choice but to trust them. She must stay well to be able to help her husband, the center of her world and the part that is missing right now.

After collecting her little white Honda Civic from its safe parking space it's such a relief there's no ticket on it, trying to push to the back of her mind everything that has happened, practicalities start to make themselves felt now as she feels concern changing into panic and the insecurity with everything changing so suddenly overnight and her now being the only income earner a reality.

Don't you even dare to think about money at a time like this, she firmly reprimanded herself for the thought, reality at the same time having a heightened sense of survival, how to pay the bills, a million thoughts that weren't there before, have come to the surface now that she has left Mason in the surgeons hands, and has time to think, she only works part- time and how will she manage the lifestyle block with all the animals on her own?

Upon leaving the Kaitaia hospital grounds and approaching the

West Coast highway she is fully aware that she's physically and emotionally not up to par and so continually watches the speedometer so that while her mind is racing through everything that has happened, and the unknown that could happen, she doesn't go over the speed limit.

Conscious of wanting to return to be near Mason and feeling the ache of missing him, she can't bear to leave him there on his own in that place. Gemma hasn't spent much time in hospitals over the years, she has been very lucky as her two kids never even broke a bone when growing up and never went to hospital for any illnesses. She can't seem to stop the intense longing to have Mason home with her.

She finds keeping control of all the emotions while driving is very difficult and she struggles to concentrate as her mind continues to go over what has happened, disbelief and fatigue threatening to take control.

Approaching the lonely little letter box standing at the side of the driveway she remembers that they bought that together because it was yellow, such a happy sunshine color and it felt reassuring as she turned into their driveway, the familiar crunching of lose metal under the tires sounded lovely after everything that had happened, and there's her reliable little friend Ombre' sitting on the back porch, wishfully keeping watch.

He hasn't been forgotten as he waits for news of what has held his owner up and why they didn't return home last night.

He must wonder why he had to spend all night sleeping outside away from his usual warm bed in his familiar laundry, his routine has been changed too, he loves Mason, and Gemma wonders if they will ever see each other again!

Rushing over to him she suddenly felt unbelievably shattered emotionally and physically. Unable to do anything she can't even make it to unlock the door and let them into the house, she can no longer stand and seeks relief by sitting down on the closest cold concrete step, wrapping her arms around his soft neck, she feels the cold tears well up and overflow as they start to run down her pale checks. At last she can cry after being brave holding off all night and just concentrated on driving home to be back to that familiar security, no one is around, and the tears won't stop flowing, at home with her dog, her body raked by uncontrolled sobbing, she clings to Ombre' and he started to lick her tears away when they dropped onto her hands. She sat holding him, inconsolable as he kept trying to soothe her with his kisses and wet tongue slurping all over her hands, she didn't have the willpower to stop him. So what if she gets a few germs anyway, what does it matter her husband is in hospital having brain surgery, he could be dying!

Who cares about the slobber on her hands? Everything seems unimportant now, the work that needs to be done on the house and the weeds she sat looking at in the garden just don't matter anymore, the tears continued to fall, and she wants Mason home, that's all that's important.

The elusive time spent as she relished the release of emotions in the comfort of her home, oblivious to how long she sat there only to be brought back to reality as the uncomfortable hard concrete surface forced her brain to acknowledge her sore bottom, so it probably wasn't long before she got up off that cold step. Finally making her way inside their home she tracked down some clean blue jeans, a top to pull on and a warm jumper. Still unable to function properly, but finally aware of the cool winter chill around her after the warm hospital waiting room, her skin feels icy cold to touch and she is also cold and numb on the inside, full of dread and fear within her soul.

Feeding Ombre' is the next thing she must do, telling herself that she needs to do one thing at a time, just keep moving and do the most urgent thing first, people are depending on her, she has to keep going and be braver than she ever has been before. The warm shower is welcoming as she stands letting the water run down her face, feeling the warm wetness on her skin awakening her senses to being here, feeling something after all the shock. Finding herself doing stuff without really being there emotionally as she watched her hands and feet moving, going through the motions but detached somehow like this body doesn't belong to her, she feels numb.

Maybe the water will wash everything that's wrong down the plug hole and life will have some sense of normality again. She decides that her wet hair should be tied up, so she can appear tidy back in the Intensive care unit where she can hold Mason's hand and lean over him to kiss his lips without hair falling onto the multitude of tubes that he will still have after surgery. Gemma's heart leaps in her chest as she dries herself and automatically dresses without any thought of what she is doing or what she should do next. Suddenly she is brought back to now with the awareness that she has a thumping headache.

Maybe a calming cup of tea, that's what people give you she decides, and toast would help ease her panic, breakfast is what she needs to help her to think straight while she listens out for any phone call from the hospital, she inwardly knows that the sons won't inform her if Mason needs her, but she would hope that the hospital would ring her cell phone, it's very quiet so he must still be okay. Her mind is all over the place as she rushes around to prepare some carrot sticks and celery, throwing them into a plastic bag to store in her handbag for later as she doesn't want to be caught hungry again and now fully aware that she won't be wanting to leave her darling Mason on his own once they're together again, she just wants to cling on to him like she hopes he is clinging on to life.

Breathe! And she takes a Panadol out of the cupboard for her headache, trying to face one thing at a time, Oh! She should phone Bridget and tell her everything that has happened while she can use the landline. It's so difficult to phone from the hospital with cell phones turned off around the many machines in I.C.U.

"Do you want me to come up to Auckland mum?" She asks.

"No! It's okay." Even though she did need her, Gemma knew that it's a long way from Christchurch and what if he dies? So being as brave as she can and trying to sound very practical, she explained. "You may have to come up later if he doesn't make it!"

The tears threaten to overtake her once more, her chest is full of pain as if a heavy block of concrete had fallen on it and weighing down on her lungs preventing life giving oxygen from helping her to breathe, the stress is huge. She managed to end the conversation without crying and hopefully she pulled it off. She didn't want sympathy she wanted her life back to normal.

There is a new reality in life now, they have never wasted money but she's acutely aware that times will now be even more financially stretched. It's Saturday but she doesn't need to phone her shop employer today as she works every other weekend and this is her Saturday off, thank goodness for that, forcing herself to stop and think about why she is wondering around aimlessly in a fog and what she needs to be doing, wake up. Just check animals and head back to the hospital.

What needs to be done? "I hope I have the emotional strength that I need to stay well so I can cope with all that's happening to us, and I pray that Mason's in surgery right now and they make him well again." She spoke out loud in desperation to Ombre' as he follows her around the house and listens to her.

Be positive, it'll be okay! They will get through this, she removes Ombre's bed from the laundry and puts it out on the back porch just in case the unknown strikes again, she gave him a big hug preparing him for what comes next, she doesn't know when she'll be back.

"I'll be back soon, good boy." She tells him lovingly, trying to sound very factual. This is affecting him too and dogs can sense when something is wrong, especially when his routine has changed.

Somehow, she arrives safely back at the entrance to Kaitaia Hospital with her cell phone on the car seat beside her, no calls! As she pulls into the hospital driveway, she can't spare time or energy searching for parking, so she heads straight for the car park building aware that they are not cheap, but she'll have to work that expense out later. Her priority is getting back to the ICU, time could be of the essence now and she's anxious to return and see if he's out of surgery.

Life now consists of having to take care, trying to focus on what needs to be done first and constantly reminding herself *don't fret the small stuff*.

On arrival at the neurological unit Dwayne and Peter are talking with serious looks on their faces, they go silent as she approaches, and this instils more fear in her.

"What has happened?" She enquires anxiously and they slowly, reluctantly look up and explain that the surgeon had come out and talked with them. "What did he say, how did everything go?" She pressed them for information.

"Nothing." Was Dwayne's reply. How can someone have brain surgery and the doctor say nothing? After her constant staring at them without answering, they reluctantly added,

"Mason is okay, and we can see him soon." Said Peter. They call their dad by his Christian name. But there is that look on their faces that shall remain etched in her memory forever, they chose to hide something they had been told, it was clear for all to see written on their faces.

CHAPTER 8

She can only imagine that maybe the doctor had foreseen some brain damage, and they were lying to her and could never be trusted. Anger burns within her as she's the one who looks after their dad, the one that he lives with and possibly his future caregiver. It's not doing her or Mason any favors to withhold information coming from the surgeon.

Back in ICU with Mason, her husband's alive and there's a nurse assigned to him, she hovers by his side continually monitoring vital signs. There is only one seat in this small machine-driven space at the end of the hospital bed, so she carefully squeezes her way towards that and sits down, feeling dreadfully uncomfortable and wondering what to do now? It's difficult to talk to Mason in this strange sterile environment with the noise of staff going about their business. She attempts to stay out of the way in a very tight space with beeping machines, as she gets her bearings and her head around this critical situation, the nurse speaks quietly to her.

"It's okay to be at the side of the bed if you want." She's kind but looks awkward as to what to say, she probably has mixed feeling about the amount of trauma a person should have to endure, and whether they should be saved at all, as she would have seen a lot of distressing things in ICU. Shuffling the few steps to the bedside Gemma's overcome and speechless, what can she say to Mason? His head has been half shaved with a blood red, raw, wound stitched from one ear that travels across his head and down the other side, it's horrific, as she stands holding his hand, she's emotional and left fighting back the tears. "Now, the struggle to bring you back to us begins my darling."

The nurse tells him where he is, asks what his name is over and over again, constantly reminding him where he is, trying to drum it into his mind, Gemma didn't understand this repetition at first. Then Mason responded and her heart jumped with pride, but he didn't know where he was, little did Gemma know but this would continue for days to come where day after day Mason couldn't grasp the facts being told to him.

It's a huge relief that he can even say, yes or no, but it's so distressing that he continues to be confused about where, who, and what place this is? There's nothing Gemma can do, and she is so grateful for the doctors getting her husband to this stage.

Helplessly watching on, unable to fix this. Watching and rubbing his hand she knows he's still here in body, surviving although still critical, she continues to have hope convincing herself that the staff wouldn't be doing all this if there wasn't any hope of a good recovery. She continues to thank staff for everything they have done to help them, the ambulance and Wilma being there with her was so commendable, simply the most unbelievable of all is that Mason is still alive!

Now that she's back at the ICU with him, the two boys said goodbye and went off to enjoy their day. It seems that even at deaths door her husband isn't important enough to anyone else, it's hard for Gemma to understand. Just the two of them together, sitting beside him in silence as the world keeps going around, there she is holding Masons hand while his brain tries to heal, several clear plastic tubes allow red blood to drain out of the tiny holes left in his head after surgery, while another clear plastic hose is dripping blood into his arm and fluids get pumped into the needle taped to his main artery on the side of his bruised neck. It's ghastly and she's grateful that he can't see what she can, her insides cry out, why did this happen to him?

Mason lies motionless looking pale but peacefully unaware of anything going on, at least that is probably a blessing that he doesn't know the trauma his body has been through, and the scars he now has, appearing to be a different person, physically present in front of her, but really not present at all, he's like a stranger sleeping.

Her heart has been wrenched out of her with unease as the pain is so real looking on, longing to hear him speak, her body, heart, and soul ache for that, just to hear his voice!

They were just ordinary people like all the others outside the hospital, people going about their day, family time together, she's feeling lost!

What will happen next, she's filled with the fear of losing her precious husband, of having to spend a day without him being in her life, her gut aches with love and concern looking down at the hospital bed. His eyes are closed, and a lump formed in her throat as she fought to gain control of her emotions. Sometimes when it's just the two of them, when the nurses go for a short break, no one is here talking and Gemma doesn't have to be strong, her mind wonders and memories flow. No one ever plans for this sort of thing to happen, it's not what you expect in life, two people like them, and she wonders how they will get over this terrible time. What could be worse than your husband having brain surgery? Isn't it something that only happens in movies? Continually telling herself over and over in her mind reinforcing that it is real, this is really happening! But she struggles to be mindful of it.

At the end of that first Saturday watching and contemplating while having munched on cheap carrot and celery to keep the pangs of hunger away, she knew that she needed her bed, she needed her dog and some solace at home. The noises and antiseptic smells of the hospital were nauseating, and she looked as bad as she felt. Mason's kind nurse took pity on her and offered to bring her a cup of tea, she needed stimulation after drinking bottled water all day, and she hadn't wanted to leave the bedside to get anything at the café.

In one way it was probably a good thing for her health that the nurse told her that all visitors had to leave at 9.00pm because even though dizziness was starting to engulf Gemma every time she stood up, she couldn't bring herself to leave his bedside without being made to by the staff. A week later and she's still keeping vigil in I.C.U. it was emotionally draining, frantic and scary when she's told visiting hours are over.

Arriving home on the cold dismal dark nights, the still air wrapping itself around her and deep inside her heart and soul a painful despair and helplessness looks to control as she continues to settle Ombre' before collapsing into bed, now becoming aware of her own frailty and in need of sleep. The nights are restless and difficult with patches of sleep derived from exhaustion while keeping one ear open all night wondering if the hospital would phone.

Sunday morning arrives and there's a chill, not only through her entire body but also the weather is wet and windy. Impatient and anxious to continue to the hospital is all she can think of as soon as she wakes, it will take at least an hour and a half, so she leaves at 7.30am after a nice hot cup of tea and forcing down a slice of vegemite toast, simply because she knows she needs to eat.

The animals are all checked, chickens and dog fed, Gemma packed a bag of wool and knitting needles for today and has decided to start knitting Mason a hat and scarf to hide the scars and keep him warm when he comes home. Arriving at the hospital before they unlock the double doors to I.C.U. again she has to calm herself and wait before being allowed in to see him, he still looked the same as last night as she bent to kiss his pale cold lips before enquiring with the nurse.

"How's he doing?"

"No change, but he slept okay." She said smiling at her.

It's a very long Sunday so she's glad of the knitting for something to do as Mason can't hold a conversation or even open his eyes today. He still doesn't know what is going on or where he is. Anyway, she has a pressing concern on her mind about their finances now, so she is reluctantly forced to steal some precious time tomorrow (Monday) to visit 'Work and

Income' to find out what financial help is available to them.

Come 9.00 pm she packs up and reluctantly says goodnight to Mason, picking up his hand she gave it a squeeze, desperately hoping that maybe he would respond with a movement of some kind.

"Darling, it's Gemma, your wife. I can't come tomorrow as I need to do some catching up with the animals at home, phoning and letting people know you are here in hospital, and I have to see your work about your sick pay. I have an appointment to see about paying the mortgage. You rest and get better, and I'll see you on Tuesday. Everything is okay, I love you." There is no response as she plops a kiss on his cheek.

Sitting knitting by his side all day gave her the opportunity to reflect on the tormented years they've endured, the stress his sons put them under, it was not fair separating them all the time.

There's so much she wants to say to Mason, she understands how hard it must have been for him to be with family when he knew she was at home alone, and he was constantly pulled between commitment to them and his love for Gemma, with his grandchildren being used as emotional blackmail. Even though she never complained and always encouraged him to spend time with them, she knew the ex-wife was often invited as Dwayne continued to push the two together.

She remembers Mason talked to her about him feeling guilty that his ex. hadn't formed any successful relationships since their divorce, and also that she even threatened suicide as a last resort if he didn't return to her, so many memories flood her mind while she is powerlessly looking on.

How uncomfortable they made his life. No one should have to put up with that kind of manipulation and huge pressure, it's no wonder his brain exploded. She can't help but blame the boys for that constant relentless torment, and she shall always loathe them for creating that huge amount of stress in Mason's life. Gemma won't waste her life on them, as she sits alone watching her husband struggling to survive it has brought it home to her, she believes after that amount of stress, this aneurism was their fault.

It's only 9.00pm as another day finishes but already bitterly cold and dark outside for her long drive home, so reluctantly with a wary mind and fatigued body she is told to leave again and as her lips touch his cold lifeless cheek, her heart longs for him to kiss her back, she whispers.

"Get well darling, I'll see you soon, have a good sleep."

She does know going home to get some rest is the right thing to do, but she's afraid to leave his side, subconsciously aware that it will be a long road out of this one, and she must stay well for him.

A quite loneliness cradles her as she makes her way out of the Intensive Care Unit and getting out of the confines of the hospital lift, she'll never know why, maybe the blank emotionally exhausted look on her face prompted the stranger to ask if she was visiting someone.

"Yes." She explained her husband had a brain aneurism.

"Don't worry." In a concerned but not a very convincing tone, "My friend had one and he copes okay he even goes to work now."

Oh, is this man an angel or what? It is wise to remember that a few words of kindness can mean so much and costs nothing to give. As she proceeds to collect her car from the parking building she has gained a little bit of hope and reassurance because of his kindness, paying the all-day parking cost of nine dollars to the machine and making the long trek home her mind returns to the day and the time spent sitting with Mason, her eyes start to fill with tears, and she tries to blink them away.

Facing another night at home alone without her other half, exhaustion and a small drink of wine helps her get to sleep, emotionally and physically shattered it feels like she has just finished running a marathon, her legs are heavy, and she has no energy to even think, that will have to wait until tomorrow.

What about Mason's job? Monday morning she contacts the bus company he drives for, holding back the tears is extremely difficult under extreme pressure, she doesn't know who to talk to, and it doesn't feel like her place to interfere or speak on Mason's behalf. They need to know what has happened and that he won't be able to work for a while, finding out how much sickness and holiday pay they can help with is also a major now that their main income has just stopped unexpectedly, there is so much to do while her mind and body are numb. All of it is difficult to face, plus she's finding it challenging to talk to people without getting upset.

It's a morning for necessary phone calls, the next being to her eldest brother Stanley in Australia who she can talk honestly to and tell him that Mason might not make it and that he's in a critical condition. She has to prepare him in case he needs to come to New Zealand because if something happens, she's afraid she will fall to pieces, and may need help with the funeral. The possibilities that she is now confronted with are horrific, just saying these things out loud is debilitating and with a shaky voice and weak body she continues, she has to face reality even though she's hoping and praying for their lives to get back to normal.

Gemma is trying to take one day at a time and be very practical about everything, by just running on automatic and not have any feelings that will cloud her judgement. There is a fear that she might breakdown talking to people on the phone, she can't afford to fall apart because Mason needs her to take charge, she must be brave. More terrible things to come, while speaking with Stanley she finds out that he has a faulty kidney and travelling will be out of the question for a while. He will phone her younger brother Len who lives in New Zealand to save Gemma from having to explain the situation on the phone to him. Replacing the receiver, she is full of despair as Stanley is unwell, there's no escaping this and she is accepting of lives changing overnight so unexpectedly, as she continues to believe everything happens for a reason.

CHAPTER 9

It's not for us to understand the ways of the world, things just happen. Perhaps the way Mason had been so aggressive towards her and the animals during the last year was a sign of pressure in his brain. There were many times when she had to seek medical attention for domestic violence and they were recorded in her medical file which on reflection, the doctor visits and the number of police callouts increased as days got closer to the aneurysm bursting. If only someone had known the aneurysm was ballooning up, perhaps it could have been clipped before it hemorrhaged, although Mason was more likely to want to ignore it.

Had he known and disclosed it to her they would have argued about him having brain surgery, the outcome may have been the same, she's just glad she was around when it hemorrhaged because if he didn't get to the hospital in the critical time he would have most certainly died. Somehow another terrible week has ended, and he's moved to the High Dependency Unit, Mason can now sit up. At first, she was a little apprehensive that her husband was moving in with other patients, concerned that maybe he wouldn't get the attention he's receiving now, but its progress even if it feels threatening.

So now it's down to Mason, it has been explained that he runs the risk of having a stroke, for another 21 days, (where the brain could go into a vasospasm or get a blood clot causing a stroke). So, she's mentally and emotionally under stress as she starts the long countdown for Mason to make it through the next 21 days, he's not out of the woods by a long way. Gemma pleads with the doctors to watch that Mason doesn't get a clot, just to get this far has been traumatic and she doesn't think she could stand anything else going wrong. Watching him in the unit she accepts that it was pleasant for him to be socializing, he can sit up and he's on the road to recovery, they were told that when he learns to eat again the feeding tube would be removed. Every night searching for sleep, she has to stay strong and hold everything together.

In the morning on entering the unit a bombshell hits.

"Excuse me, but only family are allowed to visit." The nurse states.

Gemma can see Dwayne sitting by Mason's bed smirking as the nurse glared at her.

"Yes, we have been together for 10 years."

"Are you sure?" She looked at Gemma very suspiciously as she continued to explain, "Mr. Brownlie's son Dwayne has requested that you don't have access to visit, he wants me to ban you."

Totally stunned and appalled, the words flowed. "We've been married for nine years!" Adding in surprise, "I'm his wife!"

"Just wait here and I'll check the records for you." She spoke. She left to look at her computer screen, returning with a smile on her face she informs me that, "Yes, you are married!"

"I know that." What deplorable behavior! She scowled back and continued to push past the nurse and sit beside Mason. Gemma understood she was young and just doing what she thought was right, how dare Dwayne try to prevent her from being with her sick husband, how much emotional damage could that have done his dad. Not to be together now at this critical time in their lives, could leave him without hope and possibly cause his death, unbelievable! It just defies belief that anyone could be that disgustingly heartless, yes! He definitely is without heart!

Gemma's new routine begins, and she finds another of life's challenges loaded onto her narrow shoulders, as if she needed her life to be any more demanding, she now felt the need to be with Mason to protect him from his sons.

She witnessed them teasing and confusing their dad, it tears her apart to watch as they laugh at his mistakes and as they ask how many children he has and does he remember their names, *Dwayne, and Peter.* Gemma felt so proud of him for getting it right, only to watch them tell Mason that he was wrong and that he had four children! The look of disappointment and confusion on his face cut deeply into her and she wished she could slap them for causing hurt and telling lies. How can anyone enjoy being so cruel. It's as though they don't grasp the concept of how awful Masons struggle is, it's no joke for their father.

The nights are long, and sleep is obscure, finding that she often lies awake telling herself that it's pointless to worry about anything, it won't do any good. None! And the aching pain inside will just create a stomach ulcer and that won't help Mason.

So, she tries to make her mind go blank, STOP fretting about stuff and willing dawn to come sooner for her to return to see him. Every night rolls around in her head, how much she wants Mason to have the chance to retire, if he could just have another 10 years, she'll make him happy, and he won't have to worry about anything. She'll find a way to pay the bills, please just let him have some time to do what he wants without having to work again. It's not fair to die without ever having the freedom of retirement. This is her pledge over and over as she mentally works through the 21 days scribbled on the calendar.

Rising each morning, not just physically tired but emotionally drained and the first thing she does is hug Ombre' and pray, thank goodness she has him here to talk to, it was meant to be that Mason gave her this little companion all those years ago, he's about nine years old now and hanging in there for Gemma to love.

The usual morning cup of tea that she doesn't really want is made in a blur, feeling depressed she just needs Mason as she clings onto the belief that if she starts each day the same way routine will help to make time go faster, visiting hours will come around sooner.

Every morning she routinely feeds the chickens and then pops a slice of toast for her and one for Ombre' into the toaster, she watches two hands go about doing things automatically without the need for her to think. It's still very cold on these June mornings but her mind is a clutter of thoughts floating all over the place, so she's oblivious to having painful arthritic fingers. Being in the High Dependency Unit Mason is with a dozen others all needing help with everyday needs, the very basic necessities of life he can no longer do for himself so Gemma is determined to be there in case he can't get staff assistance.

The drive to the hospital becomes methodical and as she walks quickly towards the unit, thinking how nice it is to see him sitting up watching the people coming and going, his eyes still have a distant hollow look and his mind is not there, but the staff welcome her.

"Hi, do you know who I am?" She asks him with a big smile each morning.

"No!" Came the reply with a blank emotionless stare.

"I'm Gemma, your wife!"

On arrival this routine is repeated every day, "Hi, I'm Gemma, your wife!" Always in a raised voice as his hearing aids no longer fit because of swelling.

Sometimes it's nice to meet other wives when she visits to sit with Mason through the long days, one lady visitor Dawn imparts a disapproving frown at her continually asking Mason who she is and what his name is, she whispers under her breathe about Gemma to her family. Who cares, Gemma focuses on getting Mason better and helping him to get his memory back before coming home again.

What day is it today? Do you know who I am? Pointing to the clock on the wall, what time is it? She kept up the chatter to remind him of the most basic everyday things again. The doctor doing his rounds informs her that Mason's memory loss is severe, Gemma's heart melts and she's motivated to try to get Mason's memory back as much as possible, she'll do everything she can to rehabilitate her husband. All she can do for now though is helping to organize his thoughts for him, strangers don't understand what she's doing but she'll never give up trying to get her husband's memory back and will continue to hand feed him with a teaspoon, he's so frail and oblivious of what is going on around him. Emotionally it is a difficult thing to hand feed your husband like a baby, but the hospital staff put the food tray in front of him and no one takes responsibility for feeding when he can't co-ordinate his hand to his mouth, if Gemma doesn't do it, he will go without the nutrition that he needs to get well. Busy staff doing the rounds come to collect the food trays weather eaten or not.

While feeding Mason, Dwayne arrives, smiling politely, she offers him the spoon. We all need to work together now, and Gemma's only goal is to do the absolute best for her poor husband. She pushes away any animosity towards Dwayne as she offers.

"Would you like to feed your dad?"

He screwed up his face and said, "No way!"

A little shocked by his ignorance but accepting that he might be embarrassed by his invalid father Gemma attempted to ignore his vile reaction and try making conversation as she fed Mason carefully around the tube he still had down his throat, her thinking that if only he eats this then the nurse will be able to remove the feeding tube, all the time trying to encourage him to eat yoghurt.

Rather abruptly Dwayne snaps through her thoughts, "Why don't you leave my dad?"

She was gob smacked, taken aback as she turned to look directly into his heartless cold eyes, she tried to hide her shock and contempt for this person sitting on the opposite side of the hospital bed. She didn't feel she needed to explain what love is, he obviously has no understanding of it. "And who will look after your dad then?" She politely asked.

Silence, absolute silence! No reply or suggestions, he would let his father starve, he only visits because she's here, and he can't stand to watch the unconditional love as he's not fortunate enough to have that someone special in his life, he's never found anyone he will commit to marriage with.

Mason looks so close to death, his skin is like a dull sheet of translucent grey roofing, quite lifeless and plastic, with eyes that don't appear to have any life behind them, she reminds herself to be grateful for every small mercy these days, absolutely elated that he has retained the ability to speak even if sometimes his mind doesn't always give him the correct words, he tries. Mason's whole life has been turned upside down and her heart aches for what he's going through, he's a sad vulnerable man lying there before her.

On her travels home Gemma reflects on what has happened each day, concluding that Dwayne wants her out of the picture because she's in the way if his dad should die, this illness has made Dwayne aware of their mortality and that the boys will need to wait for her (the wife) to die before they can get their hands on Mason's assets.

People always say things like that happen, but Gemma thinks it's disgusting that anyone could think about assets and inheritance while confronted with someone you love having to die first.

CHAPTER 10

For Gemma, living on little food and managing with a lack of money to keep their home going has been a necessary evil but she continues to struggle on and go without, Mason is her husband, and she loves him and just wants to be back in his arms as she strives to keep everything going for when he returns home.

A week has passed and Gemma's finding that getting to the hospital very early she's able to fit her small car in a tiny space at the side of the nearby park, that's another saving on parking fees even if she has to walk a bit. Staying on the positive side, getting there early suits her anyway as when the neurology ward opens she's waiting at the door. She's impatient to see his smile every morning after slogging her way through long and lonely nights without him, plus the fear of losing him has never left.

Always appearing to be cheerful as she enters the HDU she's determined that her face doesn't reflect any anguish or loneliness. She's determined that Mason only receives a happy welcoming good morning smile to cheer his every day, no matter how many he may have. The reality for Mason is a day of pain and loss living in a stark clinical environment which is far worse than whatever she is dealing with, sometimes fleeing to the privacy of the toilets if her eyes start to fill with tears, never letting him see any of her sorrow, just smiles and laughter to cheer him up.

After helping him with lunch she tucks him down for a rest and walks a couple of kilometer's back to the quietness of the park, all the time the chilly winter weather biting cold on her face and trying to consume the last bit of life left in her, she continues this unrelenting routine seven days a week. Sitting on a cold park bench beside a darkened pond, the center of a waterlogged park Gemma's body is depleted, she watches the ducks as loneliness engulfs her and she's lost in memories and thoughts not always good, while the serenity and beauty of this place with its purple iris flowers waving in the icy breeze tunnel strength to her, she knows she has to keep going for her husband.

Eating the vegemite sandwich, she had carefully tucked into her handbag that morning she slowly trudges back to the comfort of her Fiat, head down watching the pavement so as not to stumble out of fatigue, it's time for her to drive to the hospital carpark building this afternoon, always aware that after their visit together she leaves at 9.00pm and there'll be few people around, so the carpark is the safer option rather than walking the tree lined pavement beside the poorly lit park.

It seems that life is all about survival now, not only in Mason's recovery but there's a constant awareness of the importance for her to stay well to care for him. How would he manage without her if something should happen and how long will he need to depend on her?

She agonizes over the future; the bus company has agreed to pay his holiday pay into their shared bank account and thank goodness the bank will allow her to pay the mortgage and the many household bills from that. They have the extra expense now of petrol and parking at the hospital and that's making yet another dent in her meagre existence, so she continues to walk to and from the local park whenever the weather permits to keep parking expenses at around $63 a week, even that is a huge extra expense now that Mason is not bringing in a wage. Cutting back on food does help, so day after day she fills her handbag with celery and carrot sticks that are both cheap and easy to carry for chomping on while she sits at his bed side for nine hours every day, the vegetables ward off the hunger pains if she just keeps chewing.

This morning she entered the High Dependency Unit through the smoke stop doors, they automatically swung closed with a bang, Mason looked up from the pillow and his face lit up! Warmth surged through her body like a radiator, just that smile making it all worth the pain of sitting for so long without a conversation, she loves Mason.

Silent words fill her thoughts as she's too shy to say what she wants with nurses and visitors arriving through the doors, she wished they had some private time, and that Mason could comprehend what she says. Gemma continued to knit the hat to cover the huge scar he had across his head, helping to occupy both body and mind with pleasurable thoughts. She stayed positive, his hat would be warm for returning home.

"Hi, do you know who I am?" She greeted him with a smile, and he replied.

"Yes, you're the lady that visits me." He said with the loveliest smile ever, just for her. She turns away as the pain of sadness that he doesn't really know her, combines with the joy she feels that he looks forward to seeing her. The mixed emotions pierced through her heart and the tears began to sting her eyes. Blinking them away and steeling herself she forced a giggle in response and asked how he was today as she reached across the bed and gave his cheek a quick kiss.

Dwayne arrived, too late to hear what was said. Today Gemma was relaxed enough to face the sarcasm in Dwayne's voice as she sat beside Mason's bed rubbing his hand.

Dwayne spoke with a smirk on his face, oblivious to Mason even being there he spoke in front of his dad as though he was too stupid to understand what's being said.

"What if he never remembers you, he thinks he's still married to my mum." He laughed.

What a cruel person, even at death's door he continues his battle to separate them, unconcerned that his father is fighting for life, he continues to think only of himself. Gemma forced out a short fake laugh as she bravely responded without showing any hurt.

"Then it will be fun courting him all over again." She said as she looked directly into Dwayne's eyes.

He didn't speak to her again during the visit. They say loving each other can win over adversity, Gemma hopes that the selfishness the sons inflict achieves nothing, she's not intimidated, and it won't stop her trying to help her husband.

She's determined to make him well again! "You'll get better my darling." Gemma whispered before leaving.

Each morning she leant over his hospital bed, and they kissed, while gently cradling his cold hand around life-giving tubes, she whispered into his ear with hope and longing in her heart.

"Hi darling, it's Gemma your wife."

Everyday she courageously summoned renewed determination to defend him and do what a dutiful wife would do, to protect him with everything in her while he's vulnerable, she continued on with faith and love in her heart and after long weeks she picked up the courage to ask him again, she walked into the ward.

"Do you know who I am?"

"You are my wife, the love of my life." Came the reply.

Stunned speechless, unparalleled happiness inundating her heart so fully she thought it would burst, she gasped involuntarily as she overflowed with love and relief. She blinked rapidly to hide her tears of joy; they hugged each other like they never wanted to let go.

"You remember me, it's going to be okay!" She whispered to her Mason.

The overwhelming relief must have been clear to anyone watching in that small hospital ward. The thrill she felt that Mason must be getting better was more exhilarating than anything she had ever experienced in her life. Next week's challenge is for him to try getting out of bed and learn to walk again.

The routine continued on with her much-needed belief that it's going to work out. Leaving her husband's bedside every night was always cold and emotional with a daunting numbness rising deep inside her, she didn't want to go, and the extreme tiredness never went away, every night she drove the silent trip home alone, her stomach rumbling and she had a persistent longing for her mind to quieten its incessant agitation. *Oh, please let me stop going over everything that has happened since his aneurism*, the tears felt cold and dismal as they ran down her face unabated while she drove for an hour and half to get home to their Panguru lifestyle block, loneliness is her every day now. There is no need to be brave without people around, that's the time that she sobs uncontrollably in the privacy of the car, and no one knows, no-one is there as she is surrounded by dark solitary emptiness, somehow she always arrives home safely to her loyal Ombre' waiting.

Waking to another day without a night-time phone call she knows he is still alive; Mason is slowly working his way through the 21 days vasospasm risk. She consciously counts down the days with one ear listening for the phone to ring, praying that it doesn't, she doesn't want that call from the hospital, any tiny tinkle of rain or strange noise outside and she leaps into action, her heart pounding so hard that it's a wonder it stays in her chest, of course it would be nice to hear a voice and someone to speak to, but she's a tightly coiled bundle of fear, afraid to answer the phone just in case!

Upon returning home each night she feeds Ombre' and falls into bed exhausted, curls up into the fetal position and silently cries until tears stop falling, eventually the night-time struggle ends, and light starts to creep through the curtains. Sleep is a challenge that doesn't seem to be getting any easier, it's been three weeks since the aneurism and he lives on, she continually tells herself to be rational about everything, stay focused and ignore the emptiness eating its way to the depth of her whole being. She tries to forget each day as it finishes and put it behind her, tomorrow is a new day and if she can't fix things happening then it's pointless worrying about them. She tries to prevent the pain as it quietly gnaws away making her feel sick, that won't help anyone she reprimands herself, convincing her mind to sleep and just face one day at a time.

Her dreams and expectations are all gone, her life has changed forever and it will never be the same again, no one can ever go back to what they had before, each day that she sat with him it became more obvious that Mason would always have some brain damage and life as they knew it was obliterated by a heartbeat and a rush of blood, all she could do was be grateful that he's still alive and hope that memories of their happy times together would come back to be his memories one day. While sitting at his bedside the field worker from a stroke organization came to see Gemma, she seemed nice and suggested that maybe later on Gemma might like to get together with other wives to form a group that would allow each individual to share what they have gone through over a cup of tea.

Gemma explained to her that she's not really a group sort of person and didn't feel like sharing their personal problems with others. Most people think that they can cope in a crisis, but actually we are never prepared for the unexpected and you just don't know how your body reacts when something traumatic strikes.

Gemma is now finding out, her body has a mind of its own these days, no matter how mentally strong she is, her emotions don't have a control switch. During her daily visit to the hospital, Dwayne turned up.

"How come you're always here?" He grumped.

"Where else would I be, he's my husband?"

"No one should have to be here nine hours every day." Sounding very indignant rather than compassionate.

She didn't feel that she needed to explain to him but hesitantly she told him that she leaves early on Thursdays now as she has gone back to work the late nights in the shop each week, they need the money. To which he never replied, and she felt an unease floating in the air, over time she has grown to distrust him.

When the doors swung open to let her through on Friday morning the nurse approached Gemma and she observed a concerned look on her face, something was wrong and panic swept over Gemma, she instinctively looked over to see her husband tucked up in his crisp hospital bed and felt a huge relief that he's still alive. Before the nurse spoke Gemma had a sixth sense that told her that someone had upset Mason, confidentiality prevented the staff member from telling Gemma, but her face was strained as she explained that Mr. Brownlie had too many visitors last night (Thursday) and that his blood pressure had gone up to a dangerous level, a look of serious concern splashed across her face she explained that Mason could have had a stroke!

Gemma intuitively knew that Dwayne had taken advantage of the evening she worked. Mason's memory of being married to Gemma was returning and Dwayne like a man possessed objected, he brought his mother to visit, at the expense of Mason's life. Anger rushed through Gemma's veins as she imagined them all swarming like greedy locusts.

Having to face his ex-wife would have confused Mason and he's unable to run or even walk away, he was involuntarily captive.

Seeing his ex-wife never promoted calm in Mason at the best of times, how dare they force this on her sick husband!

The staff in the High Dependency Unit noticed the sudden change to dangerously high blood pressure and rushed to tell his visitors to leave, probably saving Mason's life. Hearing this news, spontaneous gratitude flooded through Gemma's blood stream and her legs became weak.

CHAPTER 11

It wouldn't be right for those cruel self-righteous sons to take away Mason's life after all his struggling to piece things back together. Gemma believes that good wins over evil, but she won't leave him open to abuse again, on Monday she will go back to work and hand in her notice for the Thursday night job as any money at the expense of her husband's life is just not worth having, she's determined to protect him, what is the point of anything if she loses him?

Everything has changed as a result of the aneurism, and she's surprised at how resilient she has become. She's fighting for the life of a loved one, courageous and determined to help him get his life back, she's convinced that she can be strong and is able to do this amidst the fear that their lives will never be the same again. They came face to face with death and the unknown brings the reality that they really don't know what will happen next, they worked, saved, and found love and marriage, but it can all change. Gone in an instant like a beautiful rainbow, so perfect and pretty until you look away for a moment and it has dissolved into the amber skies that have just stopped crying. Could that be her life? Is it possible that her tears dry, and the sun will come out again after many rainy days, weeks, and months?

Finally, she can relax a little, grateful that the 30 long days of sitting and knitting at her husband's bedside in Kaitaia Hospital, have finally come to an end, Mason now has a hat and scarf and will be transferred to a Rehabilitation Unit that's a little closer to home thank goodness, the expense of travel had been huge. This nightmare has had an extensive effect on them both in many ways, she's physically shattered, like she has run a marathon and still wonders if she will ever make it to the end. The emotional strain of it has zapped her energy levels and she wakes up sleep deprived everyday questioning if she will ever feel well again, at the same time she's proud she has managed on her own with prayer, positive thinking, and the companionship of Ombre.' Spending every day with her husband, her days have started early and finished late always just confronting one day at a time.

Mason is taken to rehab by ambulance and Gemma followed in her precious little car that has always gotten her through, everything is a blur as they go through the paperwork in the small gloomy office with one desk and two chairs, then the young doctor asks Mason.

"What did you do for a living before getting sick?"

And without faltering "I'm a bus driver." Came the cheerful response and Gemma glowed with pride at how far he had come, being able to answer for himself.

"Oh, you'll never do that again." The doctor said looking down at his notes.

It's as though her heart suddenly dropped out, she gasped in shocked pain as it surrendered her speechless, she couldn't have felt more adoration or affection for Mason at that moment, feeling both proud of his ability and yet full of compassion for him in that unnecessary negativity for his future. Mason stood taller than ever before.

Through all of this adversity she has learnt to be brave, learnt that courage is a state of mind and that she can take control and be strong for the man she loves, because that is what Mason needs from her, that's all she can do for him, be strong, never cry in front of him, appear to be happy and hopefully normality will resume one day. Have hope that they will manage each day as it comes until this nightmare ends and their lives will once again be like everyone else's.

The over whelming weight of responsibility to do more, weighed heavily on her along with the desire to make everything right for her loved one, was totally absorbing. A driving force within her and an overpowering new sense of needing to protect him was very intense and completely foreign to what she was used to, even protecting your child is easier because children listen, understand, and can act appropriately but this man in her life can't make decisions and act for himself, he's vulnerable to everything, this smudging of boundary's making her question if it's at all possible to be overprotective.

Life molds us and what was traditionally the job of the man to have the strong shoulders to cry on, this responsibility now fell to her. She's determined to be Mason's strength and shoulder when he needs one and when he comes home everything will be tidy and running smoothly, he won't have to worry about anything, Gemma will be there for him.

After having a lot of time to contemplate and ask *why* this happened and throughout the whole experience, she drew on an inner strength that she didn't know she possessed, through adversity she learnt and grew in many ways, she always believed that everything happened for a reason, searching, and questioning why? She could see somehow all this horrible stuff was teaching her to have empathy for others in life, but she still wondered why this happened to Mason and questioned if it was wrong of her to still remember, even after trying so hard to forget that he tried to take her life when he strangled her. Is that why this had happened, or was thinking that being too harsh, she saved his life by calling the ambulance quickly. She loves him and constantly made excuses for his behavior, wishing that he was well again.

Cautiously hopeful, gave her renewed energy as she pressed on by the possibility that he might get home one day soon then she reminded herself it's not that time yet, to persevere, be patient and not get her hopes up. Gemma is fully aware of the reality that today he's still wobbly on his feet and she thinks of all the challenges he will face when he does come home, he might want to continue renovating when he sees unfinished things around their house and he's not capable of using power tools, not being able to hit a nail straight will frustrate him and she doesn't want him to go through any more struggles.

It's possible to visit the rehab later in the day now as Mason has occupational and physical therapy to get through each morning, he's learning to shower, dress and feed himself so that allows Gemma to alter her routine and not have to rush around so early. She is able to get more rest and take time to cook properly for herself, the urgency to stay well is more important now as he will need her assistance when he returns home, a new fear of *what if she gets sick,* has been emerging lately as she's been having a few dizzy spells.

Waking this morning a newfound protective mode kicked in, she excitedly walked around the house assessing what he might want to do when he returns home and this also helped to quieten her worried mind and stay positive as she set about phoning handymen for quotes, it would mean dipping into the little savings she had squirrelled away for a rainy day, nevertheless this is definitely that day.

First, they have a fence to be fixed around the deck which is bound to annoy him as he sits and looks out of the lounge, it will create all kinds of difficulties wanting to fix it as Rehab has forbidden the use of power tools, Mason's thinking is irrational and also forgetful. She doesn't want to become his scapegoat and be accused of keeping him away from his tool shed, suddenly remembering his fiery look. Gemma convinced herself he was sick, and he would be okay now. After careful deliberation and allowing time for the fencing to be paid off she calculated and organized for another contractor to come at a later date to replace the spouting above the deck where it continually dripped. The thought of her husband being up a ladder shot waves of terror through her and was out of the question.

Mingled hope and excitement made the day go quickly as she explained to both workers that they would need to come in the mornings before she visited Mason in the afternoons. Gemma now had a new set of goals and was looking forward to the future when Mason would come home again, the excited thrill ran through her whole body igniting a newfound surge of energy she thought no longer existed for her.

Next, she checked over the pregnant sheep, moved them into a fresh paddock to ensure they were all well fed and bucketed out the water troughs. Scrubbing the green slime off them will be tomorrow's job and everything will be looking wonderful for Mason when he's allowed home. She rushed around on a high remembering the fun years with their kids, lambs, and their much-loved dog. With love and hope in her heart she was full of determination that everything would be okay, and Mason's life would be wonderful again when he comes home, hoping she might have the placid man she first married. She was excited and had a wonderful purpose to get up for every morning, determined and motivated to make his life the best she could. Holding onto the memory that he nearly died, his life nearly ended, gone!

Life is silently plodding along not unlike the clip clip sound of her gumboots slapping against her jeans as she walked briskly through the long wet grass across the paddock with her constant companion Ombre' as they made their usual trek down to the pond, time to pat, sit and reflect and try to pull all her thoughts together as she watched the ducks float aimlessly on the still water, a tranquil sight that was reminiscent of a beautiful painting she'd once seen, the clouds overhead a fluffy silver grey letting just enough light through to sparkle the top of the water.

Two months have passed since that day when they collected Gracie, and Mason ended up having brain surgery. The winter weather is gradually dispersing and there are fine days when she can now sit in the warm morning sun and know that spring is around the corner and she allows herself to feel a glimmer of hope that everything is getting better, spring is a symbol of a new beginning when the lambs are born and the daffodils flower, everything bursts into life again and maybe happiness would return for them. Beyond the weather there are still some grey days when her life doesn't feel so positive, and she's haunted by fear of the unknown and the helplessness of not being able to do more to help her husband. Rehabilitation consisted of Mason learning to be steady on his feet, the repetition of showering and dressing himself, and of course piecing all the memories back together.

He is unable to follow a book because he forgets what the last page was about, this makes his day very boring and after his morning routine he welcomes Gemma with open arms when she visits him, he now knows who she is. Every day he remembers a little more and they go for a walk, sometimes sitting in the gazebo talking about their animals and their home. Rehab expects him to make a cup of tea for her and that's also a big learning curve, she tries to coax him to be as independent as possible while still at rehab, they always watch Coronation Street together after lunch to help initiate some memories and normality.

The two of them try to do what they always did together when they were a couple out in the world and not relying on life in a rehabilitation unit. Watching and talking with him Gemma supplies routine and repetition of those things and it's beginning to orientate him to times and dates. Tonight, they're going for a walk to the shops for him to practice ordering the fish and chips and learn how to handle money again with Gemma encouraging him, she's learning to ignore the stares of people and to be strong in her support of her husband, sometimes it's embarrassing.

He has lost so much and now he works hard to get his self-confidence and self-esteem back again.

People stare because they think he's crazy and Gemma's not sure how to cope with that, she just feels so sorry for him and wants to carry his embarrassment instead, but of course there's little she can do which only makes her feel useless. Mason is slowly understanding that he isn't well and what happened has been explained to him many times, Gemma's heart goes out to him as he struggles with the uncertainty of ever working again and the cold hard truth told to him by the staff that he can't even drive a car again after having brain surgery, she queried that with the nurse, and she scurried off to get the road rules to prove her point.

Gemma's distress was extreme when she left rehab to travel home after that news, mortified by the lack of compassion and matter of fact manner she gave the bad news to her patient struggling to come to terms with losing his memory, job and life as he once knew it.

The first thing she did when arriving home was rush to the home phone and with shaking hands she phoned the land transport authority and requested to speak with the medical officer there.

"My husband has had a brain aneurism will he be allowed to drive again one day? Is he allowed to drive passengers?" The questions tumble out as she frantically asked the person at the other end of the phone, she grappled to sound intelligent and emotionally under control preventing the desperation she felt showing in her voice.

"Has he had any seizures?" came the question.

"No, but he had surgery to clip the aneurism." Nervously holding her breath with all fingers crossed.

"That's probably okay then, as long as his vision isn't impaired, but he will have to re-sit his license through a specially qualified driving instructor to assess his reaction time and understanding of the rules, but we do assess each person individually and don't have a hard and fast rule." She exhaled loudly.

"Oh, thank you for your time in explaining it to me, I'm glad that he'll be assessed individually to see if he can drive again. It's huge to take someone's license away from them!"

"Yes, all the best then, bye." Came the reply.

Replacing the receiver with shaking hands comfort washed over her like a tidal wave sweeping away the fear and leaving a glimmer of hope, if you take a person's hope away what reason do they have left to go on, they may as well just give up. Gemma can't wait to tell Mason the good news and give him a purpose to get well. He needs all the encouragement and hope for the future that he can get, restoring his hope will definitely help towards a good recovery.

The stroke field officer caught up with her again today while she was visiting Mason and after explaining the good news to her Gemma was encouraged to share it with others at the meeting that night, there are others going through the same thing.

Being alone at home and only having her dog to talk to really isn't enough, and as time drags on she is finding that she's becoming more depressed and lonely.

There is a vending machine in one of the long corridors at rehab and Gemma hasn't had a treat for months so they make it a habit to teach Mason to count out the correct money and put it into the machine, choose what button to push and share a chocolate chip cookie, he enjoys being able to spoil the love of his life and is becoming confident having his own money, a proud smile spreads across his face when he succeeds in operating the machine and the cookie tumbles down the chute.

They break the cookie in half as they can't afford one each, sitting together holding hands on the sterile looking two-seater sofa they silently watch people walk by in this cold institutional corridor.

These are their times together now, celebrating little steps of progress and they hold a secret plan for Mason to get his driver's license back, she promised that they'll travel together around the South Island of New Zealand. Gemma hopes that she has done the right thing giving him a goal to work towards, because her inner fear is that maybe he won't get there. Pushing any doubt right out of her mind, determined he will make it and maybe, now the aneurism is gone he'll be the kind man that she had married.

All is not lost, he didn't die, and they continue to hope for improvements, they don't give up when anything goes wrong. He struggles to find his room at rehab and continually gets lost around the building, he has green 'Mason' arrows to direct him along the corridor, no one else has arrows, why is he so different? Her heart melts and she wants to help when he gets lost trying to find his room, however he has to work it out.

CHAPTER 12

It's a bitter cold August night about 10.00pm, and Gemma hasn't been home long, they spent the evening together, in front of the TV at Rehab. She lit the fire first thing after the lonely drive home and Ombre' had settled next to it after enjoying his tea, the phone rang, Gemma jumped half out of her wits as it never rings at that time of night, she's afraid to answer it, pausing to inhale a big breath in case that fated phone call she had been dreading for months has arrived.

"Hello, is that Gemma? It's the rehabilitation unit here, do you have Mason with you?" came an unknown voice.

"No, I saw him this evening but left at eight o'clock, and he seemed fine, what's wrong?" As the anxiety threatened to become obvious in her panicked voice.

"He's gone missing, no-one can find him, and we think he went out the door when the visitors left." She said quite calmly like it happens all the time.

"He wears a security anklet so how can that happen?" She questioned.

"Well, it looks like the nurse went off to have her dinner and forgot to turn her monitor back on when she returned, but the manager will look into that."

As if that made anything better! They have a duty of care, and someone had obviously failed in their responsibility. Thoughts of how confused and unhappy he might be piercing Gemma's mind, they've had to part again this evening and their closeness means they miss each other more, she can't help fearing that he may harm himself if he's upset, he's within walking distance of the coast.

"I'll come right away and drive around to try and find him." It was pouring with rain and freezing cold; she didn't need this rubbish emotionally or physically. Frantically driving to the unit that she thought he was safe in! Can no one be relied upon to care and keep him safe? It seems like it's her against the world with no support there for Mason or herself and with each new day she becomes more defensive and unable to trust others with the man she loves.

Her neck muscles tensed in her shoulders threatening a migraine as she approached the carpark, she spots the group of search and rescue officers talking strategies and looking at a map, the helicopter is already cruising above the highway with a huge spotlight shining down onto the pitch-black ocean beside it. Unable to speak through the painful lump formed in her throat, afraid and feeling sick to her stomach, a conversation with the manager is strained and uncomfortable.

"He has just survived brain surgery and now he's going to die of hypothermia." She shrieked! "Do you know what he's wearing?" Gemma is distraught and uncontrollably frantic.

"He had a grey tracksuit and sneakers on at teatime, but we don't think he has a raincoat on. We're doing everything we can to find him, the police are here, and it'll be okay." She says.

Walking down the corridor Gemma insisted on talking with other residents, she didn't care what time it was, it seemed like they didn't know what they were doing, and she had lost all trust in leaving Mason's care to them. One tall thin gent who had lost the ability to speak, (probably through a stroke) was agitated and wanting to tell her something, he was pushing past the staff member and making a lot of noise, he reached Gemma, she speaks to the staff that are struggling to restrain him.

"It's okay, what does he want?"

"He doesn't know what he wants, he has to be in bed now and you can't understand him anyway." Gemma ignored the nurse's ignorance and wanting to put him to bed, they're not children.

Ignoring her, she reached out to touch his arm quietly, patiently listened allowing him to express as much as he could in his own way, he was frantically gesturing something about Mason crying.

"Did Mason tell you something? Did he say where he was going?"

Gemma asked him gently with a calming hand on his arm, he was obviously genuinely concerned and agitated. He nodded his head pointing to a yellow magazine lying on the table.

"Yellow." She looked at him, what does that mean? Watching the frenzied nodding of his head flat out.

"We have a yellow letter box, is he trying to get home?" Smiles and the weight seemed to lift from the man's shoulders, his sigh and slow relieved nod spoke volumes. Do these staff even understand the patients or are they treated like idiots just because they have lost the ability to communicate. No one had bothered to get that vital information and provide it to the search and rescue so they could at least look in the right direction. Gemma thanked him and with a little squeeze of his arm she reassured him that Mason would be found.

"I'm going out to look for him." She mumbled to staff before rushing to her precious car, darkness, solitude, and tears engulf her again as she felt how alone Mason must feel, the panic and fear inside her created out of love for each other, he had a quest to come home, just to be together again. Gemma's heart ached for her husband enduring memory loss; he doesn't know his address just the color of a letterbox. *'Please Lord, I love him so much, please, please let him be all right,'* the pain of being apart is too much for them both to bear and as the cold tears ran down her face, she wiped them away before starting the car.

She continued to drive around the streets, straining to look through the wipers each time they swish across the windscreen, he could go three separate ways home, but the police have the highway covered so she checks out the houses he used to live at, as he might have his streets confused. Driving around and staying in contact with the unit by cell phone, there is no sign of him. What if someone has attacked him, he does look like a homeless person in the very heavy rain without a coat and he's helpless and lost.

No luck, and she's at her wits end as to where to continue to look, returning to the unit and flopping into a chair, her shoulder bag drops around her feet as she sat and stared blankly into space, what does she do now. Someone puts a cup of tea in her hands.

"Go home and get some sleep." Says the manager, "We'll ring you when he turns up."

Looking down, she had unthinkingly thrown on a pair of worn-out jeans, faded tee and a warm jumper in haste after receiving the phone call.

Only now that the adrenaline has ceased surging does she notice how tired and stone-cold her entire body felt. She looked pale and drawn, with a sore back and thumping stress headache, her hair not combed since they were together at eight o'clock. She sat in her car crying out,

'Dear Lord Please keep Mason safe, please keep him warm and help him to know which way to go, please give me the strength to cope with this pain tearing me apart, from this emptiness gnawing inside me, I have to stay strong for when they find him.'

It is impossible for her to sleep, awake all night trying not to think the worst but her mind not obliging. Four o'clock in the morning the phone rings and she lunged for it hopeful but scared.

"Hello!"

"We have him back! He's in the shower at the moment to warm up, he's okay!" And Gemma burst into tears.

"I'm on my way." She blurted out, not asking if it was an acceptable hour. On arriving at the rehabilitation unit, the rescue workers were just debriefing in the car park, and she waved a quick look of gratitude at them as she hurried to the rehabilitation unit's door. Mason is tucked up in bed looking exhausted but okay, wrapping her arms around him her whole body began shaking as she was racked with tears, not just tears but total howling and the staff closed the door and left them together. No words could express the score of emotions going on right then, the relief after she had been thinking she may have lost him forever this time. How many chances do they get in life, she will always cherish their time together trying not to take life for granted as it can be gone so quickly.

It has been an exceptionally long four months without Mason and she has had to cope, the first of the spring lambs born this morning, the phone rings and it's the field officer from the Stroke organization checking on how everything is going. Just to talk to someone was too much for Gemma and the emotions came flooding out like a dam bursting.

"What's wrong?" She asked, genuine concern in her voice, she is obviously upset so she had to explain that it's spring and a little lamb was born that morning.

"And he's not here." Was blurted out in a rush of tears. "I know it sounds silly, but we enjoy the animals together."

"No, it's not silly and I understand." She said.

They continued to talk for a few moments longer in between her trying to hold back the ever-threatening flow of tears and before hanging up she promised to go and talk about her feelings at the next support group meeting on Monday night, she said it might help to share with all the other woman going through a similar situation.

It's this immense feeling of sadness for how he must feel and the helplessness of it all that's very hard to tolerate and understand, she's never had such intense emotions before and the sense of vulnerability and insecurity with unexpected things always happening. This ordeal just seems to be going on forever and ever, wearing her down, and venturing into the unknown is so unfair, now she understands when people say that life is not fair!

But it's also what's happening internally with her mind and the reaction of her body to grief being uncontrollable that sometimes caused her to feel that life is too hard. That is when she reminds herself of Ombre' and those who need her, as they are what keep her going.

This morning enjoying their walk Ombre' and her soak up the warmth of the sunshine as it penetrates her skin and attempts to thaw the cold block of emptiness inside, strolling through the paddock and down the hill is relaxing and the depth of the sun is comforting like being wrapped in a cozy blanket, she can feel again, it's spring and a promise of a fresh start is on its way. Gemma knows she is lucky to have her dog always beside her and she tells herself not to be lonely, be mindful and grateful for every little thing.

Rehab has called a family meeting today to talk about Mason's progress and she's feeling positive and hopeful that he may be coming home soon. Entering the meeting room, Dwayne is the only family member besides herself that bothered to turn up at the meeting along with the doctor, social worker, physiotherapist, and occupational therapist, they'll each give a talk on Mason's progress and his health, and reports are read out.

It's agreed at the end of the meeting that he will be prescribed a liquid food to help him gain a little weight as Gemma is concerned at the amount of weight he has lost.

Each person speaks on what they have found, and the lack of memory is the biggest issue, rehab staff recommend that Mason go into a rest home as it's suggested that he'll be very difficult to manage and could possibly get lost if he goes home with Gemma. Huge disappointment was pushed to the back of her mind as anger turned on them and she automatically snapped into protective mode.

"It's not me that lost him!" She cried out in a raised voice. Everything went quiet in the room whether it was out of compassion for their situation or just guilt that they didn't do a good job, she'll never know. Mason had last weekend at home with her as a trial home visit and she brought him back to rehab safe and unharmed so there wasn't a person in the room that wanted to tackle her on that score.

"I can foresee us going through a lot of problems, but I'm not prepared to give up on him, I'm determined to teach him the basic needs of daily life, like finding and using the toilet.

" I'm up to the challenge, after hoping and praying for him to have a normal life again I can't just walk away from the man I love. I've given up my job because I'm prepared to give him my patience and the time it will take for him to learn everything all over again, I can only hope that with all my love he has the ability to relearn enough to lead a fulfilling life." She spoke quietly with conviction.

Nothing was said as she endeavored to explain to the specialists and Dwayne at the meeting her inability to accept the suggestion of putting a 62-year-old in with 80-year-olds for the rest of his life, she desperately tried to portray how abhorrent and out of the question that suggestion was to her.

"If it were me in Mason's shoes what would I want him to do? And my overwhelming concern is what will his quality of life be like in a rest home at his age, he could live for twenty years. A rest home would be ending his opportunity to improve and be independent out in the community." She tried to press the severity of that.

This heart felt question spread a cloak of silence across the room as the atmosphere became sickly thick with all of them knowing that she was right, with no one wanting to take responsibility for the emotional heart-breaking work involved in taking him home, the unspoken words were there in everyone's mind that the easiest solution was to sentence him to a rest home, as taking him home would be a sacrifice of her own life, with no offer of family assistance, they didn't expect that of her.

The dreadful thought of what would become of him for the

rest of his days weighed heavily on Gemma, *in sickness and in health* she had to do what she thought and believed was the best for him.

The thought of what it could do to her never entered into it, love for him burned so brightly within her it was totally unconditional, and without any consideration for her own wellbeing, her freedom and possibly even her love for this person. He might not be the same intellectually, she loved him, and he would be going home.

Gemma continued to take him home for another couple of weekends to gradually get them both used to the challenges ahead as she watched the staff whispering. A whole new life began for them both. Gemma couldn't see any other way and so resolved to care for him. The time had come to discharge Mason as all patients must be moved somewhere within three months, so she went into the office with her decision.

"I'm taking him home; he's not going into residential care." She told the doctor in charge.

"I don't think you'll be able to manage him, what will you do if we put him into a rest home without your permission?" The doctor tested the water.

"I'll go and take him out and get legal advice if need be." She replied with fierce determination so they would know not to tackle her. There was no discussion as they handed out the discharge forms to fill in. Now he's back home full time and it has become a 24 hour a day job for Gemma with very little sleep and no thanks, he gets up about five times every night, one night he got up around 4 o'clock and started to dress himself in his bus driver's uniform.

"What are you doing Mason?"

He's often very confused as to the day, year and what has happened to him, and it seems like an unnecessary cruelty to keep explaining it to him because each time he has to go through the reality and upset of having the aneurism all over again. It now seems kinder to not always tell the whole truth.

"I have to get ready for work, I'll be late." He says,

Gemma knew that it was a waste of time trying to explain it all again to him. "No, you don't have to go today, because you're still sick."

"Am I. Have you phoned work?"

"Yes, you are on sick leave," she lied. "Come back to bed and don't worry about it, just try to get well."

Five months since his brain surgery and he only just thought about going back to work, poor darling.

Gemma had visited and talked with the bus company after that fated day at the hospital when their lives were changed forever, explaining that it was probably going to be a long time before he would be able to work again, at least that's what she told them because even with all the faith in the world it's not in our hands whether he can ever drive again.

It was an extremely awkward thing to do, she felt like she was interfering with Mason's job and that it wasn't her place to inform all his colleagues how bad the situation was, but his sick leave had finished and now he's on an invalid's benefit, the outcome is bleak and completely up in the air. Being confronted with this reality was yet another stressful thing Gemma had to cope with on her own. It wasn't until she had to explain the situation to his employers out loud and hear the words coming out of her mouth that it brought it all home just how serious and uncertain things are for them.

Speaking to his manager and looking through the glass panel at Mason's work mates she struggled to stay calm and business like as the tightness in her throat threatened to make the tears flow and she had too much pride to allow that to happen, putting on a brave face while her heart went out to Mason knowing that this was the place he loved to be, with his work colleagues and he might never be back here again.

She hastily said to the manager that she would keep him informed before hurrying out to the security of her waiting car. There's a whole world out there but there she was in the busy carpark, so alone like she was solo in this saga, going about the necessities of life in a foreign galaxy, asking herself how something so extreme could happen?

They are just ordinary people like everyone else, but she will always remember how isolated from this world she felt right then.

CHAPTER 13

Long monotonous days pass slowly now she's at home, caring for her husband was a 24/7 vigil with her constantly watching this frail unsteady man to keep him safe and prevent him from falling, it was scary and quite strange to have to guide him to the toilet when sometimes he stood up, started to undo his trousers to pee on the floor. It was a strange, unnerving experience for any wife to go through and she found it impossible to have any of her girlfriends around to visit, she found it difficult to explain how harrowing it was to watch this lovely guy change into this strange vacant person and her role had changed as well, Gemma became more like the housekeeper and carer rather than a warm-blooded wife.

Thankfully with repetition he picked up the many life skills quite quickly and gradually remembered where the toilet was, she taught him how to dress again, which way up to put things on and what to wear for the temperature today, she constantly expressed how proud she felt every time he learnt something new, and she kissed and hugged him. Mason was withdrawn, distant, although similar to the husband she once knew. The humdrum of everyday existence was made easier as they talked, and she tried to motivate him into working hard to get well so that he could get his driver's license back again.

Gemma tried to give him hope as they continued to work toward his goal, he drove his van once a week for short trips up the road just to become familiar with driving again. She constantly reminded him to watch the distance from the open drains and not to drive on the footpaths as his judgment of distance seemed a bit off, and each time repeatedly driving around the same places he improved showing him potential to keep trying for another trip in the van.

The need for a holiday also the inspiration to spur him on, she remained positive around him and only shed tears in silence, alone with Ombre'.

Fear was a constant companion inside her as she wondered how completely his brain would improve, having been advised that the most improvement has to happen within a two-year period as after that everything slows down and little can be achieved.

Another foreign thing for her to get used to was the huge responsibility of keeping him safe, she learned that she must lock the door at night and hide the key so that she could sleep knowing that he couldn't disappear off into the darkness, he wandered around the house at all hours.

No one wants to visit, it seems that his old friends don't know what to say to him anymore, so Gemma persevered trying to keep him socializing and doing familiar things, she tried driving him to visit them, but he received comments like,

'You're not as bad as I thought you'd be.' Which is sort of good but with mixed feelings. Mason's life and surrounding are limited so he had very few things to have an enjoyable conversation about, and people don't ask his opinions or discuss anything with him as he finds it hard to stay on track of what has been said, because of his memory loss.

Finding it a bit embarrassing to not be the same as before with his friends he said, "I don't want to visit them anymore."

"Well, that's okay, you might want to make new friends now." No one could blame him; it must be ridiculously hard to have changed so involuntarily overnight and now have difficulty just keeping up with who's who with his memory loss. Anyway, Gemma continues to do her best to keep him from becoming a hermit. They both agreed to try to go out for tea on Friday nights and had joined the local Returned Services Association in the hope that if he had visitors or the boys came around, he could suggest that they go for a drink at the club, Gemma likes to relax and listen to music for a break on a Friday night and have an outing with Mason. However, it didn't work out as he didn't have the confidence to go without Gemma, and his sons refused to go when she's there, Gemma also found that getting him there took a lot of encouragement and prompting as the motivational part of his brain was affected and he also lacked confidence, so unfortunately those outings began to fizzle out.

Her life is mentally and emotionally exhausting, and she constantly rebukes herself to stay strong and turns away when feeling upset, determined never to break down or show her frustration when he makes no sense or is forgetful, her tears are silent.

Gemma appreciates how hard he tries and their devotion to each other is strong as they both struggle on together trying to regain some sort of normality, Masons hugs and kisses mean more to her now, he's kind and isn't aggressive anymore. The love is more pronounced, he nearly died so now they don't take anything for granted, treasuring every day with her husband is precious and she wished that he were out of the woods because now she has become this person who is insecure and fearful of the unknown wondering if this could happen again. Some days that worrying vacant look in his eyes, like no one is at home in his head returns, and it's a look that haunts Gemma as she wonders what he's thinking, what's going on in his damaged brain.

Having him in the home they've created together, she felt the heavy burden knowing that it's the most important thing she's ever done in her life, she wants to cherish and help him when no one else will, if she doesn't, he'll fall apart and never get any better than this strange half person now present, the commitment weighs heavy on Gemma's shoulders.

First thing every morning she prays for strength to cope and to help Mason gain back his life, that's her goal. Unaware of why this happened to them she just has faith and believes they will see why later, maybe years down the track.

This couple have endured many long months apart during his recovery but now only two months after leaving rehabilitation she feels that it's time! He's ready to try to get his driver's license back, it sounds quite ridiculous after the diagnosis of never being able to drive again, is she wishful thinking and not facing reality? It has been a long haul with the amount of devotion supplied him following brain surgery just six months ago, and it might be an optimistically short time to expect him to resume his driving again.

Gemma continued to go along to the meeting once a month that the field officer from the Stroke organization set up to discuss difficulties and fears with the other wives there. She has to admit that although in the beginning she was hesitant to share their personal life experiences with others, she has now come to understand that everyone there is going through similar fears and insecurities and has formed mutual friendships which provide precious time out and a release of all the things she can't talk about to anyone else.

One needs to walk in her shoes to understand the anxiety, depression, and difficulties that every day brings for Mason, and these partners are all living it as well, there is a camaraderie like going through a war together and finding out that she's not the only one after all.

The brain hemorrhage has left her husband with very little self-confidence, and she longs to be able to help him regain some sense of independence even if he never works again, which, secretly she hopes and prays that he does, not only for more income and a better life but for a 62-year-old man to be at home with nothing to do for the rest of his life is mind blowing and unthinkably sad for him. When Gemma was young she never imagined this would be her life while dreaming of getting married one day.

It's alarming for a woman to think that she may end up

being the sole income earner living with a brain damaged husband. Her husband to love and cherish in life is the ultimate dream, the thought of him vague and under foot around the house all day every day for the rest of their lives is depressing.

He questions everything she does and forgets everything she says, empathizing with his huge sense of loss, not knowing if he will ever be able to work again with the memory loss, they've talked about how he might forget which direction to drive a bus, the many streets he now finds foreign and confusing, and how well would he manage money if he worked again? He wouldn't remember the amount someone has handed him, and with the immediate loss of recall memory he couldn't remember what change he has just given them, so he would be vulnerable to all kinds of abuse.

They discussed the possibility of another job he may be able to do, but he left school young and didn't have any qualifications to fall back on, so it was hard to think of anything he might be able to turn his hand to in the future. Looking on the bright side, just getting his driver's license back would give him more independence and her a little freedom even if he could just go to the supermarket sometimes, it would be a huge help and one less thing for her to do.

Hauntingly they knew the time had come for him to have a go. It's a gigantic step and he's doing really well mentally and emotionally to attempt it, with silent apprehension it's a gamble and they never speak about failing.

If he succeeds in getting his driver's license back it will boast his confidence no end and then it could be the inspiration to begin his life over again in a world of normality. He's very reluctant and nervous but she doesn't waver in offering huge encouragement.

What do you have to lose? You don't have a license now, so you can only gain by getting it back. If you don't pass this time no one needs to know that you even went for it, it's our secret." She promised him.

Having endured many hours of persistent and relentless practice she talked him around the streets in his van. He had little memory of physically driving at first then it all came back automatically somewhere deep in his brain, he didn't need to think or remember what to do in his own vehicle and his ability had grown enough that they both felt it's now or never, just do it.

"Go on, you'll be fine, you can do this! I know you can." And again, she declared how he has nothing to lose.

They had managed to save up the $300 that was needed to have a specialist driving test and Mason drove his van all the way to the appointment, Gemma sat beside him trying to be positive and reassuring, all the time feeling as nervous as he did, maybe more so!

"See you're not having any trouble driving, it all comes

naturally, because you drove as a teenager, and it's an automatic response." She tried to reassure him.

So after explaining and assisting him fill in forms, he set off with the specialist instructor, and Gemma waited for their return. Anyone would think it was her that was sitting the test as she was struggling to stay calm and keep clarity of mind, perspiring and nervous for him she worried if the stress might put his blood pressure up. Tension was building in her neck while she continued to wait alone in the tired-looking office, her mind churned over the *what if he gets his license back, maybe he could work again*.

Time had wearied her whole body, and the tension heightened the hour that he had been gone, looking down checking her watch counting time, and hoping that he hasn't had an accident because he was so nervous and unlike a carefree young person about to sit for the first time, he doesn't have time to waste. It would be devastating if he didn't get it as she knew he would never try again. This will be the one and only time and he's taking so long! she checks her watch again, he's been gone two hours now and the stress is causing perspiration to glisten on her clammy, greasy skin, frightened that perhaps something has happened and concerned about how he'll be feeling if he fails. Was she wrong to have talked him into trying? Guilt makes her stand up unable to just sit she leaves the room and starts to walk up and down the garden path watching the road.

Gemma has sighted a familiar van in the distance and a huge wave of relief floods over her, he's okay and as it pulls up in the driveway with the instructor still seated next to him, her heart does a flip when she glimpses a smile sweep across Mason's face unable to hold it back he's beaming with pride and in his haste with no time to get the seat belt off and the door open. He winds down the window and cries out to her.

"I passed!" Her feet left the ground as she involuntarily jumped up and down. That's wonderful, he's allowed to drive again!

Unable to stop her eyes welling up she blinked faster to hold the tears back, her throat tightened and rendered her speechless, she was so proud and pleased for Mason. He's amazing.

Mason leapt out of the van and rushed towards her and all she could do was smile as he wrapped his arms around her squeezing a big thank-you hug.

CHAPTER 14

His attitude to life slowly changed, he doesn't fly off the handle at every little thing that bothers him, he has reclaimed hope again, and a semblance of patience. Happy and excited they make plans to set off on their promised trip in the camper van heading to Christchurch in the South Island at Easter. Without setting time limits as Mason now lingers, she doesn't care how long it takes they have all the time in the world as long as they're together, Ombre' is family as well, so he's traveling to offer them night-time security. The animals have a fresh paddock and troughs full of water, the gates to another lush paddock are left open for them to wander and the neighbor has kindly offered to check on the animals as well while they are away.

Since the brain damage Mason tires easily when concentrating so Gemma has suggested that he just drive until he's had enough and stop every couple of hours to make a flask of tea before continuing. The trip would probably take twice as long to get to Wellington but who cares! Acceleration filled, like being over the moon or winning a million dollars.

With all the activity of packing up the van and the excitement of heading off they only just got out of Auckland and the strain on his face was clear as he looked at Gemma with tired vacant eyes, the windows to his soul. These days she is used to his eyes being a giveaway to his health and his wishful look portrayed fear of not being able to do what his heart desired, it was torture for her to watch his disappointment as he struggled to accept his reality of being fatigued.

"Let's find a place to park." She suggested, smiling at him before he had a chance to say anything, and they agreed to rest and park up for the night. She reached out to touch his hand and smiled into his eyes, snatching a breath of fresh air through the open window it was like a new world with different air to breathe, full of promise, her heart was pounding, and she felt a shock shoot down her back as she spread her fingers through his hair. The familiar smell of his deodorant permeated the van air with sweet memories of times when they were just like other people a long time ago, came flooding back.

Staring into each other's eyes the gaze is held as they silently delve into that lost world. The intention is to leave their watchdog Ombre' with the van for him to sleep in, while it's parked safely in daughter Bridget's driveway during their stay in Christchurch. Ombre' is also enjoying another road trip down memory lane and they could hardly believe the dream was real as they arrived at their destination and are welcomed to a good night's sleep in a proper bed.

Bridget intends to drop them off at the train station in the morning where they plan to catch the Tranz Alpine Express train and enjoy a much-needed restful trip travelling through the magnificent Southern Alps on the way to Greymouth. Mason can relax and enjoy the view while Gemma takes photos of the incredible mountains, rivers, and valleys to store away for future reference. She knows, is constantly aware that any adventure they have together will disappear into the black hole of his mind once he has returned home with his incurable memory loss!

He's in awe of the magnificent yellow train carriages after positioned himself next to a window on the train, it started to move off and they waved their goodbyes to both Bridget and John standing at the station before settling down together. During the trip he's afraid to move from his seat, which was an unknown unexpected event, but it didn't matter as Gemma moved back and forth to the viewing carriage clicking the most wonderful sights high up in the snow-capped Alps and travelling alongside amazing rushing rivers with their foamy white tops glistening, clicking away at stunning vista's as the rattling train turned a corner directly into the sun after being in the depths of the mountains, it was awesome.

The whole trip was really happening, and even though no amount of encouragement would convince Mason to move from his comfortable seat, his obsessive behavior no longer mattered to either of them, this time was precious. Mason was content to look out of the window at the wondrous view high up in the southern alps and travelling through what seemed like never ending tunnels, he was peaceful, victorious in his goal and happy for Gemma to bring freshly baked hot buttered muffins from the dining car as they sat quietly eating and consuming everything, the muffins tasting more delicious because of the location, relaxed and happy to be there together.

How amazing to have come this far! It has taught them lessons in life, having learnt to be accepting of whatever comes and not fret the small unimportant stuff that we're used to doing. Gemma's life has changed, she has become a very independent person who is confident enough to manage whatever life throws its way. She watches and listens to people whispering about Mason ordering her to do things, but she doesn't look on it as being at Mason's beck and call, somethings are not worth worrying about. They're together and he drove, which is incredible in itself, a personal joy with no words to express the ecstatic emotions and feelings not shared with others, they sat blissfully without speaking, understanding each other.

After arriving at Greymouth they both jumped down from the carriage and went for a look around, a brilliant, lovely day and they're not really feeling cold while the last of the sun is pushing its bright warmth through the station clearing, it's obvious that soon it would disappear behind the mountains. Mason appears relaxed and without a care in the world, he trusted and relied on Gemma to look after him and to make sure he didn't get lost.

It was time for a nice cup of tea at the inviting small café with smoke rising out of its chimney, situated a few metres up a metal road and Gemma is grateful for small mercies; they enjoy walking together.

A nice warm sit beside the glowing fire before climbing back onto the train for the return trip to Christchurch.

Bridget stood waiting on the platform, wondering how her mum coped as the long row of bright yellow carriages rattles up alongside her, she had a happy smile on her face knowing full well that they should have had a lovely time and looking forward to having the both of them staying for the rest of the week with her and John. Gemma was keen to see Ombre' even though they have only had one long day away from him she's used to his companionship, and she misses him, they've been through a lot together.

The holiday adventure ended, and she started to think about the drive back to the ferry for the already reserved crossing, allowing plenty of time for Mason to do the driving. They decide to allow two days instead of doing it in one, that's the advantage of being able to stop and sleep in their van anywhere and anytime.

The trip had normalized their existence, which was wonderful for both of them, Mason had something to be proud of, achieving the goal they set while he was at Rehab it had been an amazing journey, and she was enormously proud of his determination. Mason and Gemma are at one with nature again just like they were before, with tranquil quiescence they began the drive home together content in silent reflection.

Parking up at the various deserted rest areas on the long journey home, Mason enjoyed cooking eggs on burnt toast held over a flame for breakfast while parked alongside the paddocks where the cows looked on, and they both fed the wild chickens in the grassed car park rest area. It was as though no trauma had happened; he was happy again automatically doing what they did before.

The incredible, sensual experience traveling in the van together created a memory for Gemma to treasure, and it was made more special this trip because it may not have happened, he was told he would never drive again. Everyday made more important now knowing only too well how life can change in an instant and Gemma continues to feel insecure about his health these days after living through a life changing event, they appreciate each day as it comes.

How lucky that they can feel, even though the more they care for and love each other the more attuned a body is to every pang of feeling good or bad, the pain they went through permanently etched in their lives forever.

It's not the past or the future that matters because that's out of their control, but the reality that life is hard when you're devoted to someone and that responsibility always remains, sometimes the pain of the unexpected is a lesson in life that they would prefer not to have learnt.

The next year monotonously crawled along, like a small car towing a large caravan up hill, she just continued on wanting to get to the end, to conquer this thing that had changed their lives. Back at home things were far from normal and as the days dragged Gemma reluctantly accepted it would never again be the same, while struggling to get to the end of all these problems on her own, Mason's sons continue to deny helping with their dad and seem to sadistically enjoy any misery they can bring to their stepmother.

Even though the dream of regaining his driver's license came to fruition Mason now refuses to go anywhere without Gemma.

He hates all the stimulation in a supermarket and cannot stay inside one for more than five minutes, it's difficult to understand for anyone not experienced in mental health, but the amount of prices jump out at him, the colors and noise are too much for his brain to cope with, it pained Gemma to see the horror on his face the first time he entered the supermarket following his rehabilitation and she couldn't ask him to ever repeat that.

Sometimes feeling depressed and emotionally worn-out

Gemma has the constant presence of fear of getting too sick to care for her husband, so she decided prevention and planning was the best course of action, she tried to persuade Peter and Dwayne to help with their dad for a night to give her a break. After the aneurysm she now had Dwayne's phone number to speak with him on the phone.

"Would you be able to have your dad some time to give me a break, as I'm in overload and I don't want to get sick?"

"No way!" He retorted laughing.

"But I know that you work from home, if I get sick then you will have to help anyway. I'm trying to avoid that happening."

"I'm too busy to talk, goodbye." And he cruelly hung up the phone dismissing her cry for help with his father.

There was no discussion, they both refused to have Mason stay, because that would be interrupting their lives and helping, and what was it that made them so abstruse? Couldn't they see how lucky their dad was to have a wife who cares? Gemma wanted to pour onto Mason all the love and support she could, she just wished it were that easy to make him well again.

Her memories and emotions they shared were all important and powerful in helping Gemma to stay strong, but she also had to stay positive for Mason and never forget that even at the worst times in their lives they still had each other, he's alive and everything will work out, loneliness and the burden of being at home with him all the time was very demanding and emotionally draining.

Gemma found she had travelled through every strong emotion imaginable since their marriage began, she has felt immeasurable love, and fear when she thought she would die at his hands.

Sometimes feeling disgusted by his selfish sons, jealousy, and rage that sometimes she felt trapped, and desperation that there didn't seem to be any escape from this commitment. Going out once a month to the Stroke club support group meeting was her savior, and she looked forward to being with the other wives that were also going through endless incarceration.

Ten partners turned up religiously and talked through all the feelings with like-minded people going through the same thing, they were non-judgmental because they all knew how perplexing it was. She forced herself to be selfish, feeling guilty for leaving Mason sitting in front of the television, warm and fed once a month while she went, this time-out was like her strong thread, binding her to whatever was left of her sanity, it was holding her together!

As Mason improved, he also had trouble accepting his disabilities. This group meeting was an outlet allowing Gemma's tears to flow and express all the emotions and frustrations at how difficult life was at home coping on her own with a sometimes aggressive and irrational human being who she couldn't be angry at. She constantly reminded herself he couldn't help it, it wasn't his fault he didn't have the brain capacity to control his feelings, he was physically unable to calm himself down. But while she picked up the pieces it wasn't Gemma's fault either.

CHAPTER 15

With the passage of time, she was now able to leave a note on the bench to remind him that she's gone for a quick walk up the road with Ombre' and that helps her to clear her head of this nonsense world she lives in. Yah! She enjoyed a brisk walk today and while walking her mind pondered over the morning's events bringing a glimpse of humor back to her face as she recalled what happened.

While taking Mason a cup of tea as he sat on the edge of the bed, she said in a matter-of-fact way. "Let's get your hair cut today."

"No." He replied without hesitation.

"Oh, are you wanting to be really mod or something?" She said jokingly, being careful not to anger him but searching for a little conversation. "It's getting really long."

"Yes!"

"Well, that's okay if you don't want it cut, do you know that you look like Jesus with your long beard and hair? It's 2012 now, when did he die?" She asked with a smile on her face.

"2012 years ago, he replied straight faced, and it took him a while to grow it, so I'll probably look like him in 2014."

"So, you're not going to cut your hair for two years then." She queried getting a little concerned that he's not joking.

"Yep!"

"Okay, will you promise to tell me if your hair gets tangled in your hearing aids than?" She left the room quickly suppressing her hysterics, happy that he might be joking or could he be trying to be annoying. But with his memory loss he'll forget his plan tomorrow anyway and want to look tidy again, he was very fussy about his appearance once upon a time.

Gemma no longer cares what he looks like, it's not important. When he came home from rehab to make him feel better, she told him that as long as he dressed well and was tidy no one would know about his brain damage, of course it doesn't matter anymore if he wants to look like the mad man from Borneo, it's not worth an argument. She never argues with him, just goes with the flow and tiptoes around to keep the peace.

Mason has a personal calendar hanging on the laundry wall, it hangs in an obscure place so as not to attract attention from outsiders now that he has become aware of his abnormalities, he's self-conscious about his struggle to keep in touch with the real world and so Gemma thinks up little strategies that co-ordinate his day for him, he has learnt to put a little dot above today's date and messages for himself to know if he has showered or not, this has proved successful in preventing the multiple showering that used to happen every day. The calendar helps him to know where he is at, and hopefully what season he's in. It's still a struggle and he doesn't understand thermals are no good to wear in summer.

Gemma wakes each morning to pause on the side of the bed and pray to be patient and strong facing another day, she tries to keep Mason to a routine and on a fine day will suggest that they go for a walk down to the pond after breakfast, arriving there to relax on the two plastic chairs which are now a permanent fixture. It's so peaceful and tranquil as she attempts to start a nice quiet talk together, this seems to be quite therapeutic as he remembers the names of the birds and trees, sometimes the huge goldfish will sunbath on the top of the water and it's always a thrill to watch as the swallows swoop down to skim tiny flying insects off the top of the still water.

This is the thirty-minute space in her day that she can sit and breathe without him asking the same questions over and over or hovering around asking when the next meal is coming. Constantly repeating everything to her husband many times over, all day every day is challenging.

Sitting at the pond together watching in the still quiet she's appreciative of their special times together, it's such a merry go round of feelings and even though life is tough Gemma is grateful for what they have and know that some people don't get this extra time together, a special time to sit and reflect.

Day after day, every day the same, life has become very lonely and just as Gemma thinks she's about to go crazy living this uneventful lonely life things miraculously fall into place! What a blessing, she might be able to return to her school job she worked at prior to Mason getting ill, after discussion, the school is accommodating her by juggling student lessons to allow time to put Mason into a rest home for day care for only four hours a week! It's not much, but it's something special for Gemma to look forward to each week.

Each time, it was difficult to pull herself away from caring for him, but after a firm talk with herself, she was convinced, that for such a small amount of time apart they would both benefit from moving forward. Gemma knew he would be in a safe environment and so hoped he would go there amicably; it'll be good for him to get used to socializing with people again and a wonderful chance for Gemma to be a productive member of society again. Talking with the principal at school he understood how significant Gemma's work with the special needs students meant to her and how pleased she was to be able to have a normal conversation with work colleagues again.

This private school Gemma felt was very lucky to have Mr. Selwyn as principal, a man that shows great compassion and insight which is so different from many people Gemma had encountered that don't really have any understanding of what's involved in being confined in a building with a brain injured person. Some days Gemma associates herself pretty much like a prisoner and just to be able to have a conversation with normal people again gives her the motivation and continued hope to go on. She had kept in touch with a few of the staff just to let them know how Mason was doing, and she's really looking forward to seeing them all again! The day arrives for her to go back to work and even though they talked about how useful the extra money will be and Mason has agreed to a short stay at the rest home like it's no big deal, she is anxious. Now the day has arrived she's nervous as emotionally and financially this needs to happen.

"Mason, this morning we're dropping you at the Rest home around the corner from my work, put on your tidy jeans that are on the bed and I've bought you a puzzle book to have a look at while you're there."

"How long will you be?" He asks nervously.

"I need to be there at 11am, so you can enjoy a nice lunch and read your book, then I'll be back straight after school." She explained carefully. "It's only for one day a week." Quickly adding as she felt the angst and got the look.

"Get ready and we'll go and have a look." Making light of it and acting like it's happening whether he likes it or not.

Relieved when everything went well at the rest home, the staff helped introduce him around the residents and she seated him on the deck in the morning sun with a cup of tea.

"If you want you can sit out here away from everyone and just do your puzzles, I'll see you later, won't be long." Giving him a big kiss and a hug she rushed off while the going was good.

Telling herself he'll be fine, and she mustn't think about him while she's away at work, she has to trust that the rest home will ring if they need to. Stunned as she walks the bustling corridors she can hardly believe it, she's back at work. Looking forward to four whole hours a week having conversations and teaching. Time away from Mason where she doesn't have to worry about his safety and the threat of depression that she could have fallen into has now paused, now she battles with her conscience, feeling guilty and horrible about the desire to escape from her home life, she's pleased when her workday arrives.

The district health board (DHB) has a needs assessor allocated and she's coming around today to see how everything is going. Gemma is deep in thought this morning wondering what she will say as she nervously awaits her knock on the door, will she be able to suggest any more help or will she tell Gemma that she's not coping with her precious husband, acid eats at her stomach afraid that they'll want to take him away and put him into care and she couldn't bear that.

There's an insecurity about life that keeps creeping in that wasn't there before his brain surgery. After the first ear piercing welcome from Ombre' Sue Woods takes a seat at the dining table she wants to use to write notes, Gemma feels that request disconcerting and she goes to make a cup of tea for the three of them. Sue begins to read out multiple pages of questions on how they're managing. She's very nice and easy to talk with even though Mason and she are justifiably very defensive after the trouble they encountered at the rehabilitation unit; they feel threatened that they may take Mason away if he can't manage at home after she insisted on taking him home.

Sitting at the dining table Gemma relaxes as her concerns are shown to be unfounded and the meeting goes well, then a frown wrinkles Sue's face showing her depth of concern as she becomes fully aware of the situation, she expresses concern that Gemma is his full time carer not getting any help from family and it is obvious that she needs some help, that's her new title these days, in all the paper work Gemma has suddenly become not only his wife but now his carer as well! Sue is supportive and insistent that there must be carer support time out and she will also arrange for free incontinence products for Mason to wear at night which will help prevent all the washing and expense. The meeting is highly informative, and Gemma is appreciative as Sue notes down her constant anxiety and concern that if she gets sick then there's no one to look after Mason and he remains very dependent on his wife.

It is still a major concern of Gemma's, a responsibility that sometimes wakes her at night in a state of panic as it threatens to overwhelm and brings sleepless nights knowing that her husband would be lost without her.

The stress Gemma carries causes her arthritis to flare up resulting in terrible migraines. When that happens, those days are especially hard because she becomes bedridden and feels guilty and difficult to have the patience required to explain to Mason to get himself a piece of toast now he has learnt to use the toaster, fortunately she relies on her anti-inflammatory drugs to fix it fairly quickly and the following day she is usually okay. Thank goodness she hasn't had any real flu or illness preventing her from looking after him so far, some of the others in the support group have the same fear of '*What if something happens to us carers.*'

During the meeting Sue is adamant that Gemma must have a break from caring, running all the animals and working, it means that she is always working.

Sue carefully explained that Mason is eligible for 28 days a year stay in a rest home so that she can recharge her batteries and stay well. They can split the 28 days however and whenever they decide to, but there's no response from Mason when she looked at him, he's motionless and solemn faced, perhaps he can't comprehend that it's just a holiday and he would come home again. It'll take careful explaining to make him understand, so she won't go into it now with the assessor there and will explain it carefully after she's left. There's nothing else to discuss as his health is good and he has no complaints, so she makes her way to the door requesting that Gemma lets her know which place she chooses for Mason's respite after they look around the various rest homes together.

On the weekend they both set off to look at the local rest home now he understands that she's frightened of becoming sick and not being able to care for him. They need to prevent that from happening by giving Gemma a short break, he reluctantly agreed to just one night. Gemma will take anything at this stage and maybe she can just stay in bed one morning, the chickens can wait to be fed. Oh, a lie in would be nice, she longs to be able to get up when she's ready just for once, without all the running around organizing what Mason is to wear and ensuring he has something to eat. He doesn't know if he has eaten or not with his lack of memory, he continues to get up four or five times every night and wanders around the house early every morning not knowing what to do with himself, and crashing and banging attempting to wake her up, he is become more demanding now.

The local rest-home has an empty bed on Saturday night so they booked it, how strange that excitement rippled through her as she looked forward to something so simple, but she can't wait to have the day and night to herself just to stay home. Not have to go anywhere and stay in bed all day if she wants, not that she would, but she certainly needed the break. Saturday arrives and he has his pajamas packed in a small bag ready to go.

"I'm not going, I've changed my mind." He says to Gemma after hanging up the phone from talking with Dwayne. Questioning him why he'd changed his mind he refused to answer. Patiently explaining to him that she needed a break was pointless, as it's obvious that Dwayne had said something to put him off going.

"Why do you need a break? You only work 4 hours a week." He snapped at her as though he couldn't believe it, ideas have been put into his head and he's lead by what Dwayne has dictated. He wouldn't remember that it's only 4 hours. All the discussion and explaining around the table with the DHB to both of them has gone up in smoke because of that short conversation with his controlling son.

It does sound silly to want one night without him so much and she is really surprised at the depth of unbelievable disappointment she felt that he won't go.

Gemma phoned the rest home to ask their advice and help but they explained there's nothing they can do if he won't go.

Desperate tears running down her face and disbelief as she can't comprehend that she has broken down over such a small thing, she is totally distraught and emotionally out of control which just proves how much she needed a break. Going to the bedroom she throws herself onto the bed and sobs uncontrollably, full of questions, she queries if her life will ever improve. Will she be changed forever, tired and worn out, will she have the ability and strength to ever get over this when she's afraid that all the stress of caring for him is shortening her life. Gemma remembers when the biggest worry was having a job and getting a warrant for the car, but these days it's the everyday running of the home and caring for Mason. Praying that she won't get sick because she doesn't have any energy to go on each day, she worries what the future holds for them both if she fails. Guessing over her ability to put these tough years behind her one day, start life a fresh and move on and wondering if she'll need a shrink to sort her out and physically her whole-body aches so much. How long can she survive like this? Humanity is meant to have one day off each week, everyone needs a day off and she believes what she's asking for is fair and necessary.

Since first going to the stroke group and talking to the other wives there, (actually, it was mainly crying) she continues to look forward to that outing once a month even though she's fatigued and it's a huge physical effort to get there, it has turned into a lifeline for her, and she has become so dependent on talking with the others that sometimes the wait between meetings seems intolerable.

Enjoying an evening where she and Mason are both happily cuddled up on the old familiar sofa watching the TV, a special report flash comes across the screen, there has been a massive earthquake in Christchurch, pictures of broken and crumbling buildings and people wondering aimlessly around in a confused state flash across the scene. Panicked, Gemma ran down the hall to the bedroom where her mobile lay beside the bed, she has to phone Bridget and check they're all right. Displayed on the front, there is one missed text message.

"We're ok mum x." It reads.

Carrying the mobile tightly gripped in her hand she collapsed back onto the sofa her body suddenly heavy as she continued to follow the news report on the television and try to explain to Mason that the earthquake is where they had been visiting in the van, but that Bridget and John are uninjured. They watched the destruction and chaos, people crying and frightened, tears started to roll down her face as she felt their grief, fear, and their helplessness in Christchurch.

"What's the matter with you?" Mason snarled back impatiently, unable to feel anything.

"I can't help it darling; this is happening in New Zealand! It's terrible." Mason looks on without showing any emotion and she had to remind herself that it's the brain damage that prevents him from behaving like a caring human being, he doesn't have any human instincts anymore and in amongst the turmoil of what's happening in Christchurch with her daughter she takes time to silently pray that he will be normal again one day.

One year on from the brain aneurism and following the Christchurch earthquake Bridget and John have decided to move to Auckland, it's meant to be, she just knew it in her heart, she believes that we're never given more than we can cope with and she's not coping. Gemma is elated to be able to talk with her daughter even though it's a sad time for them both having to leave their home because of the aftershocks, it's nice to have the presence of someone that cares about her and listens, they're struggling in their own way after the traumatic shock of the earthquakes and the effect it had on them. These two young people's jobs are gone, and their home life disrupted leaving them shaken and so they have decided to stay with Gemma and Mason while they look for a new home, living together Bridget begins to understand how difficult it is to live with Mason.

"Mum, I didn't know he was so bad." She said apologetically to Gemma one day over a cup of tea.

"That's okay, it's not until you live with someone that you can see all the issues that arise from memory loss and brain damage."

Gemma has so much unwarranted hostility fired at her from Mason's family and no help at all but even though Mason isn't Bridget's real dad she's amazing with him and shows great compassion and patience.

It's so lovely to see this compassionate person in action around the house and it fills Gemma with pride to know that she did well raising her. They stayed for a few months and then bought a home in Auckland closer to their new jobs they both managed to find. Thank goodness they're here, Gemma needed her daughter living nearby, even though it took an earthquake, (an act of God) to get some help.

CHAPTER 16

Surviving the next two years is challenging. Waking each day Gemma looks for any improvement in Mason and praises him for little achievements that she finds. He isn't aware that in reality everything is still a problem for him, he doesn't realize that they are now Gemma's problems, she lives with it when he leaves farm gates open, it's Gemma who chases the sheep and puts everyone back in the right paddock, he is oblivious to any problems he's creating and wonders what's going on if she complains to him. He doesn't remember even going through the gate let alone leaving it open or where the sheep ought to be. He doesn't remember the hot tap being left on all day and it's not his fault when the huge power bill arrives, the fact that his wife has to go without something so she can pay for it doesn't even register.

Gemma finds it exhausting to live with someone who has memory loss unless they have a disposition of acceptance that their partner is trying to help them, but Mason's inability to recognize that, means he wants to take his frustration out on her, it takes a never-ending supply of unconditional love and patience to live without any consideration coming from her husband. She knows through the support group that in some cases the husbands do appreciate that the wife is only trying to help and she's not there to be abused and frustrations to be taken out on. No one gets married to go through these injustices' day in, day out.

Everyday things are emotionally draining now, everyday things such as when she relaxes to watch a favorite program together, he continually asks '*What's happening*,' of course when she patiently repeats and explains everything because of his memory loss and lack of understanding it means that she misses parts of the program which spoil the story for her, it definitely isn't relaxing anymore, plus she feels a deep sense of loss for the couple they once were and the closeness they enjoyed together when she used to cuddle up on the sofa next to him after cooking tea and tidying up. That enjoyment has gone now as it has for him along with his memory and lost sensuality for the closeness they once had, it's just another little bit that dissipated like mist floating into the air following the brain aneurism.

The consolation being that he didn't die, they are cuddled up next to each other and watching television together and she cherishes that.

This person sitting next to her is now completely different he's not the person she married, she's living an illusion, wishing it to be how it once was even though she has accepted who Mason has become.

Life is full of subtle changes not obvious to anyone else; it's living with this brain damage every day that becomes so emotionally draining and the continual repeating everything to him four times because he forgot what she just told him, she knows he can't help it, but neither can she and she can't make it better for him! There are the misunderstandings now that they didn't have before because he doesn't remember what was said, what day it is and that she asked him to dry the dishes two hours ago.

After another harrowing day bedtime arrives, and she leaves Mason watching television in the lounge after telling him she's off to bed to read a book.

"I'm coming too." He says so they turn everything off before going to bed. She jumps into bed with her new romance book for a quiet read, then he demands the television on in the bedroom. He's grumpy when she explains.

"You can watch it in the lounge if you want." (He doesn't remember her saying she wanted to read). So she reluctantly puts her book away as the fiery anger glares hot from his eyes, time has taught her that it's best to tuck down for an early night before he physically lashes out, sometimes he pushes her out of bed, thump!

Without warming she lands on the floor. No quite time for her as now they are watching television in bed and answering the many questions he's firing at her. Gemma has lost her freedom of choice, and she can't turn off the light to sleep as Mason wants it on to watch until late. Giving up every shred of freedom is her reality, even with children she could put them to bed and have some time alone but not with a brain injured adult who is mature enough to have a say.

Confusion often causes him to become verbally aggressive and if he can't understand things he will become cruel and irrational, sometimes doing things like the time he physically prevented Gemma from coming into the bedroom because he didn't want her to go to sleep, he gripped her arm so hard he hurt and bruised it.

Afraid he could escalate into a worse situation she had to call the police for assistance. Mason was given a strong talking to by police and Gemma recommended taking out a protection order but how can that work when he lives there? He can't work and can't manage on his own, so it just doesn't seem to be an option. Gemma is told its domestic violence, when in reality it's Gemma just accepting that he doesn't know what he's doing wrong, he's like a child wanting his own way and it's trivial to complain. There doesn't seem anyway out because she loves him. The more she complains the more snarled and angrier his face becomes, it's safer to say nothing.

The next day walking with Ombre' down to the pond her heart is devoid of any feeling, her world just a hollow existence now, with her head down, thinking and trying to remember something that brings some pleasure, some beauty in this darkness of constant depressive comments, there's never any gratitude in what he does or says, Gemma's whole world is consumed with caring for him, her every moment is him.

Something must change because she's sick and losing her

identity as a person, maybe she should ignore her anxiety and apprehension in search of someone to housesit. Will he become angry and violent towards her if she takes a break. Between the fear and internal numbness, she endeavors not to start crying again from desperation and indescribable emptiness and all she has is her dog to cuddle.

As for the rest of the week, Wednesday night Mason goes to have a shower and a bit later he comes into the lounge and complains that the floor is wet, she leaves the news she is watching to have a look, the water was still dripping from the shower head, he had just turned it on to have his shower, but he obviously hadn't had it because he was still dressed and dry. The floor was wet from Mason just turning it off.

Looking at him still dry, tired, and expressionless she explained, 'You turned it on because you said you were having a shower and seeing the water running you turned it off again. You've forgotten to have a shower.'

The tedious up and down and continual explaining is exhausting Gemma, abruptly turning to go back to the television for a bit of time out now she's fed-up, disillusioned, and depressed with her life when her program has finished. She's fearful to say anything that will make him angry again.

Two days later Gemma decides to only leave one wall light on in the lounge as Mason watched television and she sneaked off to bed, just tucking down cozily starting to fall asleep when he comes in loudly announcing.

"Something funny happened, the room went dark and then the lights went bright again." He said very concerned.

Startled she reluctantly roused herself out of sleep mode. "Let's have a look." Dragging herself into see the 5 candle-type bulbs hanging from the central chandelier were now glowing creating a very bright lounge.

She quietly explained to him "You turned the wall light off and then turned the main centre lights on when you found yourself standing in darkness and you don't remember." Adding that "You know that lights can't turn on by themselves."

His face displayed a blank look of confusion as that much explanation is too much for him to understand, she didn't wait for more questions she wanted and needed bed to try to get some sleep, physically and mentally exhausted.

Just getting through every 24-hour day was difficult, at times there were little glimmers of a normal person somewhere in there, but it had been two and a half unbelievably heart wrenching years. When he's having a good day she's forever hopeful that he's recovering and everything will be better next year, the other days Gemma is lost in a solitary life just her and Ombre', essentially non-existent to others as they all go about their business and she just continues on privately, who could possibly understand if she did talk about what he's like to live with and the toll it took from her. Someone would need to walk in her shoes to understand.

"Let's go out for a nice drive somewhere today and find a bakery to get lunch." Gemma suggested.

"Okay, I want sausage rolls."

Driving past Preston Funeral Directors, she commented that it was really nice inside when she attended a neighbor's funeral.

"Yes, I know because I went there for my stepdad's funeral." he said.

"Who?" She queried.

"Steve that your mum married."

"My mum married Harold, he was my stepdad, your father-in-law."

Mason sits in the car confused and not speaking while he tries to correct his mistake.

"Oh, I was thinking about my first wife's mum." He replied after a long pause before he realized what was going on in his memories.

Does he now think that Gemma is his first wife? He's unaware that this funeral director has only been open about a year, so he was never there anyway. Gemma's not the sort of person to complain, she just gets on with it the best way she can because she loves him, she's torn between her devotion and caring for her husband and the guilt she sometimes feels for wanting out, wanting to run away, to give up and feeling guilty for being that way, she reprimands herself that it's selfish, but she wants to be selfish, she wishes someone would look after her. Someone to care about her!

There is an inner longing to cry out and make people listen and see what her life is like but then she thinks what's the point. That won't make it all go away, she is stuck in a situation she can't do anything about and wondering how many people are out there living this torturous life? Gemma is resolved to just conquer one day at a time and never frets the small stuff.

Anxiety and nervousness have become a constant thing as she's unsure of his mood swings so much so that walking on eggshells being careful not to upset him and cause him to push her around is the way she survives, his behavior is changing her into a different person, and she sits with Ombre' in solitude down at the pond and wonders if life will ever be normal again. Did she bring all of this on herself for wanting to help Mason and not taking the effortless way out when the professionals offered to put him into a rest home?

Her awareness becomes clear that love really is blind, and she was ruled by her heart not her head. Gemma has discovered a coping mechanism, when loneliness and desperation and when life's struggles are getting too much and she's at her wits end, when she can't stand it anymore, she begins to write things down on paper.

It gave her a way of letting go of it all, when his behavior became impossible to deal with and her patience has flown out the window she finds some strange kind of relief, meditating upon her thoughts and gains strength and clarity, she can't speak to him about her frustrations, but she can express the hopelessness and loneliness in her written words as she disappears into her private thoughts on paper with the warmth of a loyal friend lying up against her leg.

Writing the day's events down definitely works, she can't turn on the computer and type because he watches and hovers airily over her, reading everything she types. Writing with pen and paper he leaves her alone; probably just thinks she's paying bills or doesn't think at all. The words flow fast when she's upset and writing furiously to get it all-out, pent-up anger, love, hate, they're all such intense emotions. Love and commitment, allowing someone to destroy and hurt so much that the love blends with hate for the things they do and the way they behave. She realizes that she is the scapegoat for this brain injured person, someone to take all of his frustrations out on, no one gets to see him when he's frustrated with life and needs to blame someone, but Gemma is always there.

She is the person to blame for all of his health issues, he doesn't write his concerns down as she does, and he channels all the angry words and violence at her. Doctors did recommend that Mason seek counselling, but he doesn't see any reason to. Sometimes all of Gemma's feelings mingle into a jumbled mess, like a ball of wool being played with by a kitten, maybe to remain tangled forever, always damaged, and never to be a ball again. Does she throw away every wonderful moment they have ever shared? The gentle times, loving and happy memories and the sometimes-sad closeness they shared, being in awe of their connectedness with the earth, enjoying new life being born together now lost forever in their past.

Some days walking as strangers would, with him not having

any memory of the things she speaks to him about, of their life in this little bit of the world, living on this property and sharing a home, she is sad and sometimes grieving as she tries to jog his memory by talking to him, but his brain now has a physical black hole where everything was once filed. There is still hope that tomorrow will become just a little bit clearer, maybe.

Driving down the road this morning to work and the quietness being alone in the car, she asked herself when she last felt happy, she can't remember how it feels to be happy!

Gemma is hopeful that others can read about her plight and know that they're not alone in the fight to help a loved one and the struggle Gemma's going though. One thing she has learnt is that there are a lot of partners feeling the same loneliness and separation from society, because people are busy going about their everyday lives, they are struggling along unnoticed.

Gemma is mindful of the emptiness inside like a huge dark cancer is eating its way through her, and she's powerless to stop it, she knows that to survive she must just go with the flow, taking control, one day at a time. Without her love for Mason and the memories, she wouldn't have the motivation to go on fighting this battle. She's certain that her husband would be lost if he had to go into a rest home, his recovery would stop, missing out on the precious times they sometimes have being at home together. She continually pushes herself to stay positive, forcing herself to find little things to be grateful for every day to keep going for his sake, to provide him with the best life possible. Looking hard to find the good moments and making a list of everything that is good in their lives.

About eight months ago, Gemma decided to look for cheap help, in the way of somewhere for Mason to go to so he could socialize, develop some independence for himself, make some new friends and have a change of scenery while she does some shopping knowing that she doesn't have to worry or rush back for him because he's having fun in a safe place.

It's a very stressful experience trying on a new bra in the women's changing room while wondering if your husband is getting lost out in the car park. Caring for anyone whether it's a child or adult with memory issues, is hard!

CHAPTER 17

Gemma has evolved into being very protective and Mason totally reliant, so she feels that the need to have some distance, even if just for two hours a week when she's not working is so important.

Discovering the right senior group of people is difficult, not just for Mason but there needs to be an understanding by the group and an acceptance that Mason has difficulties with activities and fitting in.

Finding the energy to keep looking and not give up has been disheartening some days for Gemma. It's taken a lot of determination and a few months of visiting various groups, but Gemma stays positive that the right place will come along. Then she reads the advertisement in the local paper, what a lifesaver! They need more members to meet and play indoor bowls each Tuesday morning until lunch time, Gemma's not at work on a Tuesday morning. It takes a bit of persuasion, but Mason finally agrees to go with her just to have a look.

After a few weeks of Gemma going with him, he soon gets enough confidence to go it alone after everyone is welcoming and accepting of him, this has turned out to be one of her best ideas as it provides him with companionship and her some time out. Gemma is elated with Mason's progress back into society and satisfied that it has been a success for someone in his situation.

Continuing to attend her support group just once a month to talk with the other ladies about how things are going, she often wonders how she copes between meetings as the socializing helps a great deal and she goes home more relaxed, there are no more tears at the meetings and they all have a therapeutic laugh together with like-minded people, it sometimes means that she's more tired the next day for work and some evenings she can't convince herself to leave Mason on his own, they have been through so much together but surprisingly most of the time he's okay with her leaving a note by the electric jug saying where she is and leaving the 111 number for emergencies next to the phone. He's happy to watch television in bed with a promise that on the way home she buys a treat from the drive through, hamburger and chips is the usual welcome back on her arrival home and his face lights up with a big smile, she's unsure if it's the food or her he welcomes but he always seems very happy, and her time out enables her to continue in her quest to help her husband.

Maybe there is light at the end of the tunnel when she thinks of how far he has come, he can write now, read, is very good at puzzles and seems to be happy which has always been her goal. This year she has increased her hours at school and although he's able to cope at home alone for a few hours each day, she remains afraid of what she might find when arriving home, usually she's greeted with,

"I'm hungry." And on inspection of the kitchen finds his lunch that he put into the microwave to heat up at lunch time has gone through it's time and is still in there after 3.00pm he forgot to eat it, one of the many little things that she tells herself aren't important and he will learn to deal with in his own time.

The biggest problem is his possessiveness, and he resents that she's capable of working when he can't, with him often resorting to using delaying tactics. After popping bread in the toaster and rushing around to finish getting ready for work this morning, she returns to find him eating her toast with a smug smile on his face.

"You had your toast already, did you forget?" She asked while tolerantly dropping another slice of bread in to cook, intending to eat it in the car.

"No!" He replied, "I just wanted to have yours." Honestly, men can behave like children sometimes.

He has learnt to use the scrub cutter with Gemma's help,

and it now needs a reconditioned engine because he insisted on managing the petrol himself, forgetting to mix oil in the petrol. Up until now she had been mixing it for him and supervising the use of it. The verbal abuse had become so bad and scary that last time she thought he would hit her if she kept doing it for him. After feeling threatened and confused as to how she could help him without hurting his feelings, decided that maybe he was embarrassed and needed the space to work it out for himself, she decided to leave him to cope on his own, hence the resulting quote of a $900 repair bill that she will struggle to pay. The pointless and futile rush of hopelessness as to what is the best thing to do for him when they don't have that kind of money to spend on his mistakes spreads over her entire body.

Since his aneurism she has always told herself not to fret the small stuff and just let him do things even if they are wrong, things don't matter, she loves him and he is what matters, not material things. Now this costly exercise has her thinking maybe she has to draw a line, not only because of the repair cost they can't afford but also because this failure will also impact him and results negatively on his self-confidence, his face shows the sadness and disbelief with what has happened to one of his favorite power tools, he was doing so well working with his tools and being the man about the house again, possibly becoming overconfident. Now she treads carefully as he always reverts to aggressive behavior when something doesn't go right.

Gemma knows that it's a balancing act and she needs a degree in psychology, perhaps the carer does have to intervene even if it's embarrassing for Mason and difficult for him to accept at the time, to outsiders it may look like she molly coddles and bosses him around but to prevent an accident or damaging his self-esteem and the wonderful progress he has made to date means that she might have to tread persuasively around the power tool issue in the future.

Her heart went out to him when she explained what had

happened and how much it cost to repair, he looked so deflated, and she felt his pain and disappointment as much as he did. Carefully positioning the scrub cutter back into her car boot after paying the money for the reconditioning they set off home and on the way she again carefully explained what has happened to the engine and why (in case he has forgotten), suggesting that he write on a sticky label when he puts oil in the petrol so he mustn't use the petrol if there is no label saying the oil has been put in and she has bought the exact size jug for the oil, so he doesn't have to measure out anything. Hopefully, this will give him some responsibility to take charge of it without her guidance.

"We know you forget what you have or haven't done, so we just have to do things differently, that's okay." She quietly reassured him with a fixed smile, deliberately hiding her deep concern. Secretly praying that he won't blow it up again and wondering what they will eat this month with no money. Only a month has passed when she arrives home from work to find him pulling the motor apart because he couldn't get it to go! After carefully persuading him to show her how to start it she found that he's forgetting to pump the petrol and move the choke, now she will have to take it back to the shop along with the many pieces he doesn't know how to put back together again.

Gemma's entire body wants to scream with excruciating chest pain and anxiety, longing for an end and release of this constant turmoil rushing around in her head. But still there is no respite. The following week he's angry with his electric drill because it won't go when he pulls on the trigger, he thinks it's broken, fortunately she arrives home just in time as he started to pull it apart.

"Let me check before you pull it to pieces." She pleaded with him.

When she checked the problem and showed him that he hadn't

switched the extension lead on at the power source.

"It's plugged in, I thought it would go." He said grumpily semicontrolled.

Everyday tinkering with stuff that men enjoy doing is difficult for Mason, and the more she tries to help solve the problems for him the more hostile he becomes towards her. The distress hurt her insides, her love for him putting an ache in her heart so much so that her throat burnt as she attempted to hold back the tears, she felt sad for him that he's not normal like the other guys, and she was here for him trying the best way she knew how to sort it, but his pride gets in the way.

Sometimes her desire to run away returns if only to let everyone see the mess he'll get himself into without her present, but she can't! There's no-one to see to the animals, they'll starve or get out on the road when he leaves the gates open and who will move them to another paddock for fresh food because he doesn't have cognitive capacity to think of that. Gemma's days are spent rushing between work and home praying she will find that everything is okay when she returns home, the constant tiredness, stressed and often afraid of her husband's temper continues.

She feels trapped, and can only pray for someone to help her, to be more patient, a better person and to understand what she should do to help him get well. Every day is swallowed up with Mason's issues and her world is engulfed in a thick mist of dark despair most of the time, it has become a massive web of entanglement with no end to it.

Keeping to a caring routine for Mason seems to help a bit, sometimes when arriving home from school he has been chopping firewood and stacking it which he seems to like doing. She grabs the kitchen scraps as usual and heads down to feed and pen up the chickens for the night. They get locked in the hen house and then she feeds and let them out in the morning before going to work, that way the eggs are always in the boxes and not lost in the paddock, as she walks along wishing that Mason could learn to do this task as young children do.

Gemma is grateful for her cozy warm gumboots as she treks along the track, the grass is knee high now and she makes a mental note that she needs to let the sheep in there again. Her foot is about to touch the ground when she catches a glimpse of something shiny sticking up between the long clumps of grass, there's a fleeting moment of fear and a sense to NOT take the step, *don't put your foot down* as she is left standing with one foot in mid-air, moving to the side of the track before losing her balance.

Searching through the long grass for whatever it was that she had glimpsed, she finds the rake lying on the ground with the spikes in the air, she had come so close to stepping on it, and she knew it would have gone through her boot with the handle hitting her in the head!

Sitting in the long grass to collect herself, aware of the serious close shave she just had. What is the rake doing here? Looking around to see what it has been used for, there's nothing but paddock, no lose sticks or soil or anything that one would need to rake up. She's so lucky not to have stood on it, and stayed sitting for a moment, a bit shaken from an accident being so close to happening. Walking back to the house to ask Mason. "Did you use the rake?"

"No."

"Have you used it recently, because I found it left down in the paddock?" She insisted.

"I don't know." He said sounding a little harassed.

"Well, you know I have always told you to put the spikes into the ground and don't leave it sticking up." Then she didn't say anymore so as not to rile him and is left suspicious to know why the rake wasn't in the garage and wondered if it was innocent or deliberately hiding in the long grass on the route that she took every day. His moods and lack of understanding are making her paranoid, she hoped not but every day she saw in him a lack of any ability to reason and be safe. Oh well, if life was always easy, it would be boring.

It's been wonderful that Mason has continued to go to bowls on a Tuesday morning and can drive himself there and back home again noting that he needs to renew his driver's license this week so he can continue to do so. It is with trepidation that she phoned to make the necessary doctor's appointment for him to pass the medical needed before he can relicense, Mason is insistent that she didn't need to go with him as he had done this many times before. Nervously, she understands that for him to be normal she must let him do things, so loosening her grip she goes off to work hoping that he will manage. On arriving home, he proudly updates her as to how his day went, it was a big event for him.

He successfully managed to get himself to the doctor's rooms and he remembered to tell the receptionist he was there before sitting down.

He continues to tell her that he kept an eye on his watch that she had insisted he wears when he goes out and it showed that he sat for two hours.

He never saw the doctor, Gemma immediately went to the phone and inquired with the receptionist what had happened. Apparently, they called and called his name with no success so thought that he had gone home. Gemma thinks he probably sat waiting and was so distant and vague that he didn't notice the nurse calling his name, he has poor concentration. That was a wasted experience with her now having to phone the doctors rooms as soon as arriving home and getting an appointment for the morning, she needed to ring work to take time off so she could take him back to the doctors, who are being very accommodating to get Mason sorted.

Thank goodness he passed his medical, blood pressure and his health is good apart from his pride being hurt. Sometimes memory loss can be helpful. Tomorrow they will take the medical certificate to the Motor Vehicle Association to relicense him after Gemma knocks off work at 3.00pm as there's no time to travel there today and he's too grumpy anyway. It's just a difficult emotional roller coaster, keeping him safe and trying to save his pride, with her always being his scapegoat for his moods.

CHAPTER 18

The evening sun is setting a bright red glow in the west, a glorious sight from the lounge ranch slider and after clearing up tea they settle down to rest while catching up on the six o'clock news. A broadcast comes on about an airlines plane that has been shot down, they watched the details and bodies being recovered, hundreds of people line the road as each coffin is taken off the plane and she's gripped with compassion seeing the grief of the people.

Mason says "That's ridiculous! Why are we watching this as they flew over a war zone, it's their own fault." He shows no sympathy for the people on board the plane or the families who have lost a loved one through no fault of their own.

"The news will be finished in a minute." Gemma said, not wanting to get into it.

The lack of compassion is a continual shock, even though she makes excuses for him because of his brain damage and shows him as much love as possible, she just believes that that will teach him to learn to feel something, but it doesn't! She has difficulty accepting that he can't consider other people's feelings, even if he can't feel emotions, surely, he can show some understanding to people who are visibly crying and upset, can he not compare his devastation from the loss of the scrub cutter (losing something) or someone he loves as being similar.

She continues to plod on one day after another with armloads of patience and oppression, with a heart full of love, compassion, and hope that tomorrow might be the start of a new beginning for them.

Waking to a stream of sunlight shedding brightly through the thin bedroom curtains she's ready to take her morning walk with Ombre' down to the pond, to move the sheep and feed the chickens on the way down the paddock then they'll have time to sit quietly, soak up some tranquility while she strokes his silky coat, talk, and reflect on life before going to work this afternoon.

These days Mason doesn't often go with them to the pond and Gemma finds that what he plans in thought, and what he actually does are two different things, it needn't be reality because he lives in a world of his own.

Like a dream he plays it out however his disturbed mind dictates, it's difficult to get her head around, because in reality his actions often cause him more frustration and confusion. To be a sound, capable human being we need to act and be responsible for our actions, this doesn't apply to Gemma's husband! Mason goes about every day with little understanding of the consequences for his actions. Being forever watchful she looks on with a feeling of helplessness at the wasted person before her, wishing she could fix everything and that he could enjoy life even more, he came close to losing his life and yet that fact is lost on him, and he is not motivated to make the most of any day.

Mason tells Gemma that he doesn't want to work again, he's happy because he has her to do that for him, saying "Why should I work?"

Gemma struggles along with this deep sadness, her eyes reflecting a broken heart and unbearable loss because she perceives something inside him has perished.

He is like an injured animal and it annoys her to watch his life pass him by as she would have thought that self-preservation would prevail to propel him on to better things, but it doesn't appear to, even though she is glad that he's happy while she takes on any problems it also strikes her that he's not living in the real world, not feeling highs and lows of life, surely if you live in a protected bubble all the time you can't appreciate how wonderful anything is without the down side to compare to. Gemma accepted a long time ago that his aggressive manner is because of the trauma that changed his life, whether that's reality or just her making excuses for him it doesn't really matter, because she has unconditional love for him and continues to care and help him to be the best he can be. He's like a lost soul, even a wounded animal would fight to survive but sitting by the pond with her furry friend lying up against her leg the realization is that it's not her job to be in charge of lost souls. It's not her job to judge or ask why this has happened, but just to keep on believing that everything happens for a reason.

Time for her to sprint back up the hill to the house as Mason will wonder why it's taking so long to check the animals. The afternoon is slow to arrive but then pushing her home life into the background she finds motivation and is smiling while enjoying her half day at work helping the students strive to achieve great things.

This giving her a purpose to go on. It's just a short afternoon before arriving home to Mason standing in the kitchen, he starts yelling at her that he can renew his license by himself, and she doesn't need to go with him. He has been stewing on it all afternoon as she had left a written note on the bench telling him to be dressed ready as they would do it when she arrived home from work. This is not worth arguing about and she decides that she'll not bother, not wanting to keep protecting him at the expense of her own safety. Let him find out the hard way.

"Okay, do you know where to go?" Gemma queried, "Beside the Panguru shops like we did last year." She prompted.

"Yes, piss off, I know what I'm doing." He replied gruffly.

Insuring that he left with the paperwork and the money he needed, a big hug and a kiss she reluctantly waved goodbye before going inside to put her feet up smiling at the prospect of a peaceful cup of tea.

It's been over 3 hours now and he should be home. She was getting worried as she turned the stove off and put their tea on hold for when he arrives back, she wonders if perhaps she should get the car out and go looking for him, maybe he got lost or had an accident.

Constantly checking out the kitchen window she eventually spots his van totter into the driveway, a huge sigh of relief and butterflies start to settle in her stomach, she can't wait to see him, she doesn't want to appear too anxious by going outside to greet him even though she longs to rush out to hug him. Telling herself just try to act normal and don't let on that she had been concerned.

"All done?" She casually asked with a smile when he came through the door.

"It was closed at the council building in Kaitaia." He said.

"You went to the wrong place." She gasped, shocked that he went to Kaitaia she tried to make light of it.

"You don't renew your driver's license at the council, that's only for rates. Never mind, we can do it on Monday as you don't need the van until Tuesday for bowls."

He's driven over 80km to Kaitaia instead of the local Panguru Automobile Association, he's tired, so she doesn't speak in case he becomes violent.

It's just lucky that he hasn't come to any harm, and he had enough petrol. She does hope that he will think twice next time he yells about doing everything by himself.

Two and half years since his operation and he can't manage on his own. He can't shop in a supermarket, pay bills, renew his license or his car registration, banking, cooking, or anything without supervision? His sons tell Gemma he's normal and he doesn't need her, according to Dwayne she molly coddles her husband. In reality he needs constant help, and she wished Dwayne would get his head out of the clouds.

Preparing for Mason's Tuesday bowls is one of the few things she looks forward to now as she has the whole day off work and can spend time to help him get ready to socialize with the bowling buddies, he's made friends with. While he's away she sometimes bakes hot scones and surprises him by arriving with them in time to share a cup of tea and a chat with everyone when the games are over, his face lights up when she arrives and pride spreads across his face as he rushes off to get her a cup of tea, with such a lovely welcome warming her insides more than the tea, other times she can't wait to have that two hours on her own away from constant complaining or repetitive questioning, because now that he has learnt the way there and back he's able to drive himself, it's wonderful that she can go to the shops or if finances permit sometimes get her hair done without the stress of having to be back in time to collect him.

"Can you bring the van up to the house this morning so we can plug it onto the battery charger for a while before you go out, you haven't used it for two weeks, so it won't do any harm to charge it up." She suggested over breakfast.

"I have, I use it all the time and it doesn't need charging." He snapped back very aggressively in a loud voice. He finds going out is a bit challenging and that's probably why he has mood swings, but he'll be fine once he gets there, she's sure.

"Okay, well where have you been in it?"

"Ah, I don't know but I use it all the time." He snapped at Gemma.

"Well, you have bowls today so drive it up to the house, you will hear the fan belt squeaking if it's trying to charge the battery up." She tried to remain calm as she coaxed him because she wants to encourage him to go to bowls, he didn't go last week, and she needs the break from him. It's a concern to her that the van needs to be reliable so he can get home again, when he goes out, he doesn't have a cell phone because he can't use one. The debilitating tension is mounting in the back of her neck, she knows it's just stress and it will disappear when he has left.

Fortunately, he walks off down the drive to get the van without the need for further explanation, he's probably determined to prove her wrong. The sound of the squeaking fan belt was obvious all the way up the driveway which was about 60 metres away, so nothing is said when he arrives back in the house, they are able to attach the battery charger leads to the battery without having to remove the heavy thing out of the engine cavity, out of the blue he starts swearing and calling her names because he can see the gauge registering that it's low on battery and he hates her being right. Gemma knows that verbal abuse won't physically hurt her, but it does do psychological and emotional damage as he slowly destroys the confident woman she once was.

Sometimes the dark despair at this life threatens to overwhelm her as his sons don't seem to appreciate the effort made for their dad and all she ever gets these days is abuse, if only someone could appreciate that she's just trying to care for her husband and she longs for a glimpse of that quiet man she married a long time ago or even just a normal life like other people have, she strives to be positive above the painful memory of their lost love, yearning for him to be well again.

After checking to see he has put batteries in his hearing aids and is dressed appropriately for the weather, she kisses and waves goodbye with a smile, he drives off and it's a chance to tidy the kitchen and make the bed in the quiet calm of an empty house with Ombre'. He enjoys having Gemma home on Tuesdays as they walk down to the pond and she spends some quality time with her affectionate little dog lying across her feet as she sits on the soft grassy bank watching the ducks idly floating around the pond talking all about her worries, Ombre' is a good listener.

They watch the birds skim across the pond catching insects and hear the peaceful singing of a Tui at the very top of a huge gum tree. It's a lovely place to sit and ponder over everything.

Unfortunately, even here in this beautiful restful place has been tarnished with bad memories for her as she goes to look at her favorite May tree that Mason had chain sawed down, for no other reason except he wanted to be mean to someone on one of his bad days. He knew that Gemma loved this tree more than the others because of the changing colors of the leaves in the Autumn from green to golden yellows followed by pretty little white flowers in the Spring, she has been nursing the remaining stump and can see new growth coming back to it, she won't let him see her looking at it and then hopefully he'll forget it's there, Gemma and Ombre' share the secret.

All of these things Mason forgets after he has had one of his crazy rages and even though she tries to forget the horrible way he treats her and the animals, unfortunately they are etched in her memories causing hurt. Sometimes she thinks it must be great to lose your memories like they were just a pair of old shoes lost at the beach. Never mind, she tells herself there is a good reason for all of this and she knows that he would be lost without her. By the time he gets back from bowls she has managed to pull herself together again just to have the occasional breather and cuddles with her devoted furry friend is what was needed.

Another day, while watching something on television together he points out a guy and explains that he has since died, and Gemma thought good that's progress because he's right, but then disappointment strikes when Mason continues to explain,

"But these days he's put on weight."

"No, Mason he's dead now, this program was recorded years ago before he died." Looking confused he can't get his mind around it.

Another Saturday arrives and Mason has been wandering around the house since 6.00am, Gemma suggested that he go and do his 1000-piece jigsaw puzzle in the lounge while she make tea and toast to take back to bed for hopefully a peaceful morning lie in.

Putting two slices of whole meal bread into the toaster for her and Ombre', she decides to take the kitchen rubbish outside to the bin while it's cooking. Mason appears in the kitchen, she wonders why her toast hasn't popped up yet, Mason is spreading something, and the toaster starts smoking.

“Have you popped the toaster up Mason?” She asks rushing over to stop the smoke.

“No, I just took one out to give to the dog.” Ombre’ longingly looks on.

“So, you popped mine back down again and burnt it.” She carefully tried to explain while taking out the remaining black slice.

“No!”

“Yes, you have cooked it twice!” She said with diminished memories of her having a lie in and toast in bed, her stressful day has already begun. He doesn’t understand how it happened.

“You stupid bitch, it’s not my fault you burnt your toast, stop trying to blame it on me.” He yelled furiously at her.

Her throat tightens as tears start to pool in her eyes and she turns away so he can’t see them. She knows it doesn’t even warrant a reaction to his insults, so she tries to ignore it and say nothing as she is safer that way.

After wafting the smoke away out the kitchen door so the alarm wouldn’t go off she decided that she may as well get dressed and press on for another day with Mason, oh where did her dream of a peaceful Saturday go to!

Gemma’s life is just one long monotonous ordeal now and this is the start of another horrible day, she can’t wait to go back to work on Monday to be with normal people, after dressing, trying to relax with her cup of tea she grabbed two crackers from the pantry cupboard to eat as she wanted him to forget about the toaster. She hurriedly hid it in the cupboard while he’s out of the room and left a note on the bench saying she had gone for a walk.

Of course, she understands that he can’t help that everyday things confuse him, but if she tried to explain things to him he got grumpy, if only he wouldn’t swear and be mean to her, they could deal with problems a lot better.

Walking clears her mind but unfortunately also gave her time to fume over stuff and become aware that she could have given up on him and started a new life, so many people would have gone along with the medical advice of putting him into a rest home and not given up their independence to become his caregiver, loving him and commitment to their marriage makes her vulnerable to compassion and desire to help rehabilitate him and she believes that she is doing the right thing.

Mason knows he had brain surgery, and the doctor has explained to him many times what his problems are. So why can he not be more appreciative of her efforts, she just needs a little bit of kindness. She's not worried about the things he can't change, but he's able to control his manners, she has noticed that he's aware of what he's doing when other people are around and he behaves well in front of his sons.

Time crawls along with tiny improvements but he's quick to anger and his irritability is worse. These days she carefully guards what is said, and tip toes around so as not to upset him, knowing full well that she has changed into this frightened person. One cold afternoon in May arriving home from work driving past the five-wire fence around the paddock next to the house she noticed it's tipping over. A dark feeling of dread plummets from the sky before she even gets out of the car, now what? "What's happened to the fence Mason?"

"Nothing." He scowls.

"Have you been fixing something?" She broached the subject diplomatically.

"I haven't done anything you stupid cow." He replied.

"Well, the whole fence is tipping over; I better go and have a look after I change my good trousers and grab by gumboots. Do you want to come and have a look with me?" She asked politely.

After entering the paddock, she discovers that the fence is

just sitting in place, all the staples have been removed from five long stretches of wire. It must have taken all day to pull that many staples from the battens on what was once a nice fence, there was no reason to alter it. Mason arrived behind her.

"The horses next door must have pushed it over." He says and she can hear the doubt in his voice.

"No, because I can't find any staples on the ground anywhere and the whole fence is falling over, not just a little bit." She explained to him, and he looked very guilty. He removed them; it couldn't have happened any other way. He knows it himself without her saying any more.

"I haven't touched it."

"Well, I'll go and get the hammer, and can you give me a hand to put it all back before the sheep get out, it's going to be dark soon." Not even waiting for a reply she ran off to the shed and sitting on the work bench was a plastic bowl full of used staples next to the hammer. Picking them both up and rushing back aware of the urgency to get the fence back up, before the sheep are all out on the road.

"Look I found this container of staples; you must have taken them out of the fence today for some reason." Explaining without trying to antagonize him as she needed some help to hold the wire up while she nailed.

"I can't remember doing that so I'm not helping, it's getting cold, and I want my tea."

"No Mason, I'm sorry but this fence has to go back up tonight. The sooner its up the sooner we can eat." She started to work on the fence, and he stands watching for a few minutes before realizing that she is serious and not going inside the house until it's all up.

CHAPTER 19

Whenever Gemma arrives home from work now she has made it quite clear that she intends to walk the dog, Mason is getting to know that is her routine, he doesn't realize that walking with Ombre is her escape where she can be lost in her thoughts and dreams, forget about home life and no one can condemn her for trying to keep fit and give Ombre' a walk. Mason doesn't want to come or help walk the dog during the day, so he doesn't object to her doing it.

Dwayne is bringing Adam, Mason's grandson around to see the sheep and chickens on Saturday, he's only seven so it should be a nice visit for Mason. Gemma has written it on the calendar in the laundry for him and will remind him again on Saturday morning that they are coming around 1pm. The morning has arrived, and he doesn't seem bothered one way or the other, not showing any excitement or feelings of any kind. They arrive as expected luckily after her doing all the preparation for Mason.

"Do you want to come for a walk down to see the sheep and feed the chickens Adam?" Gemma asks.

"We'll all go." Snapped Dwayne gruffly insinuating that he didn't want Adam to be spending any time with his grandma. So, they all headed outside to put old gumboots on, the shed has a lidded drum full of chicken food already down at the hen house and they all came running for extra food. After spending a little time at the henhouse and Adam collecting some eggs in a bucket, they sat them down to collect later on the way back from seeing the sheep. They all continued walking down the grassy race under the big old pine trees which lined it and followed the fence line to the paddock with the sheep in.

"We'll have to help Adam to get over the fence." Mason explained.

Looking up from the ground, "Why don't we just go further

along to the gate? It will be easier."

"No!" He snapped back at her. "There is no gate."

She said nothing as she felt Dwayne's demonic stare shoot her way.

After they all managed to climb over the fence unnecessarily and pat the sheep she walked over to the gate and opened it for them to leave the paddock and return to the house, on the way back Dwayne sarcastically said to her.

"Mason's fine, there's nothing wrong with my father."

She asked him, "How do you think the sheep got into a paddock with no gate. Do you think that's normal behavior?" There was no reply, he doesn't want to accept anything is wrong with his father it's a case of '*If you don't accept it, then it doesn't exist.*'

The relief after they have gone was bliss as the tension in the air had been choking her, at the same time tolerating them and hoping that Mason enjoyed his visit, she wonders what Dwayne's motive was for coming around, she's trying not to be paranoid, but he only visits once or twice a year and he's never pleasant to her. They had Mason's favorite pie and chips for tea tonight, so she also put on a pot of frozen vegetables to boil, without her noticing, Mason saw the vegetables boiling and turned them off. Gemma sat down for 25 minutes in front of television and returned to the kitchen to see if everything was ready, the pie and chips are nearly crisp, but she found the pot on the stove with the vegetables still cold and hard.

"Mason, you'll have to wait for tea a bit longer now because you've turned off the vegetables." She finds its better these days not to ask him if he has done something because he denies it, so now she just tells him instead, which he accepts, and it keeps the peace.

"Well, they were boiling." He said.

"Yes, they have to boil for them to cook, if I am cooking

then you need to ask me before you touch anything. I promise that if you are cooking then I will ask your permission before I turn anything off okay?" He didn't reply.

Gemma's voice came out a little firmer than expected as she's getting exhausted with having to watch every single thing he does and maybe she's also a little stressed after tolerating Dwayne's comments today, he needs to walk in her shoes to see his dad's behaviors and memory loss before making judgements.

Mason has been trying to learn how to work the washing machine for three months now, she stands, watches, and says nothing as he said he can do it now. Putting the clothes into the machine, he sets the water temperature, the water level and how fast to spin. He forgets to put the soap powder in. The next week he was so intent on the soap powder that he forgot to put the clothes in. He has had 12 attempts to get it right and each time he forgets something. She has written it in large black marker pen on the dials, but he cannot use the machine, when she mentions it to anyone they don't believe her because it's such a simple task people just don't believe he can't do it! With all her patience and good intentions his sons still think she's exaggerating and making his disabilities up.

It's one of those small things that are not worth worrying about and she just does the washing for them, it's not a biggie. Remembering Dwayne's quote '*There's nothing wrong with my father*!' makes her laugh out loud.

Thank goodness she wakes to another fine Saturday today so she can paint the outside of the garage, she decides to have morning tea before she starts, discussing it with Mason he says he is happy doing jigsaw puzzles in the lounge and she's thinking it's all okay to get this job done. Having completed only a small amount of painting and he comes out to ask shall we have a cuppa.

"Nice thought darling, but we just had one and I want to get this wall finished before I stop." He took no notice and came back with two teas, without saying anything she sat and drank it outside with her hands covered in paint. Maybe he's trying to be useful and nice to her, so after thanking him she started again anxious to have a fresh look on the old garage, 20 minutes later he comes out again, its 11.00 he says.

"So what! Can you please leave me to do this painting, or you can help if you want, but stop interrupting me, you're making it take twice as long." At 11.45am he comes back,

"It's nearly lunch time." He says,

"Oh good, will you put the left-over sausage rolls that are on the bench into the microwave, and I'll have something later."

"No, I don't want to. I'll wait for you to do it." He replied.

This seems to have worked as he went inside and didn't come out again.

What a nightmare she's thinking, minding a bored adult acting like a child, constant nagging and attention seeking. Then 15 minutes later when she reached the corner of the garage she felt guilty and sorry for him and goes inside to get lunch for them both. Everything takes so long and becomes a chore when she is babysitting as well, but after finishing just one wall they go out for a drive together and enjoy a pleasant walk around a local park hand in hand.

Monday comes along again and it's a welcome relief from all the work at home, before leaving she collects the hand operated hedge clippers from the shed and tucks them into the kitchen porch, turning to Mason for some help.

"If you want something to do today darling while I'm at work, you can help me by clipping the hedge which would be lovely to come home to." She smiled at him.

"Okay, I might." He said before she gave him a big hug and sloppy kiss said her goodbye and headed off without too much trouble this morning. The day with the students is great and she loves helping them, on arriving home small droplets are just starting to land on the windscreen but between them she can see a little bit of the hedge done, pleased she can't believe it, rushing inside to praise him for his lovely work. Warm hugs are given and he's really proud of himself with smiles all round. There is a flashing glimpse of hope in her soul.

"Where have you put the clippers darling?" She enquired, "It's started to rain, and I don't want them left outside."

"I don't know!" Came the reply.

Still in her good clothes from work, hardly in the door and she rushes over to where the hedge has been clipped, looking around all the obvious places, checking in the shed but finding herself having to look the whole length of the lifestyle block, it turns out that he had wondered off with the clippers still in his hands down into the gully, that's where she found them after she was soaked through. It's not a big issue, however because of the rain and little money she didn't want them to go rusty. On the way back up the hill to the house she's quietly fuming, partly brought on by fatigue and partly disheartened because nothing he does turns out to be of any assistance as he never finishes anything except jigsaw puzzles and doesn't stay focused on anything for long.

They keep his focus because of the changing pictures and colors, he can sit and do puzzles all day but only half the hedge.

Gemma's sadness and frustration is building as there is no outlet for her disappointment with life, she says nothing to him about her feelings as she becomes afraid of falling further into this dark hole of depression. Her husband looks too young for a rest home, but intellectually he would be far worse than a lot of the elderly living in them even though physically he's quite capable. Some days it all gets a bit much for Gemma and the tears threaten to flow she holds them back and mentally makes excuses for him, he can't help it and it's her own fault for getting tired from working, managing all the stock, shopping, cleaning, mowing the lawn and still trying to help Mason by teaching him days, times and keeping him informed of what's happening. She finds it impossible to contemplate a rest home for him as she loves him too much and it feels like giving up on him.

Oh, when is the next support group meeting with the stroke club for her to off load all the frustration? The stroke organization have allocated some carer support for Gemma to have a break but Mason refuses to have anyone in the house so she's not able to have a whole day out, that's why she only works part days each week, she's fortunate to work at a school where the principal allows her to have Tuesdays off when Mason goes to bowls, these breaks are short but are a welcome relief for her, she tries not to do housework instead choosing to look around the shops.

Occasionally the bowling group go off to a restaurant for a lovely lunch, so she goes and enjoys that outing time with her husband and his friends, they sit and chat with all his bowling mates over lunch and he glows with pride introducing his wife to everyone. At these times she does feel that her efforts are worthwhile as quietly he shows that he is appreciative of her.

It was such a good idea for him to join a group, his self-esteem has improved, and he has to socialize and try to hold a conversation as they discuss likes and dislikes of various food. The seniors say that he is getting very good at bowls, and he helps roll up the mats after the games giving him some responsibility, going out once a week is providing him with a bit of independence and an interest now that he can't work. Gemma is warmed and pleased that he's happy.

Tuesday finally rolls around again and hopefully after getting him ready Mason will go to bowls, she suspects that he's getting harder to manage, or is she just getting worn out? Her nightmares are starting to haunt her again, like they did before his aneurism because he was unpredictable, and she never knew what he would do next. To manage this fear and cope with always walking on eggshells she has started going for more walks or leaving him in the car when she goes shopping. He doesn't like her going out without him, and the abuse is getting worse. Driving the car and listening to him going on at her about nothing important is very difficult and dangerous, she thought he was going to hit her again like he used to and she's becoming more nervous not knowing what he will do next. Gemma is throwing herself into work, and trying to get the house sorted with painting, she's tired and anxious whether he's going to hurt her, wondering if he's going to have another aneurism because his actions are reminiscent of the years of abuse she had before he strangled her, she wonders when this behavior will stop and how long before their lives will be normal again.

Peter phoned last night and asked if he could take Mason to watch Len (his youngest of four) play soccer as he supposedly plays well, during the call she found out that Peter had given Mason his home phone number, but it hadn't been passed on to her, they still refuse to accept that Mason has memory loss! Peter wondered why she hadn't contacted him about whether Mason would like to go and watch 9.30am this Saturday, she explained that she would ask Mason if he wanted to go and phone him back. It took a while explaining and making it clear that he understood she wouldn't be there with him.

Peter assured Mason he would look after him and Gemma was not needed. He'll pick Mason up at 9.30am and the game starts at 10.00. Gemma is a little worried because it's been 3 years of caring for Mason and all this time Peter had only seen his father in the hospital and once at rehabilitation. She has been trying to get him as independent as possible, which means he appears normal to people and they don't understand the effort that goes on behind the scenes to make sure he's ready and how much his memory loss effects everything.

Gemma schooled Mason to repeat his phone number on Saturday morning before leaving, reminding him to let her know if he needs help. It had taken 18 months of repetition from her before he could retain it in his memory. It is a concern that he can't use a cell phone so is reliant on using Peters, what if he gets lost? As they wait 9.30am has come and gone still no Peter.

Mason said to her, "Don't be surprised if he has forgotten to pick me up."

Her heart melts as her arms reach around his neck, "Let's have a cup of tea, maybe he's running a bit late, and they'll turn up after the game and you can see your grandson then. Never mind, they have busy lives, and we have each other, I love you."

While making a nice hot cup of tea for them to have sitting by the window watching and hoping, Peter eventually pulls into the driveway at 10.20am.

"Quick, grab your coat darling." She says with a smile. "I've made you a thermos of hot soup in case you want it because it's cold out there today."

"Oh, thanks." He says.

Mason isn't like other people and rushing him isn't good, he needs to follow a quiet routine. It takes so long to just get him ready on time for an appointment in a relaxed atmosphere, with all the explaining that has to go on about what to wear and preparing his hearing aids. He no longer has the ability to hurry, it confuses him. She isn't pleased about them telling him a time, and then arriving late. Seeing Mason upset and insecure pains Gemma, showing her their neglect and ignorance.

Gemma was looking forward to doing her housework knowing he was having fun, now Peter will have to earn her trust in the future as she doesn't want Mason upset and under pressure like this again, it would be better for him to be at home relaxed and happy rather than risk having a stroke through the actions of others. Peter has always been unreliable, and history has shown that she picks up the pieces if his dad gets sick, she's the one that has to live with the consequences of their actions.

CHAPTER 20

After the vacuuming is finished and she had a good go over everywhere with the duster she looked up from the cupboard as she put things away, to see Mason, Dwayne and his son Adam arriving in the kitchen door.

Surprised, "How'd it go?" She asked.

"I got there when it started, Dwayne said, but Mason didn't arrive until half time, Len was side lined before that, so my dad didn't see him play. I suggested bringing my father home as Len was cold and dirty, and needed a shower, Peter didn't take any dry clothes for Len, and he couldn't come here with dirty shorts on." It was said in an accusing tone.

"Oh, that's a shame he got there too late, it wasn't Mason's fault that he didn't get picked up on time. After all that waiting he didn't even get to see Len play, never mind, thanks for bringing him home." She explained.

Gemma is genuinely grateful to Dwayne for bringing Mason home safely, he looks a bit tired and dazed as to what is going on but is happy to have a coffee with his son and pleased to have his grandson as well. Overall, it wasn't a very successful outing and a poor idea trusting Peter to take his dad out, he can't even organize his own son's dry clothes.

The builder has now finished cladding the deck around the pool, so after they have both left she talks to Mason about having his grandchildren around sometime for bar-b- ques, in the hope of cheering him up and giving him something to look forward to after this exasperating day. He didn't want to talk about it and just shrugged as though it was neither here nor there and he couldn't care less, which might be just a cover-up for being very upset. Waking to a dark cloudy morning in June and with mixed feelings she looked forward to the first of her school holidays, memories of June being the month when their lives changed forever three years ago and here they are with Mason acting crazy today. The weather is getting worse with loud thunder crashes and flashes of lightning piercing the dark clouded sky along with heavy horizontal rain.

Mason comes rushing in yelling, "The drain's blocked."
"What drain?" She asked.

"You know, the rain can't get into the water tank." Anxiously yelling at her to have a look out of the window.

"Oh, the spouting is overflowing on the house, don't worry we can't do anything about it until the weather improves, it doesn't matter it won't hurt anything." She calmly reassures him.

He wants her to help him get the long ladder and hold it while he cleans out spouting, he's hysterically yelling at her.

"Mason, I'm not going out in a storm, this time every June you try to make me a widow, one year you fell off the roof. You need to just calm down and we'll have a cup of tea, everything is okay it won't rain forever."

"No!" He yelled back.

He's really out of his mind in panic and if she was at work he would be up a ladder in the storm again, but this time she's here to tell him how stupid that is, he could repeat the fall he had years ago, imagine how terrible it would be if it happened all over again.

It just goes to prove that she's not overprotective as she sometimes thinks, he really can't think logically, things freak him out, so he becomes frantic. He's a danger to himself and he continued to be loopy, hyperactive, and very demanding all day until the thunderous weather ceased.

Well, it's taken over a week for Mason to be semi-normal after Peter took him out, but today is Tuesday and he's getting ready for bowls and is back into his routine. With Gemma being on school holidays she decided to watch him play. He's looking around everywhere for something before getting into the shower.

"What do you want darling?"

"I can't find the pink towel I like." He replied.

"You used it last night, it's in the washing machine, just grab one from the cupboard and I'll make us a cuppa after your shower, before you go out." She calls back.

"We have two!" He yells back from the shower (he's getting worked up)

"Just use another towel, we have plenty."

"What have you done with my towel?" He screams as he confronts her in the kitchen. She stops what she's doing and without speaking calmly goes and finds the other pink towel on the clothesline outside, handing it to him wet and gently explaining one is in the washing machine and this one was on the line.

He refuses to have a sit down and doesn't want a drink he starts to storm off to go to bowls without a shower.

"You have plenty of time." She calls out to him and repeats, "It's too early to go yet, you have plenty of time to have a sit and have a drink then you'll be relaxed before you drive the van."

Mason physically shoves her out of the way as he rushes past in a bad mood and storms off to bowls, he'll be there too early and she can't help but think, who cares, she's only human and there's only so much patience a person can have. He's becoming quite paranoid (thinking I have hidden two pink towels) and also gets worked up over nothing.

Well, after making some hot scones to take for them all to enjoy at bowls and having a bit of a breather for herself, she's ready to go and watch him play. Looking up from his seat he appears really pleased when she walks in with a big plate full of cream scones setting them down on the table, he must be feeling hungry and as she takes a seat to watch him step forward from his team, bend over to bowl she sees this lovely man focused as he gently rolls it down the mat, he plays his last round very well. Watching on as butterflies flutter through her she's convinced of her love for this guy, she is still attracted to this man she married. A smile of satisfaction spreads across his face as he appears to be feeling very proud of himself. It's one of her few happy moments when she feels pleasure because he's enjoying life and that's what she has been striving to achieve for him. Gemma's smile beams from the warmth and love deep within her.

Back to her students after the holidays and it would be true to say that she throw herself into helping others as an escape from her own problems. She returns home to find Mason has left the gully gate open sometime today and she is looking at 20 sheep in the orchard which is full of flowering daffodils now being flattened and walked over. Thousands of daffodils she sells at the gate for a little extra money have been destroyed and he explains to her that he tried to get them out and had been chasing pregnant sheep through the flowers without any success.

Now she's worried, lambs are due in 4 weeks' time, and she hopes they don't miscarry; she doesn't know how much stress he put them under knowing he throws things at them. The sheep had come out of the gully when he left the gate open and then wondered into the orchard, Mason would have panicked and gone so crazy at them that they scattered everywhere and wouldn't come out.

She walks slowly around the edge of them and herds them gently through the gate without any trouble, but the damage has been done, all the time thinking *please let the unborn lambs be okay*. She is reluctant and anxious to come home some days now, as she never knows what she'll find.

Morning comes and she doesn't want to face today! Another day she wants to thwart happening. She is tired, feeling a sick gnawing in her gut, struggling to face the day. Day after day they just keep coming, and she's so terrified of what they might bring. Time keeps moving on and she must face them, she has no other choice, there's never a holiday for them to look forward to and even if they could afford to go out for dinner occasionally, Mason prefers to stay home, and it's not worth arguing.

She looks forward to the meetings with the stroke club group, the 10 of them have been supporting each other emotionally for 3 years now and it keeps her going, just to have a cup of tea and hear how everyone is getting on with their husbands who are all in various states of disrepair after their strokes. They've become good friends and like to have a shared tea sometimes. One partner had a stroke at 52 years old which they all thought was young but have since discovered that strokes are happening to younger and younger people these days.

Sunday, sometimes when organized they both go off to church and have made it a habit to stop at the bakery after, to get his favorite sausage rolls for lunch. Today she doesn't feel she has the energy to go out to church and just wants to have a day in the garden followed by a bit of baking time later this afternoon, to fill the tins with goodies for Mason to eat all week while she's at work. Time slipped away quietly while she enjoyed weeding the garden, suddenly the realization hits her. She's used to him hovering around her so now she becomes worried, he's been gone for an extraordinary length of time, panic fills her tired body as she goes to find him.

Down in the paddock she spots the top of his warm knitted brown hat she knitted for him just showing on the crest of the hill, relieved, she walked across the long-wet grass to see what has captured his interest while she still has her cozy purple gumboots on.

"What are you doing darling?" She called out to him with no response as the cold wind blows away her sounds, she gets closer and sees he has an old crowbar in his hands and is heaving away trying to leaver up the sheep hut in the paddock.

"What's all that wood doing in there?" she exclaimed. "We have a woodshed."

The woodshed is large, standing height and keeps wood nice and dry so she is flabbergasted as to why the firewood would be in a low sheep hut that wasn't built for the weight, now resulting in it slipping sideways off its posts onto the ground, and has a broken floor.

He looks up with an angry, distorted face. "Piss off!" He curses at her, and she pushes her luck to try to get it sorted for him.

"Can I take out the firewood first and then you'll be able to lift it back onto the posts?"

By his behavior it appears he has been stacking firewood in the sheep-hut down in the paddock which is meant for the upcoming new lambs to shelter in. Stacking the wood in there creates an unnecessary lengthy distance to go to get firewood and there is no logic in putting wood in there..

Understandably upset with her for discovering him, and realizing the silly thing he has done; Mason swears angrily at her. Throws the crowbar to the ground and storms off.

She's sorry for him as he has probably spent the morning moving firewood, but they have a woodshed so why did he put it in there, of course he doesn't know why he does strange things, there is no reasoning behind what he does. Now that the floor is broken he's frustrated because he can see with his own eyes the damage that he has caused. He will want to use Gemma as a scape goat but that's not possible as she is here to see that he did it and he can't blame her. One good thing though is her relief that he didn't hit her with the crowbar.

He has brain damage and doesn't think right, it's nonsense when Dwayne said, *'there's nothing wrong with my father'*. There is! Whether he wants to believe it or not. But it doesn't help Gemma emotionally or physically to understand and face the facts because no-one else can understand what it's like to live with this strange person. He has wreaked the sheep-hut with lambs due in a couple of weeks, it was built because it's needed as a place for lambs to go in bad weather or to aid sick ones at this cold time of year. Giving the lambs dry feet and a place out of the chilling winds prevents problems and saves lives.

This is all very upsetting and stressful for Gemma as there's no way she can fix the broken hut, standing there in the paddock pondering what to do, deciding as a last resort she has a few cold plastic drums lying around that she can gather up and lie them on their side if she has to, for the tiny vulnerable new-born to get out of the rain on a stormy night. Gemma hopes they won't need them as they won't be very warm and there's no room for the mother. Oh dear, I hope the lambs will be okay.

Mason has his van keys in his hand, and she moves out of his way as he rushes past, she's reluctant to ask where he's going as she doesn't want to antagonize him, so she doesn't say anything. He drives off disillusioned with everything, and one look at her he would see the strained face, she is so tired of all this and doesn't know how she can keep going. She was already sick this morning and this has now been added to the stress, one day it will be the last straw.

Gemma can't see anyone wanting to help her, this is their life now. Mason is her husband, and she loves him very much, but he is also her problem. Most people don't want to know and are too busy to notice and the others, the look on their faces reflecting they're just glad it's not them.

The phone rings, it's Norma and she finds out Mason has driven to Norma's, not remembering that she and Peter are no longer together but she took him around to see Peter her ex-husband and was ringing to sternly tell Gemma not to let it happen again. She just politely thanked her for letting her know that Mason is okay and ignored her complaining before Norma slammed the phone down in her ear. With a sigh of relief and dismay Gemma reached for the edge of the bed to sit down.

Her best friend walked over to stand next to her and she stroked his coat, he knows the watering eyes and the strained look he has seen so many times before, so he does all a dog can do to console her, lots of licking. “Let’s go for a walk little guy.” She said smiling.

CHAPTER 21

Spring is here and the remaining daffodils are all flowering in the paddock, lambs are frolicking and chasing each other so while sitting on the damp grass taking it all in for a moment she reminisces of times gone by when they were both overflowing with happiness, now just to be able to pause, find the time to breathe it all in, is challenging. She's feeling quietly positive with the change of season, Mason comes and sits next to her, and he looks surprised when she plants a kiss on his check. Spring always brings new beginnings in nature, convincing her that everything will get better from now on.

On Friday after work, they set off to have a look at The Country Valley rest home, Mason thought it looked okay just for a short stay and has agreed to go on the waiting list for respite that the assessor said Gemma must use. Mason straight away phoned up Dwayne when they got home, and he demanded to speak to her. He wanted to know what she was thinking of, putting her husband on a waiting list for a rest home and she explained about the needs assessor recommending some respite care to give her a break, the home doesn't keep an empty room available so he can only go when a room becomes available and it's not permanent just two days to give Gemma a short break.

"What do you need a break for?" Came his nasty scoffing laugh.

"I look after your dad 24/7, he gets up four or five times every night to use the toilet and that wakes me up leaving me sleep deprived. I also have to get up for work the next day and then come home to find fences down because he was home all-day causing chaos. You work from home. Why don't you take your father out one day when he's home alone? Maybe next time you take Adam fishing it would be nice for Mason to spend time with his grandson." She suggested.

He wouldn't commit to anything, didn't agree, or disagree just rudely ignored her before he hung up. He doesn't want to look after his father because he knows the work involved but doesn't want to admit to that fact!

Mason has agreed to stay at The Country Valley rest home for a couple of days after the assessor had stressed the importance of it to him. It's all arranged as they have a room available until a permanent resident arrives out of hospital. They pack a small overnight bag with his puzzle book and everything he needs, after a cup of tea together and a happy atmosphere with no pressure she gently explains to him again that it's only for the weekend so she can laze around, not cook or clean for him, while he can treat it as a holiday before she picks him up on Sunday afternoon to come back home again. There is no reply from him and he's not moving as she busies herself at the bench with the teacups and attempts to talk, without showing emotion in case he's doing this deliberately to upset her.

"You need to go because the needs assessor wants this to happen to keep me well, it's also the right thing for a husband to do. You've seen husbands stay in to give their wives a rest, the day that you stayed at a rest home when I first went back to work." She desperately explained "This time I won't be at work; I know you'll miss me, but you can ask for help to phone me any time you want, and the staff will dial it for you."

"Okay." He said with a sad look.

She can't believe how her heart is pounding and her hands are trembling while they get into the car to set off. She's aware that in reality it's just a small thing but to her it's huge! She's looking forward to having a lie in bed, watching television in silence without any questions being fired at her during the entire program, it's been a long haul since he got sick and hopefully, he's getting well enough to understand she's tired.

The respite discussion obviously got back to Peter as he

eventually managed to come around two weeks after the phone call, just to show off, he was taking a two-week holiday and needed a break because he works hard. He says that he'll catch up some other time but for now he only has time for a quick cup of coffee. What a prate! If that's not rubbing salt in the wound. He doesn't know that Gemma's already had a couple of days on her own, Mason must have kept it secret, so looking exhausted she said nothing about the respite he went on. Gemma works hard at school with children who have special needs, at home with the sheep, cooks all the meals, does the washing, shopping, cleaning and never gets a few minutes peace.

Their confused father who she loves dearly constantly asking the same questions over and over, so she doesn't feel it necessary to justify herself when the boys obviously don't care and go out of their way to be obtrusive. Before leaving, standing in the kitchen doorway with Mason waiting outside, within hearing range Peter turns, with piercing eyes glaring at Gemma he calmly states,

"My father's not being fed enough and doesn't look well." He said in a nasty manner aimed to hurt.

"He eats what he wants, and his doctor is very happy with him, he's an adult and can speak for himself." She replied.

He left and she sat down wondering what that was all about. What a joke! Just because his wife left him for another man he has to have a go at their relationship by making ridiculous accusations during this terrible time they're going through. He deliberately placed doubts in Mason's mind so he will question if she is looking after him properly. It's not her fault that their dad had a brain aneurysm, but she is doing her best to get him over it. Her love is unconditional and her resolve to stand by her husband in sickness and in health is commendable and not easy to keep going, every morning Gemma prays for strength to go on.

She vows that she will never again ask Peter or Dwayne for any help with their dad as they are uncaring, selfish and show no love for him, they have shown themselves to be only out to get any money they can from her poor husband. He was a great dad to them, and this is how they repay him in his time of need. They go on holiday and throw it in his face that they don't have time for him. She pledged in her heart, *'I love you and I will keep on trying to protect you and look after you for as long as I can.'* She promised.

The couple of days he went for respite was a great stress relief, he should go once a month but he will never do that, so the only time out Gemma gets is by going to work, some days it seems that she is in remote control, just humming along like a well-oiled machine doing the same old things, a laugh along the way sometimes at work with the teachers and students is a welcome release but at home she faces a blank canvas, like a hard black slab of solid stone.

On the outside appearing to be a solid rock able to cope, unable to be broken or penetrated but the reality is she has built a lifeless cold wall of survival around herself that appears like everything is fine. She misses her lovely husband that she had for such a short time, and she misses her daughter in Christchurch, feeling isolated from the whole world and her life is not meant to be like this. Today, she is sitting down to make a list of all her friends and family to keep with her so in times of loneliness she can look at it and remember all the times they have had together.

Life is very hard now as she struggles to stay positive because of the emotional strain of the love that is not reciprocated, created by his inability to control, or understand his emotions since the brain damage, and her physical challenges of sleep deprivation and pain are a never-ending part of Gemma's everyday existence.

It's 2011 and a sense of warm pleasure fills her not only because it's a beautiful October day in Spring but because she has her darling man next to her offering to walk down to the pond with her and Ombre' today, he's happy as they sit and chat while watching the Swifts swoop down and snap up the tiny insects from the surface of the cool clear water, the exquisite amber goldfish are perfectly silent as they glide away to the opposite bank escaping the ripples in the water.

"I know where Peter lives because Norma took me there, I left my van at her house one time when I was grumpy and drove off." He murmured.

"That's great darling are you sure you remember the way to it?" She asks supportively while feeling so proud of him for trying.

"Yeah."

"Maybe your memory is getting better with time." Giving him a reassuring smile while putting her arm around his shoulder for a hug. It's a rare time that he wants to come and sit at the pond and is reminiscent of the lost years that seem like a lifetime ago. They share some relaxed time together, but the sun has gone down behind the hills, and it has started to get a bit cool, so they decide to walk back to the house. She slips her tiny hand into his larger one and their fingers automatically intertwine.

How comforting it is to have contact with him as they walk back hand in hand she feels like she can breathe again convinced that she must never give up hope.

There is no more discussion on the way back up the hill as they walk along silently soaking in the closeness, maybe he too is aware of the physical warmth his contact has created, and she hopes so. They drift off in different directions as she goes to check the animals are well.

Later in the afternoon when she goes to call him for a cuppa he can't be found, going into the garage she finds the van is also missing, while she's down in the paddock checking the lambs he has taken the van and driven off without telling her. It's a concern when someone just disappears without saying anything, but welcome to Gemma's world. Taking time to think about it, when he talked to her about remembering going to Peters, shows her that it must have been on his mind to see Peter. It's heart-breaking to think how he must miss his sons; she feels compassion and is protective towards him.

Gemma wishes that she could take away all of the emotional pain and loss her husband feels, she has tried to put herself in his place and often feels empathy for him now he can't work or remember things, he has experienced such a huge loss in his life and maybe he wants to seek out the remaining few distant memories of when he was a dad to his young boys. Happy times that fortunately he still retains in his damaged brain. Gemma guesses that he wants to see if he can find his way back to Peters flat.

Trying not to worry and hopeful that he will find the way to Peter's place she subconsciously notes the time, he must have left about 2.30pm and she convinces herself not to worry and to make use of this little bit of alone time in the garden, while she has a quiet time to enjoy it. Time disappears too quickly when she enjoys the garden and coming back inside to wash her hands, she considered planning their tea, hunger is making itself felt as it's 6.30pm. Now a bit concerned she decides to risk abuse by phoning Peter to find out if Mason is coming home for tea or having it there. Confirming that Mason did arrive okay thank goodness, even though no one let her know he was safe.

Peter boasts "My father has driven himself here twice now with no problems, he's quite normal."

"Mason told me that your ex-wife Norma drove him there last time." She replied matter of fact without any emotion.

Peter refused to accept it and began arguing with her at which point she didn't have the energy, or patience to bother so told him to spend more time with his dad and he would see all of the problems. Explaining that when Mason visits him all he does is sit in the lounge all afternoon being waited on so how does he know what Mason is really like? Did he have to make a cup of coffee for himself? No!

She believes Mason about Norma taking him the first time because there was no reason to make that up, and he didn't have the new address so why is Peter lying to her. Gemma just can't stand anymore deceit from the boys as its childish rubbish and a hindrance to caring for Mason. She has no time for either of them and can't be bothered arguing over something they know nothing about because they refuse to have their dad to stay with them.

Anyway, feeling a bit defensive she explained that she was calling because it's getting late and she doesn't think Mason should be driving home in the dark, it's finally agreed that Mason will be on his way home for tea (probably because they don't want to feed him.)

Gemma hung up, feeling her life was horrible, all she does everyday is try to keep Mason well and happy, she thinks it is time they recognized the love that she has for their dad and surely he deserves to have a loving relationship of his own choosing, they must know he will never go back to their mother. Mason told her he finds her repulsively fat, and their marriage was well and truly finished before he met her.

CHAPTER 22

How wonderful waking to another beautiful spring morning, so Gemma decides to leave everything else that needs doing and get straight outside into the warming sunshine, hoping to achieve all the planting that she has been wanting to do for ages.

While toiling away in the vegetable garden which is under the kitchen window, she's feeling very satisfied to have managed to plant out all the vegetables that they like to eat, hoping all going well they will not have to buy any if they keep up successive plantings right through Summer. The last of the winter vegetables, cauliflower, broccoli, and peas are nearly finished so she has now planted for their summer salads. The delicious smell of Mason's toast wafts down from the kitchen window as he descends the three steps from the back porch, to stand beside her on the worn-out concrete path.

"I've planted some lettuce, carrot and radish seeds." Pointing out the rows freshly dug to him and suggesting, 'I want to buy some tomato seedlings to put in, maybe you can push the sticks into the ground as supports for them to grow on.'

"Why aren't you planting flowers?" He snapped back angrily while still munching on his toast he held in his left hand.

"You told me you wanted this as a vegetable patch, it has been for some years now and it works well for picking stuff, being so close to the kitchen." She smiled back at him.

When they bought the house it was overgrown flowers and remained as flowers for a couple of years as they had so many other things to worry about, but a vegetable patch was perfect there, if she had kept planting flowers he would have complained about that as well, he suggested vegetables. It would be nice to be appreciated sometimes, instead of him coming out this morning and enjoying her efforts he upsets the tranquil mood and grates on her self-esteem. Gemma is sick of his loss of ability to recall memories, this constant explaining. Six times over everyday, and wishes she had the romance and physical contact back in their relationship again, she misses him.

The planting is finished now for a while and she thinks it will save them money, she goes to pack the spade and garden fork away in the shed because it's time for a cup of tea and some toast, while in the shed she notices the battery to his cordless drill is in pieces hidden behind a board against the shed wall, where she was to hang the spade up. Oh no! This was a dangerous thing to do, and she quickly returned to the kitchen to talk to him about it.

"Mason, what's happened with the battery I found in the shed?" She reached for the electric jug to add more water to it.

"I don't know, what battery?"

"Come out to the shed and have a look so you remember, it's important for using your drill." As she pushes open the ill-fitting old door and he sees the bits she laid out on his bench, it's as if a light goes on in his head as he remembers.

"Oh, I tried to fix it because it wasn't holding a charge."

"Maybe it just needs recharging more often than you think with your memory's inability to compensate for time." She suggests. "But anyway, did you read on top it tells you not to open it, it contains acid and caustic substances that can cause serious burns."

"It's alright, I was careful anyway." His face looks startled as he begins to read the clearly written warning.

"There's no way you can fix a battery, so I will order another one for you. You cannot put this back together again it's too dangerous."

Making herself a mental note to write down the number and size she will order one ignoring his protests as she has stopped listening, silently thinking how lucky he was that he didn't get chemical burns while she was at work. This will be a challenging

Thursday night, he needs to fast from eating any food or drink as the doctor just wants to have a routine blood test done in the morning, she carefully goes over the instructions a couple of times. Explaining that he can't eat after tea tonight until he has the test done in the morning.

At 5.30am he wakes her up. "It's not six o'clock yet is it?" He asks.

Willing her tired eyes to open she replies, "I don't know, have a look at the clock." The clock is in full view but he's out of bed just blankly staring down at her.

"Why do I need to know the time darling, I don't have work today, I'm on school holidays."

"I can have breakfast eh?"

"Did you see the note on the bench with your prescription for a blood test?" (Luckily, she thought to put that there last thing before going to bed as an extra backup for him to see, if he went to make toast.) He has obviously been out to the kitchen and that's why he's now hovering beside the bed.

"No, you can't eat or drink until after the test, no matter what time it is. So you might as well come back to bed, we'll go to the laboratory as soon as it opens in the morning before you have anything to eat or drink, you'll be fine until then."

It's astonishing what time he wants to eat just because it's on his mind that he's not allowed to eat, however, he accepts that he has no choice but to come back to bed and they eventually get up and go for the blood test without her having anything to eat or drink either.

Everything went well and his results have come back all normal, contrary to what Peter would have preferred.

Both waking to another brilliant sunny day, and she's still on school holidays, so they decide to have a nice day at the beach. They pack a green salad lunch and drive along the West Coast Road until they find a soft grassy spot for Mason to revel in the warmth of the sun sitting on a car rug. Ombre' and Gemma enjoy a short run along the shallow water's edge. All three are having a lovely relaxing day and all is well with the world again for just a little while. On returning to have a lie down on the rug next to her man the sun is just the right amount and not too hot, Mason has a beautiful smile and seems to have forgotten that there's anything wrong with him as he chats and cuddles her amongst the sand dunes, the day at the beach is magical.

At times like these it's easy to believe that things will come right with him again one day in the future, but then she psychoanalyzes herself. She just longs for everything to be okay and doesn't want to face facts, after a lovely day out in the sun she's pleasantly drained, physically, and mentally and plans to go to bed early, it's only 9pm but it's been an emotional day.

Mason comes into the bedroom and wants her to check why the outside light at the end of the house is still working.

"It's a sensor light, if you keep going out to see, it will come on."

"But it's still on." He's just been out there again.

"It'll go off if you stay inside." Again she tells him. "If you stay inside you can look out of the window and watch it go off, but it does take a minute." He doesn't understand, is becoming agitated and argumentative, she supposes the day out has been exhausting for him as well.

Getting up and turning off the main light switch on the laundry switch board is probably the easier solution for her. No sensor light now on the house but hopefully she'll be allowed some rest. Early to rise again tomorrow no doubt. This is a school holiday for Gemma but not a holiday from her life, just a short break out at the beach. Given a glimpse of closeness again causing her to wonder if that's worth seeing and feeling? or does it only make coming back to reality and straight back to the confusion more upsetting. Oh why can't normality last a little longer?

It's a rare thing, finally this Saturday the boys have arranged to take Mason fishing, they were due to arrive last week when she got him all prepared and waiting but no show, no phone call either, no explanation all week and then they get a phone call last night and they will supposedly come this time at 9.00am. Gemma hopes they will this time!

Mason has been sitting in the kitchen wishfully watching the driveway for them to arrive since 8.45am, it is now 10.00am and still no one has appeared. It's so disheartening to see him sitting patiently waiting, which is difficult for him to do, and especially after he had made such an effort to get ready for a second week in a row, Gemma silently prays that he will not be disappointed again.

Placing everything he needs on the bench at the back door so he can't miss it, then she explained to Mason that she's not well so has to leave for her doctor's appointment soon, and if they don't come before she goes he will have to pull the locked door closed behind him when he leaves. She had hoped that they would have taken him at 9am as arranged and she wouldn't have had to tell Mason about the appointment.

Better late than never, he returns home from the fishing trip, Mason comes into the house alone, little is said, he's withdrawn and doesn't want to talk, she doesn't know what happened, but they haven't heard from either Peter or Dwayne for two months now, she suspects they saw how difficult their dad is to manage and are not in a hurry to talk about how the fishing trip went. The boys remember another person, the dad that once took them fishing when they were little now has a fear of water.

CHAPTER 23

It has been a peaceful couple of months, so Gemma is not complaining, the school year has finished for her, and Mason appeared happy having her back home, baking for him. Both of the boys have arrived unexpectedly just as she was going out to do some last-minute Christmas shopping and she reluctantly leaves Mason with them. She drove along hoping he could cope without letting them stress and influence him too much. Goodness knows what she will find on her return home.

They face this Christmas knowing that it has been over three years since their lives were turned upside down. Since Gemma saved her husband's life and he had to endure months of rehabilitation following brain surgery, he continues to have challenges and to have days of hope, and he has made many improvements along the way. He's a different person now and she lives on her memories of the man he once was and has grown to accept that he can't help being the confused soul he now is, Gemma continues with hope, courage and understanding.

Mason has given up on the movie they were watching on television and has gone to bed, which was unusual. Deciding to go to check on him she finds he is sitting on top of the bed *'studying'* the road map. He is obviously distressed and anxious and it's 10 o'clock at night. "What's wrong?" She is aware that whatever is on his mind is so upsetting to him that he couldn't finish watching the movie.

"Dwayne wants me to visit his new house at Christmas and I'm worried about how to get there." He spoke quietly. "I asked if he could take me there one day, but he said it was just around the corner from his old house and that I could find it."

The panic clearly visible on his face, when will they learn that the stress they put him under will kill him one day! Gemma's so annoyed with that lazy b... they go home to their partners and live their lives and she is left with the results of their thoughtless ignorance.

She recommended to Mason to just forget about the visit and enjoy Christmas with her, explaining that she would drive him there if they would tell her the address.

"Dwayne said you're not invited."

It's just another effort from them to cause high blood pressure and possibly a stroke, poor Mason, they plan to keep them apart at Christmas time. Every Christmas she can have with her husband is precious time for them! Gemma has tried to trust his sons with Mason, but they do too much damage to his health, it would be her that loses him if he died, not them, they rarely see him. It would not change their lives at all if he was gone, but it would break her heart to let that happen after all their effort for him to retire happy.

Mason did nothing about visiting them, she assured him that they could come around whenever they wanted over the holidays but of course they didn't bother. He and Gemma both had a lovely Christmas day on their own with all of Mason's favorite foods and she enjoyed a couple of glasses of bubbly wine before spending the afternoon cuddling in bed together.

A New Year has arrived, an uneventful seeing in of another year, as she looked out of the lounge window she could just catch a narrow glimpse of fireworks and wondered about all the people out there in the world all celebrating while Mason slept. Although physically not alone it felt like she was with an emptiness and something missing.

The night before starting back to work is bumpy. She has explained that she is at school tomorrow, and so he is up and down all night, banging things, and slamming doors and making sure she didn't sleep. Regrettably, he is nervous about being alone when she goes back to work.

“Darling come back to bed, it will be a short week as I’m not working on Tuesdays and having a half day on Fridays, I’ve cut my hours back so the week will go very quickly.”

“If I can’t work then you shouldn’t either.” He mumbled sulkily before getting back into bed. He tucked down and she comforts him by resting her arm over his waist while popping a wet kiss on his check.

“Good night darling, have a good sleep.” She whispered.

During the Christmas school holidays she worked hard to bring the house up to date, painting around the old wooden windows and the fence around the new deck, this caused her arthritis to flare up from holding the paintbrush too long, making it near impossible to manage any more painting. So she has decided they need help to finish the last of the house, she will just have to find the money for it. There is no other way, the old house needs to be maintained.

After getting quotes and arranging the starting date, the cheapest painter set up his trestles early this sunny Saturday morning. He had started to paint the most difficult wall of the house; Gemma is really pleased that he has turned up and it is all happening during the beautiful summer weather. After greeting him she goes back inside to finish her breakfast and cheerfully informed Mason that the painter was working on the highest wall.

Sometime later while at the kitchen sick cleaning up she could see the painter with his trestles going back to his van, which is weird! Heading outside to see what’s happening he explained to her that he has stopped work because Mason had told him that no one will pay him, so he may as well go and save himself the work.

“You will get paid.” She exclaimed shocked, “It is nothing to do with my husband, he doesn’t work, and I will definitely pay you. Please start work again. I can give you a deposit if you like.” She pleaded with him.

"No, I don't like the guy, I'm sorry if he's your husband but I'm not going back up a ladder with him around, it's not worth it to me." He finished packing everything away and that was the last she saw of him.

Gemma's eyes started to blur from approaching tears and the stress of not having the house painted before winter, looking up at it with the paint curling off and exposed weather boards the fear of having to do everything herself with sharp pains in her hands overwhelmed her, full of panic and distress because she's unable to do it! Ombre' has been sitting and watching as if he listens to what is going on, he nudged her hand with his soft little face to remind her that he's there for her, she bent over to acknowledge and thank him.

"I'm okay, let's go for a walk." She said as they began to walk to the pond with tears streaming down her face, she tried to prevent any sound escaping, wanting to protect her concerned furry friend now her day had turned very grey. Sitting on the dew-covered morning grass beside the pond she poured out her soul to Ombre' with her arms around his neck, explaining to him that she does not know why Mason does those things.

Mason didn't say anything to her about the painter although she is aware of his jealousy, and when he can't do things he doesn't want anyone else to do it either, resenting her being able to work, she has had to explain to him many times that someone has to pay the bills.

Never mind, she will find another painter who she will warn first about Mason's brain damage and not to take any notice of what he says because he is not the full quid, she is so angry and disheartened now it's going to cost more.

Mason has adjusted to her being back at work, following a couple of weeks with reduced hours, he's used to being at home alone with their docile old dog for company, and she still leaves notes on the bench every day to remind him of her work routine. Walking past the summer vegetable garden she is pleased it's coming along quite nicely with loads of lettuces beckoning for their salads. Going inside to make a cup of tea Mason walked from the lounge to the dining area to get his coffee, he crashed his leg against a chair that had been in the same place for 12 years.

"Why would you put that there? You stupid cow." He demanded.

"I haven't moved it, it's been there for years, just watch where you walk." She replied rather unsympathetically being offended by his verbal outburst.

Now he's in an absolutely foul mood and wants it moved because he's embarrassed that he tripped over it. These days he misjudges distances, and his co-ordination is not as good. One of the issues she has with his behavior is that now with brain damage the neurologist explained to her that he cannot regulate his moods and she finds that she must be prepared for anything, he can fly off the handle and push or hit her at will, completely unjustified and unexpected.

Gemma again tried to teach him to use the washing machine to give him more independence and better self-esteem but that's proving to be an impossible mission. After going over it three times and with numbered instructions on the machine with black marker pen, he cannot do it by himself. Sometimes he does not put any soap powder in, or he tries to force the dispenser lid in the machine upside down. Turns it on, and off again and then got angry that it will not go, or he doesn't adjust the water level correctly, he puts low level water with a full load of clothes, most of the time he couldn't get it to start and has never managed to get anything washed properly as yet.

Pondering whether she should give up trying, or will he master it if she repeatedly shows him over and over. Gemma just didn't know if it was worth letting him get all frustrated when he failed to achieve the task. When a partner has brain damage why don't family get any training on how to manage them, so partners know if it's possible to learn with repetition or not? It's all very hard to cope with when you're emotionally involved by wanting to do the best thing for one's poor husband and she's sure it's easier to teach strangers that you don't have any feelings for.

Desperately thinking of a way to stay sane, Gemma hatches a plan. It would appear that the only holiday or break they could afford would be to fly to Australia to visit family. She is really looking forward to visiting her two brothers in July because she has not seen them for a few years and desperately needs a break. Being amidst her family will seriously help her emotionally. Gemma finds it is with trepidation that she broaches the subject to Mason about them having a holiday together, pointing out the added bonus of staying with her brother, they won't have to pay for accommodation while enjoying the warmer weather. He refused to fly, he yelled at her and was quite adamant that he would not be getting onto an airplane until hell freezes over, he also refused to go into rest home care for that week. Leaving her completely distraught and emotionally crippled with disappointment yet again.

He is trying to control and isolate her from her brothers, he knows how devoted she is to him, so he attempts to use that to believe that she will not go without him, determined, she explained that she is definitely going to see her family. So he needed to make up his mind if he was going with her, he threatened that if she goes he will not feed Ombre'. Gemma has found a neighbor who will keep an eye on Ombre' for her and hasn't told Mason that.

Making plans to go, she starts to label and add meals to the freezer, ready for him to microwave if he won't go to the rest home, but his inability to do any washing remains a problem. Mason still believes that she will not go, but he fails to understand that she's at her wits end and can't continue, she has to have a break it's no longer a choice.

Recently, on one of her visits the needs assessor got Mason

to agree to her arranging for a lovely lady Lee-Anne for home help once a week while Gemma's at work, giving Mason company as well as her not having so much work to do when she gets home. Gemma going away is off the discussion list and she's hoping Mason will get used to Lee-Anne being around vacuuming, so she has booked the air flights to go away to her brothers in July as discussed. Lee-Anne has agreed to look in every day, clean plus do the washing while Gemma is away, frozen meals are left for Mason to heat up and Bridget will phone every morning to remind him where Gemma is and also to check on him to make sure he takes meals out of the freezer every day to thaw for his tea, so he doesn't forget to eat.

All the flight information, when Gemma will be back and instructions to be ready to answer when she phones at 7pm every night will all be written down in easy-to-read days and stuck to the fridge for him to keep looking at, she has put measures in place so hopefully she can relax and be back refreshed in 7 days time.

It is a hugely difficult thing for her to leave Mason on his own and her stomach was more than butterflies, it felt more like bats flying around inside making her quite sick, but she knows the importance of actually doing this! He has to learn to fit into society again and allow her to see family.

CHAPTER 24

During her stay she attempted to phone Mason every night at 7pm New Zealand time but never got to speak with him, whether it was deliberate, controlling, sulking or didn't understand about the phone she never knew, but Bridget said every morning the home help arrived at the house the phone was off the hook until she put it back on again. Obviously not being able to check on him made Gemma quite frantic about how he was, chatting with Bridget she said she believes he is doing it on purpose because he thought she wouldn't go without him. Bridget is fantastic, she had left everything with her to mind, animals to check, dog to feed and food for Mason, she dropped Gemma at the airport and arranged to pick her mum up.

The holiday could have been more stress free with phone contact, sometimes wondering if he will put her into an early grave. Mason always went mad if she requested a holiday, and she explained working people have several weeks off every year and they don't live under these conditions, this is the only stress-free break she's had in 4 years. Gemma pauses to appreciate every Christmas they have together and wonders how many years they'll get.

April has arrived and Masons sons haven't been seen for the entire year, so life is finally ticking along in a relatively nice routine, Mason is relaxed, and everything is good. Then Dwayne phones, he wants to arrange to take Mason to the beach up by Ruakaka on Tuesday. Mason spoke up for himself as he enjoys going to bowls and it's written on his calendar, he explained he doesn't want to miss bowls on a Tuesday, so they decided to go 12.30 after he gets home from his bowls.

Tuesday came around and when he arrived home from his morning with his bowling buddies the rush was on to have some lunch together and put his feet up so he could be refreshed for going out again. Gemma was about to make a flask of coffee for him to take when Dwayne phoned to say he will be an hour late, what's new! But with bated breath she's relieved that at least he will go through with the outing even though the day was wearing on. Gemma doesn't understand the point of going to the beach this late in April, she says nothing and remains cheerful for Mason while putting his warm jacket by the back door for him to take.

They sat and watched TV for a wee while, looking over to Mason he's snoozing on the sofa so she got up to do some baking, another phone call from Dwayne to say he's busy with his mother's computer and would be another 15 minutes. Time came and went, Dwayne turned up at 3.00pm and didn't come inside but looking at his dad he asked, "Have you got your swimsuit ready?"

"It's April! It'll be too cold." She exclaimed shocked, while Mason looked on with an agreeing nod of his head. Probably Rose (Mason's ex-wife) had suggested swimming at the hot pools or something, she's the reason Dwayne is over two hours late. She never gave up flirting with her ex-husband. Gemma doesn't want to have a conversation with Dwayne because her concern is that her poor darling has been mucked around for the whole afternoon, he is always tired at this time of the day. Luckily, he had a short cat nap in front of television but his flask she made ages ago won't be very hot now after all this waiting.

Life continues to be all about their ignorance and Rose's conniving to flirt with her ex, Gemma is convinced they really have no understanding or respect for Mason's feelings, he's now 66 years old and not a well person. On his birthday last month no-one came to see him, Andrew, the oldest grandson phoned to wish him a happy birthday which was nice, and Peter phoned a week later when he remembered too late and Dwayne not at all. Time and time again they prove their father is not even a tiny part of their lives and Mason notices it, he keeps track on his calendar. He sat and waited to hear from them on his birthday and Father's Day and nothing happened, he found it difficult to hide his upset and it's Gemma who picked up the pieces, she sees what they do to him.

Finally, Gemma is thrilled for Mason reaching retirement, which was one of the goals she really wished for him, he got his driver's license back being another huge achievement. He has come a long way while still living with cognitive deficits, still gets confused about time and when he needs to eat, what day it is and what season it is, so what to wear is still a problem. Unfortunately, they argue more now because he's more confident and self-assured over things, like when he sees the long wool on the sheep and remembers that they need to be shorn but fails to accept it when she explained, it's not the right time in the middle of winter!

He's looking well at the moment, but everything changes so rapidly with him that it made life so unpredictable, he has managed to gain ten kilos since last year, so now she worries in case his blood pressure goes up. Both he and Gemma have a silent awareness and fear of possibly having another aneurism, they never talk about it.

Whether the fear was justified or not, after his life changed so suddenly and dramatically that day in June they've only talked about it once and she is sure they will always wonder and feel insecure about his health. Gemma being home for the winter school holidays will be a good thing because they think perhaps he eats all day when she's not home. That might be why the increase in weight. The phone rings, it's his grandson Andrew to invite Mason to watch Len play soccer, she remembers last year, and her heart skips a beat.

"Darling, its Andrew on the phone, come and talk to him on the landline. He wants you to go to soccer on Saturday." There was a long pause while she held the phone tightly in her hand because it's not cordless.

Mason called out, "No, I'm busy doing something on Saturday." And he refused to go to the phone. Last time was obviously so upsetting for him that he remembers and doesn't want a repeat, Gemma knows that he's not busy on Saturday.

Hesitating before conveying the message, Andrew says that they would all come around after the game. So after hanging up the phone Mason decided he wants her to bake muffins for them all when they come, she reluctantly agreed.

He was happy, they turned out yummy and after setting them on the baking tray to cool she turned to him. "I wouldn't hold your breath they probably won't even come, but it won't matter because we'll enjoy the muffins anyway." Gemma said with a smile before packing them away for tomorrow.

She was right, Saturday came, and they did not turn up. They waited and waited Gemma put off starting tea in case they turned up. They didn't even bother to phone Mason to say they weren't coming after all, and she just wondered if it was in retaliation to upset him because he didn't go to watch the soccer.

He looks forward to seeing his grandsons but again they have little or no understanding that soccer might be too long for him, or maybe it was because he didn't want to be disappointed after last time when they didn't turn up at all. Gemma finds it all deplorable behavior and tries to make it up to him with a nice tea together chatting about other things in the hope that he would forget about it, unfortunately memories that hurt him deeply are more likely to stay filed in his brain.

Bowls again today, Mason is in a routine of going every Tuesday and he enjoys the welcoming friends he has made; he needs help to get organized, dressed appropriately and to leave on time but it is always worth the effort, Gemma's reward is to see him happy and socializing once she gets him there. Work has been particularly good to her, and she feels lucky to have an employer who lets her have every Tuesday off so she can help her husband to be part of a community and make friends.

Wednesday night and she is off to her monthly support group with the stroke club ladies, she has continued to go to it most months for all of these years. She can empathize with the wives and husbands going through similar issues as herself and it's good to talk and discuss new ideas and successful ways of managing their lives such as the bowling club which has worked for her and Mason. She strongly recommends that others who have a disability seek out a group activity even though it is different then going to work every day, it does provide companionship and allows for social skills to be learnt while allowing for the caregiver to have time out.

Others at the meetings have different concerns such as one wife who has had a stroke and refuses to shower, her husband is at his wits end, as not only is it unhealthy but after ten days of not showering she smells. The partners that have had strokes are adults, people who make their own decisions, and there is a big drive these days about individual rights even though those at the support group meetings talk about how the person often doesn't understand the consequences of what they're doing. Carers run the risk of being complained about by family members who don't see what is happening and don't have to live with the terrible consequences of brain damage. The caregivers struggle at times just to explain what it is that they endure. Sometimes defensive and wanting to protect the loved one or sometimes out of embarrassment, when this man moved his smelly wife into the next bedroom because he couldn't stand to sleep in the same bed until she had a shower, he was condemned by family members as not being understanding enough. One should try to walk in his shoes before passing judgement.

It has long since been a commitment of Gemma's to try to help make her husband as independent as possible in case something happens to her and she's not around to care for him. This is a fear that is shared by all of the support group members who often express a concern of *'What if I get sick and can't manage to look after him, what will happen to him?'* If she's not here who will look after him, pay the bills and make sure he eats properly. This is one reason she encourages him to pick up bread from the local dairy on the way home from his bowls on a Tuesday, even if she doesn't need any, she simply puts it into the freezer and thanks him, it seems like a small thing but it's scary for Mason.

"Don't forget to pick up two loaves of bread on your way home please." She called out to him as he dressed in the clothes that have been laid out on the bed, she has ironed a shirt, checked his trousers as they needed a wipe down from chalk dust from last week and put money into his wallet. Gemma also wrote instructions down on a post-it sticker and got him to stick it onto the dashboard of his van, that way it's impossible for him to miss seeing it on his way home after bowls and he can't forget to pick up the bread.

Over the years she has had to learn to make sentences into statements not questions, as he becomes worried if she asks him to do something like picking up the bread, and it's easier for him to argue instead of confronting his fears. It always has to be a positive statement in order for him to be happy to do it without discussion then he does it routinely. The post-it notes explain what shop to go to when he drives passed the block of shops. It must sound very bossy to outsiders and Gemma doesn't care, she has found that this is the only way to communicate effectively with Mason and it prevents any anxiety.

The washing beckoned to be hung out piled high in its yellow basket and she left it to make Mason her priority, everything had to wait to ensure that he was organized and relaxed before he leaves home, so she set about making a cuppa and getting out the banana cake left over from the weekend, they had a nice sit down together beside the window overlooking the garden before he went to get his van out of the garage.

"Don't worry if I'm not home when you get back as I'm going to go and pay the house insurance." She smiled at him.

"Well that's a good idea," he says with a smile, "You can get the bread as well while you're out."

"This is my day off; I want to stay home but I can't ask you to pay the bills." Gemma replied, "I'd love to stay home if I could as I'm out every day. You only go out once a week."

This explanation seemed to work, and he doesn't question anymore. He had enough intelligence to understand he's getting off lightly, he didn't want to pay the bills as well! She laughed quietly at his improvement, sometimes he sounded so normal and a fuzzy rush of love and pride for him warmed her heart as they kiss goodbye.

He walked to the top of the driveway, the driveway gate was closed so he came back to the house and continued to walk through the back door across the dining room and out the ranch slider to get to his van and drive it up the driveway to the gate, that's weird.

Then he stopped to get out of the van to open the gate, drove through and would have to close it again. Why didn't he just open the gate to start with, walk down the driveway to collect the van and continue to drive all the way out the open gate. The mind boggles, everything is a challenge for him, and he can't work things out in his mind and yet how could she explain this to his boys, they don't live with him, and they refuse to listen.

By the time he drove off in the van she's mentally tired from watching he got away okay. She hadn't even drunk her cup of tea that she made for them both, so busy making sure he was looked after with money, sunglasses, and hearing aid batteries in his pocket, but she's happy knowing that he's sorted for another fun Tuesday.

The bowling day provided her with a little respite even though it was challenging work to get him ready, on time and looking nice, socializing with his new friends was really important for him as they accept him as he is now, unlike his past friends who felt uncomfortable with this different person, and never come to see him anymore.

It also gives her opportunity's to make little tasks for Mason helping him to gain a little more independence.

"Mason can you see if the warrant of fitness has

expired on your van please?" He came back and said, "It doesn't need one until January next year."

"No, that must be the registration, you haven't had a warrant for ages. Just have another check."

He returns and says it expired last week, so she quickly reassured him not to worry, they will go together on his way to bowls. There goes her morning off!

"We'll put some air in the tyres as well, while we're out." She suggested.

Parked at the garage to pump the tyres up he got out to do it, Gemma waiting in the car as wives do. No! she should know by now not to take anything for granted, she needs to be aware of everything he does as it dawns on her he is deflating the tyres and trying to pump them up with the vacuum cleaner! She rushed out to help him pump up the tyres again, explaining about the bell dinging when they reach the right pressure. It is devastating that so many things have been lost from his memories.

CHAPTER 25

The world around has not changed, the sound of the birds and the chilly winter wind in the trees is like it has always been, the sun still shines, and new babies are born, rain still falls from the sky as she ponders how life has gone on just the same, but not for them. Her life is sad, hard, and often an endurance test, and she still believes she did the right thing bringing him home, he's happy, has had time to retire and to be free of responsibility, at the present time from where she sat, that's the best thing you can ever give a person.

Wednesday morning and she has a half day at work, after finishing in the shower she walked into the dining room to have breakfast with Mason and her precious Ombre' is silently waiting, patiently sitting, and watching to see if she has a moment to feed him in between Mason's consistent demands.

"Where's my toast?" He yelled all the time she was in the shower under the warm welcoming shelter of the water she'd retreated to.

"What's wrong?" Looking at him?

"You can get it darling."

"Do we have any peanut butter?"
He demands.

"Just look in the pantry Mason while I get ready for work," He's watching her and asking more and more questions to keep her in the room, she started to feel worried about his behavior and went to get the peanut butter for him. While handing it to him he snatched it in one hand and gave her a sudden big shove with his other, she lost her footing and flew across the room landing on her bottom with her elbow hitting the corner of the solid wooden dining table on the way down. Lying on the floor she hesitated to move too fast in case something was broken, consciously checking how she felt, slowly getting to her feet while Mason just stood watching, her elbow was sore, and she hoped it wasn't damaged.

"What did you do that for Mason?" she inquired in a state of shock.

"I don't know, just get up and stop making a fuss." Came an angry response. As days came and went it didn't get any easier, getting up and pretending it never happened, carefully walking on eggshells and being afraid to move from her chair.

He didn't want her to go to work, while he's spreading two slices of toast she gingerly asked permission. "Shall I cook mine?"

"Yes." Came his abrupt reply.

While getting her toast out of the toaster he became angry because he now believes that the two he spread were apparently for her.

"I didn't know, I asked you if I should get my own and you told me yes."

He stormed off to the bedroom swearing and she's relieved, definitely not going to follow and ask what's wrong, what just happened? Gemma had no idea, and he would not either as these days he got so confused. She's perplexed as to how to handle him, he acts irrationally, and she has to keep from annoying him, but anything on his mind sets him off.

Quickly crunching her way through two slices of hot toast and peanut butter as fast as she could and keeping watch as he passed the doorway on route to the bathroom, her nerves are on edge, she watched and listened, fearful of what he might do next.

After having her shower, she had dried the floor with the half-wet towel before putting it in the laundry basket, he storms back into the kitchen and standing too close for comfort. "Come with me." He commanded loudly and beckoned for her to follow him into the bathroom, which she did very reluctantly.

"Look!" He yelled. His face was stern with fire in his eyes.

“What?” she asked sheepishly.

He points without speaking at the dripping shower head, which is turned off and will stop eventually, but the floor is naturally wet from the drips.

“You haven’t dried the floor of the shower.” He’s enraged and fiery eyed, but she has to bravely answer, he deliberately went looking for something to have a go at her about, he’s a bully and no good comes to them.

“I have dried the floor, and the window is open, what more do you want me to do? I am concerned about getting to work on time, I’ll see you later!”

Frantically rushing to the bedroom, grabbing her bag that was ready on the bed, she quickly gave her wee Ombre’ a big hug right around his entire body aware of the pang of pain in her elbow, she can’t wait to exit through the back door and straight into her car before he comes at her with anything else.

It is horrible going off to work with him feeling upset if he tried to cook toast for her but didn’t succeed, life is unpredictable, and she doesn’t like to leave on a negative note. It’s so hard living with brain injuries, not just for the individual but also for those that live with them. All she could think of was Ombre’ didn’t get any breakfast and she was sympathetic for him as she drove to work grateful that she’s okay and didn’t break any bones in the fall. It’s a half day, Ombre’ will be okay until she returns home but does wonder if maybe all this bad behavior is the sign of something worse going on inside Mason’s head.

Focusing on her students’ work, she tried to forget about her home life, what is he doing while she’s not there? Is he okay, it’s difficult to push everything out of her busy mind while she worked, he’s home and there is nothing she can do so she tells herself to forget home and enjoy working with these lovely children who are growing and learning, people who she can help. Eventually she will have to go to the doctor to get her elbow checked out, sometime this week along with her hip as it's very painful as well.

It had been a very cold day in more ways than one and on returning home it was nice to walk into a warm house, he had lit the fire in the lounge. After leaving her shoes at the kitchen door she walked through to see him sitting on a comfy upholstered stool stooped over a coffee table doing a jigsaw puzzle. Smiling down at him she states how lovely it was to come home to a warm house and she didn't have to light it. Then looking over she saw a black melted blob stuck to the flue of the wood burner, he obviously burnt his track pants while apparently warming them on top of the fire, the dread of him causing a house fire was something she has stressed over for a couple of winters now.

Don't fret the small stuff she desperately tried to stay calm, he's still alive and they still have a roof over their heads, she will have to talk with him again about not putting things on top of the fire but for now, today had given her enough to cope with, she longs for time with her dog and a cup of tea. Memory loss is a huge safety issue, asking herself was she wasting her time telling him over and over when he forgets again and again, but what else can she do?

Gemma's life was tough during the winter months feeling trapped inside the house with Mason's unpredictable mood swings was claustrophobic, like being in a rocking boat in the middle of the ocean surrounded by nothing but water threatening to drown them. She can't wait for the rain to stop falling from the sky and the tears from her eyes, while she clung to memories of being free to sit beside the calm pond again with her dog and watch the clouds move overhead in solitude and safety. Sitting on the end of the bed and looking out of the window in the hope that she'll be able to do that again soon. Gemma is oblivious to how long she sat watching the rain trickle down the windowpane before looking up to see an amazing rainbow with arches of beautiful color appearing in the sky overhead, she felt positive that someone, somewhere sees all, he knows her tiredness, her every emotion she believes that he wants the best for her.

Waking to a sunny clearing appearing between the clouds it promises an improving day, she's sixty-one years old and has received cards from family that are now sitting on the side table. Mason picks them up to read as she excitedly tells him they're having a roast dinner together for her birthday celebration. The phone rang and Gemma greets Dwayne, she passes the cordless to Mason before sitting down, while talking he was heard saying that he couldn't, because it's Gemma's birthday today, however after a lot of silence and quiet mumbling, he didn't appear to be very happy when hanging up the phone and going to the kitchen to inform her that Dwayne wanted him to go and visit the new house he hadn't seen yet.

"It's my birthday today and we're having a roast tea especially." Sad, anxious and annoyed because she knows Dwayne controls her husband.

"I know, I told him, but it didn't make any difference, he told me how to get there, I've written it down on a piece of paper." Mason said apologetically with a hint of regret.

Gemma's immediate concern was for Mason while pushing her disappointment out of her mind she wondered if he could manage the task set.

He seemed to be sure he knew where to go this time, as he had written directions down and she watched as he carefully tucked them into his wallet. Dwayne has instructed him to charge up his 10-year-old cell phone, Gemma tried to explain that it didn't work anymore so not to rely on it, he was never able to use a cell phone anyway, concern and frustration was building as she can't believe how stupid Dwayne is in the way he manages someone with head injury and memory loss.

He has sent his father off with a mobile phone on the old CD network that doesn't exist anymore and hasn't checked to see what directions he wrote down. If he needed help how would he access it? Dwayne rushes through his own life not caring for others, to him ignorance is bliss, and everything was left to others to pick up the pieces. It's Gemma who suffers the stress and worry for the one she loves. Mason has no way of contacting anyone if he gets in trouble.

"Do you have to go today? Why not next week?" she asked him.

"He said I have to go today."

After hearing that it was her birthday, he would have become very insistent on taking her husband away, but she didn't want to worry Mason about that so said nothing. She doesn't fret the small stuff anymore and accepts that her enjoyment is not relevant.

"We'll charge up the battery for half an hour for you, but it won't be able to phone anyone. Then you'll be able to leave at 9.30am, if Dwayne said it takes around 40 minutes to get to Herekino you should be able to get there and back before we have my birthday tea tonight?"

He's ready to go, kisses, hugs and she reminds him to be careful as he set off on what Gemma knows to be a challenge for him. Hopefully, he would find the old house and the neighbors might be able to redirect him because the new one is supposed to be just around the corner from there. All these thoughts buzz through her mind leaving a heavy weight on her shoulders as she knows Mason better than anyone and doubts he can follow the directions he wrote down and was told not to show her, she can't help but worry.

On the bright side it's a beautiful day now the rain has stopped, and the sun is brilliant, she's on her own from 9.30am so she'll just have to swap her birthday celebrations with Mason for a whole day doing other things, nothing will destroy her happy day where she can always enjoy the peace, quiet, and walk with Ombre', finding joy wherever she can and being grateful for as much as possible. She's heading off to the support group evening later on tonight, so she had that to look forward to, they've organized a nice birthday supper.

Gemma reflects on how sad it is that so many milestones happen while they are in separate places, so many years of Christmas's and New Year's being on her own while Mason has been deliberately taken by his family, deciding to separate them had prevented likely memories.

As she feared, it turned out her darling man did get lost, he parked the van and wondered around the streets until he met a postie who was kind enough to show him where the street was, luckily she wasn't aware that this horrible thing was happening to him until later on after the trauma had stuck in his mind and he came home and told her. No one contacted her when he hadn't arrived for ages and before he left to return home he didn't use the landline to advise he was on his way home. As the darkness threatened she became worried that he should have been home for her birthday tea before it got dark, afraid that if she made enquiries the name calling and verbal abuse to mind her own business would be more than she could stand. Her emotions again fraught while waiting and wondering what has happened to her husband today.

Well, with the time fast disappearing and Gemma expected at the stroke club group for her birthday she made the decision to leave home at 6.30pm praying he would be nearly home, she wrote a little love note and left it on the bench with food in the fridge for when he arrived, hoping that he had a good day out with family as she drove off.

Returning home later at 10.00 pm pitch black surrounded her as she turned into their noisy metal driveway and drove past the yellow letterbox. Rushing panicked into a shadowy house and looking everywhere with her heart pounding she calls out, there are no lights on and he's nowhere to be found, panic hit hard like a brick on the head aware that he had been gone all day and if something has happened to him how would she explain that to anyone looking for him.

Guilt permeated her every cell for not looking after him.

Gemma has to make the unavoidable phone call to Dwayne to tell him Mason wasn't home, he's missing! She is staggered by his reply,

"He'll be there somewhere, he left here at 7.00pm, just wake up and open your eyes you stupid bitch." Came the reply.

"He's not here, I've looked everywhere in the house but it's not my problem to go looking for him in the dark, he was with you, so you find him." Speaking very calmly and assertively she had no more tolerance left, she was worried.

Wondering through the house not knowing what to do next she decided to make a cup of tea and sit to let her heart stop pounding. Someone was coming through the open kitchen door, it's Mason! He has been walking in the dark, through the cold dark evening. Rushing over to him Gemma flung her arms around his neck elated that he was okay, he looked so tired.

"What happened?" She wipes away the tears of relief running down her face.

"The van stopped, luckily I was just off the highway and able to walk home. I got the battery out and it weights a ton to carry." He says.

"Put it on charge and I'll make you a hot drink, you look frozen. You didn't take a jacket with you this morning. I thought you would be home hours ago."

After putting the jug on to boil she rushed outside to the garage to check if he could manage, she found him looking exhausted. Dwayne turned up! He got worried when she refused to go out in the dark looking for Mason. Mason turned to him and explained its good he's here because he can help run the battery back to the van in his car around midnight when it had enough charge in it, Gemma offered to hold the torch. Dwayne was reluctant to stay that long and started to complain, obviously he had no choice but to help.

It was probably a lesson for Dwayne as he must realize now

that Mason probably got lost both ways when he arrived home so late from what should have been a 40-minute trip, it was a miracle that he was alright, and she hopes Dwayne has learnt something from it. *Know Your Limitation* is something that Mason needs to apply and not be bullied into doing more than he should by his son, she would talk to her husband about that.

Another morning of rain trickling down the window pain as Mason and Gemma reluctantly rise after their late night,

"Are you okay?" Observing his sallow skin, he looked ill.

"I'm exhausted from it all, it was a long way, and the battery was too heavy to carry."

"Don't worry, you can have a lazy day doing your puzzles, just don't go next time if you don't want to, there's no reason why your sons can't come here to visit." She insisted.

Both of his sons are just a selfish pain in the back side, they didn't make things any easier for them and she can't help but wonder where an earth he drove to last night that took him so long, lucky he didn't run out of petrol. Gemma hopes that Mason will remember how sick he feels today and might think twice next time.

She looks forward to spring days while longing for Mason to come and sit peacefully with her at the pond again, when asked about it he openly explained that he spends every day at home and can be alone by the water when she is at work. He prefers to spend time chopping down gorse to burn rather than take time for sitting, he loves to light fires.

Communication is also a big part of their home life that has been affected since he became sick, even just watching television together he will sit in front of it and not discuss which channel to watch making it impossible to find something they both enjoy, she suggested to him once, if he didn't like the program let her know and they could change channels. He held the remote in his hand so she thought that it might be on his mind to do so, without speaking he hastily stood up and angrily stormed off. Gemma went to find him and explained how to communicate if he likes this program or not and suggested that it's okay to just ask if he wants to watch something else. Stating that she isn't a mind reader!

CHAPTER 26

September weather has arrived bringing with it hope that as the weather changes so must their lives improve, however she woke up with a really severe pain in her neck when getting out of bed a few days ago, it had now progressed down her back and her energy levels have begun to decline. Trying to rest on the weekend is impossible, with Mason being more demanding than normal, he hates her being sick. On Monday she had to phone in sick to work thinking that she must have flu and becoming worried enough to go to the doctor, now she can't eat, and has extreme fatigue.

After a thorough check-up he says her lungs, heart, throat, temperature is all good! Gemma's completely exhausted and he gave her a week off work, telling her not to do anything but rest. Dr Stone warns that any energy she used up meant it would take that much longer to recover. Gemma felt even eating was taking too much energy, it's difficult. She's that tired she has difficulty walking and can't drive the car.

Frozen food from the freezer popped into the microwave for Mason and a plate full of mandarins for her on the bed was all she could manage to do.

Will she get through this time in her life or is living with Mason slowly destroying her bit by bit, she knows something has to change as she dragged herself back to work and asked the very accommodating Principal to reduce her hours still further, she's so fortunate to work in such a wonderful school and he has arranged for her to go in late on Thursday mornings so that will help, (not the finances through). Feeling that her survival is priority now, and never mind about the money. She eats little.

Simple things like picking up Mason's hearing aids that had been repaired was too overwhelming for her at the moment. The

Audiologist worked from his home, and they had driven there many times before, so Mason insisted that he could go and pick them up.

He's gone for several hours when it should only be 30 minutes down the road. When he arrived home, he said he went on the highway, goodness knows why as he only had to go down West Coast Rd, perhaps he travelled to Pawarenga where his old Audiologist was, she didn't know but she was concerned that he's getting lost and so decided to have a careful chat over a cup of tea.

"Thanks for getting the hearing aids for yourself, you seem to be going the long way around to get anywhere these days though, perhaps you're getting a bit confused in the car, now that I always do the driving, maybe you shouldn't drive if you can avoid it. I'll be back to normal again soon."

"Oh well, we'll see." He said,

The exhaustion and inability to be able to eat didn't seem to be getting any better for her so the Doctor has ordered that she should be taking 30 days respite from Mason every year. Gemma explained that Mason won't go, and she can't keep asking for her daughter's help, that's not fair.

Life goes on and she pulled herself together once again, despair at life sometimes so bad that it sapped all of her will power to keep going, she never before experienced such a contrast from the strong committed lady, to becoming so emotionally debilitated from the constant abuse, sarcastic comments, and ingratitude for trying to do the right thing.

Saturday morning and Mason has decided to drive a short distance down the road to see Peter so she asked him to get a 2-litre bottle of milk on his way home, expecting him to be gone a while but no, he's back in a couple of hours and came back grumpy but wouldn't say what was worrying him. He bought butter instead of milk, but she said it didn't matter they can use that later for some baking. Something happened there to really upset him at Peters as today is Sunday and he's still upset and swearing at everything. He continues to withhold any clue as to what had upset him, but it must be bad for him to remember a day later.

Managing to get to November without any major problems was fantastic for Gemma's recovery and they were starting to think about Christmas. Dwayne turned up to visit, she finds it increasingly difficult to even bother to talk with him now. She pointed out to Mason that he made several cell phone calls on the home landline during the visit so that she would have to foot the bill.

Venting her anger she needed to explain her feelings to Mason, after 14 years of marriage his son had never even made her a cup of tea, going on to say she thinks if she's not allowed at his house then he's not welcome in hers, that's how she felt about his son! Going on to say that she has always been excluded, she will not be welcoming to him anymore! Mason simply said that he hadn't realized.

Sunday 22 December 2013 and Mason looked at his calendar on the wall, he can see that they haven't heard or seen from either of the boys for a month now. With Christmas around the corner Mason was feeling irritable and emotionally deprived.

"You know how to get to the house now so why don't you drive over to see Dwayne, maybe Peter could turn up as well for you all to catch up." She suggested over a morning cuppa.

Life had been fairly good lately as they ventured out a few times to cafes now school had finished for the year. When they arrived home from anywhere, at only 66 years old Mason always fell asleep in an armchair, he needed to sleep after every outing and then he woke up amicable.

"Okay I'll phone him up and see." He says looking hopeful before yelling out from the phone that he can go round.

"Can I talk with him while he's on the phone please darling?" She holds out her hand to take the phone.

"Hi Dwayne, can you text me when your dad arrives

there safely please?"

"No problem." He said before hanging up.

Mason left at around 10am and three hours later still no text, she phoned up to check on Mason, Dwayne was unfriendly and didn't want to talk but confirmed yes, Mason is there, so she can relax now (Dwayne is a vile creature). Time went on, she again waited and decided to eat tea without Mason, reassuring herself that it's nice if he gets to have a meal with them. Mason arrived home safely at 8pm and was starving as he hadn't had anything to eat before they let him drive home.

Later on in the year Mason's birthday came around and he wanted to go out to a smorgasbord restaurant, he loved choosing from a whole variety of food to eat that he no longer remembers, it's great fun and Gemma ordered him a non-alcoholic fancy drink with sparklers going off in it, he was happy with a beaming smile, and she's pleased to see him that way. No word from his sons they obviously forgot his birthday, but Mason's had a great time with Bridget and John to visit, so he didn't even miss them.

Four days after his birthday he began to get a bit upset and moody and declined coming for a walk down to the pond for a sit with her and Ombre'. While stroking his furry back and watching the swifts swoop down to skim insects off the still water Mason arrived with a machete in his hand and started to slash every tree in sight.

"Oh darling don't break the trees that we've been growing for 18 months now." She calls to him.

"I don't want them!" he shouted back and went to attack the most beautiful May tree that stood nearly 2 metres tall. Wanting to protect it Gemma rushed over closer to the tree and again pleaded with him.

"Please don't kill the trees, just calm down and tell me what's wrong."

He lifted the machete over his shoulder and glaring at her, with fiery eyes he swung it.

She was just out of reach but heard the swish of the blade through the air beside her head, distraught she began to run as fast as she could uphill in long knee-high grass. Struggling to keep going, but afraid to look back in case the last thing she sees is the blade before it killed her, she prays for safety as she kept running and did not look. On reaching the house she was relieved that Ombre' had kept his distance as well and she quickly locked them both in the house and bolted for the phone. Three police officers arrived while Mason was outside, after making light of it he said Gemma exaggerated it all, returning to speak with Gemma the constable explained that something wasn't right because Mason had given them several different versions, like he didn't know what had happened, they confiscated the machete after he said he had hidden it to protect himself from Gemma, and they made him go to Peter's for the night.

This is the stuff she lives with, all caused by not hearing from his sons on his birthday! The frustration and anger had built up and he exploded because his brain damage doesn't allow him to calm down. He takes everything out on the only person there.

The following week Mason could not sleep so Gemma is woken up by banging of doors around the house, she doesn't say anything and ignores him pretending to sleep, he stands in the bedroom doorway and switches the light on and off, on and off until she gets up because he won't allow her any sleep, it's 2 o'clock in the morning.

Sleep deprived for a few days now and she felt like she was running through rain, cold continual discomfort, and misery soaked through her never letting up, something had to give. After another night of no sleep she's at her wits end, as imminent darkness spreads through her entire body she has mentally had enough, and at first light she throws on some old clothes to make her escape walking to the local beach, leaving her car behind no one will know she has gone. As she continued to walk away only certain of one thing and that is she had done everything she could and nothing matters to her anymore she cannot feel, can't think and is too tired.

There is no room for thought just a never-ending bleakness, not knowing anything but sadness, she is alone walking towards the sea. Morning light is rising but she cannot feel any warmth, awareness has left her as everything is obscure and cold, mechanically walking without understanding what she's doing, not realizing how far she has walked only knowing that Hokianga Harbor is 16 km from Panguru.

Her legs hurt but sea is in sight now. A car pulled up beside her and the driver called out of the window.

"Can I give you a ride somewhere Miss?" he asks.

"No, it's okay." She called back.

Somehow, one foot in front of the other she keeps going, arriving on the beach to find people already there, she hadn't thought about that. Desperate to seek relief she plonks herself down on a distant sand hill looking out to sea, waiting for the people to leave. She didn't bring food or water, so she just lay down in privacy, sand made a comfortable spot, she shuffled around, and it molded to her shape.

Waking to hot sun overhead she had no idea how long she slept for and there's no cell phone coverage, but looking out at the water there were more swimmers and lifeguards now. Oh no, they are a barrier, what if they try to save her, how will they feel if they cannot, and she dies on them? She didn't want to leave that with someone for the rest of their lives, she started to cry from desperation, and she asked why. Sitting up waiting, she recalls her devoted little friend and starts to wonder what will become of him. He will either have a terrible abused life or he'll be put to death all because of her selfishness, she has to go home to him.

Starting the return trip home was slow as everything hurt, her head was clearer though as she rests along the way. An empty bus pulled over and a concerned driver got out.

“I passed you walking on my first run, that’s a hell of a walk, can I give you a ride?”

“Okay.” Silently taking a back seat she didn’t want to talk but she was eternally grateful for the Lords help.

Sinking into a comfortable seat the driver kept looking at her in his rear vision mirror, not in a menacing way more of a concerned face like he thought she was going to pass out or something.

“Can you let me off at the corner please?”

“I’ll take you all the way if you like, where do you live.” He enquired.

“No, it’s not far from the corner, I can manage thank-you.” Once the bus came to a standstill she carefully negotiated the stairs.

“Thank you for the ride.”

“That’s alright, are you sure you can get home?” the driver asked.

“Yes, I’ll be fine.” Giving him a reassuring smile. He will always be remembered for his kindness; he was there when she needed some help. Arriving home, she could barely walk, her hips were struggling to move so she couldn’t have made it without the ride.

Ombre’ heard the click of the gate as it opened and ran to the kitchen door, he saved her life today!

“Hi, I bet you’re hungry aren’t you?” Unable to bend down as her legs had stiffened up with pain, she dropped two slices of bread into the toaster for them both.

“Where have you been?” yelled Mason who had just come into the kitchen.

“Out walking do you want any toast?” Gemma asked, reluctant to spend any time on him.

“What’s for tea?” He growled.

“Anything you can find for yourself as I’m sick and going to bed.”

He didn’t expect that! And there is no reply as she looks like hell warmed up. There is no comment as she takes toast to lie on the bed and watch television, everything else could wait, and if she wasn’t here it would have had to anyway. Maybe he’ll let her sleep tonight.

CHAPTER 27

Sunday morning and she struggled to complete the household chores with little energy after sleeping. She managed to do some baking and made three large chocolate cakes complete with shiny sweet chocolate icing, then squirreled one into the freezer for a rainy day and tucked the other two away in the pantry for her spoilt husband to enjoy some scrumptious goodies while she's at work next week. Today, she needed to just cruise along and do whatever she felt like doing, emotionally drained and physically exhausted she needs to slow down and take more time for her. Ombre' her forever watchful little companion has other plans, sitting very stately right in front of her while she enjoyed a quiet time and a cup of tea.

Piercing eye contact from those big brown eyes watching with a questioning gleam induces more relaxation and gratitude for the love she does have in her life.

"Okay, she says with a reassuring smile, let's go for a walk." He leapt up in the air flinging himself around in a circle nearly up turning that cuppa! She held onto it tightly and figured she had better finish it quickly before going to fetch his well-worn lead from the old laundry, all the time hearing the sound of four paws skidding on the polished tongue and grove floor beneath him. Well, that has cheered her, it is surprising what a good laugh can do for you, now more relaxed and hopeful that she can make this a good relaxing day she called out to Mason.

"See you later, just going for a walk, won't be long." Before setting off along the newly metaled road, Ombre' sniffing at every other blade of grass, the world is at peace, life seems good today.

As she walked past the second house at 9.00am on a sleepy Sunday morning there were few cars, and she leaves the road to cross onto the grass verge, the open drain had been cleaned out and was much deeper now running alongside the rural road edge.

Suddenly a wave of indescribable extreme agony smothered Gemma at the same instant as she could hear a horrific scream escaping involuntarily. Not fully aware of why she was now sitting on the ground her left foot bent under her body and it refused to untangle from its position.

The obvious conclusion being she had slipped off the road edge, lose metal still rolling from under her, a drop of around 90cm. Still holding on tightly to the lead to keep Ombre' safe she tried to understand what had happened.

"I'm okay Ombre." Trying to reassure him as he licked her face, trying to right things, unconvinced and with enough intelligence to understand this was not how they normally go walking.

Feeling optimistic she knew that she must get her foot out from under as it was going numb, and instinct told her that's not good. So after leaning to one side it still didn't want to move, she bravely took hold of the shoe with both hands and getting ready to endure some pain slowly, carefully pulled her foot out from under her bottom and tried to stand, telling herself she's just a bit stunned and her ankle with a foot facing the wrong way would untwist in a minute, she would pick herself up and limp home, it's not far. Pain surged through her leg and another howl escaped into the silence as she was forced back to reality, she's unable to make her foot move and this may not be what she planned for today, but the fact is it was happening, and she needed help!

Holding one arm up as if drowning she reluctantly waved as a car came scrunching along the road, out for a Sunday drive. There was no doubt in her mind this couple would stop to assist, she believed it. They pulled over to the opposite side of the road and ran over to see her, Lynda a nurse, and her husband.

Pain, the word didn't describe it, kept washing over her as

she struggled to deal with why she was sitting on the edge of a gutter, her foot is pointing the wrong way and everything below the knee had a mind of its own, she was unable to go anywhere, definitely couldn't get up and would have gladly crawled home if it were physically possible, it wasn't!

Gemma's rescuers were amazing, Lynda took charge while looking straight into Gemma's eyes to get her attention, forcing her to stay conscious and strong for the dog as her husband held tightly to his lead keeping him safely off the road. Other cars were appearing around the corner and traveling approximately 70km.

The speed was concerning the three of them while Gemma was still helpless on the edge of the road, Lynda waved frantically at the first one to slow down, it did, thank goodness! But the car behind it didn't, it continued on with a loud crash and began to shunt the back of the first slowed car which was pushed forward, careering across the road towards Gemma still unable to move out of the way.

She screamed, "I'm going to be run over." As she peered into the underneath of the approaching car she couldn't believe this was happening, would she die with her head under a car?

"No." Lynda yelled back, "It'll stop in time." You could hear the doubt and fear in her voice and with it a rush of adrenalin, just for a moment the pain in her leg was obliterated. The careering car stopped less than a metre from them and the two driver's faces showed more shock than surprise at their damaged cars, they exchanged details and then drove off, probably realizing how lucky they were that they hadn't run Gemma over.

A sudden high pitched howling noise sounded again, a sound that she had never heard before and never wanted to hear again informing her she needed an ambulance, it's not a sprain like she had been hoping. Lynda phoned Bridget and an ambulance, she then ran back to the house and informed Mason what had happened, he arrived about the same time as the St Marks ambulance and Bridget turned up. It seemed like an eternity waiting for the ambulance but what amazing men as they gently and swiftly lifted her straight out of the ditch. Any fear or panic she held of being moved proved to be completely unfounded as it all happened very professionally in an instant, without any further trauma to her foot or leg before they sped away with the siren going. Travelling to hospital in a morphine assisted trip while Mason took their bewildered little Ombre' home and Bridget followed the ambulance, thank goodness she's here, Gemma won't have to go through this alone.

The drive was a mix of pain, drugs and vomit and Bridget was a welcoming sight at the Accident and Emergency department. After being rushed away in a haze the doctor later appeared with her X-ray's showing both the fibula and tibia were broken, Gemma was adamant that she didn't want surgery.

Unfortunately, they explained the bones are spiral fractured and they won't line up without surgery. After some discussion and convincing she reluctantly agreed, Bridget settled her for the night and assured Gemma she'll go home and make sure that Mason knows what's happening and has tea organized for tonight. Gemma's worst fear had arrived, who would look after Mason and how will he manage now that she's sick.

Today, Gemma has a steal rod through the tibia and the smaller fibula bone was left to repair itself. Her ankle has been realigned and six screws have been put into her knee and ankle to hold the rod in place, she hopes that they can be removed at some later stage when the bones have knitted strongly again.

Ten painful days are spent in hospital worrying about Mason and how he's managing, what a blessing that Bridget had recently moved to live locally and could help because while Gemma was doing so much healing, she needed good nutrition, and all Mason could provide was cheese sandwiches and cups of tea for which she was very grateful but it's not an adequate diet.

After a few days of surviving at home putting on a brave face and not wanting to ask for help she woke up feeling desperately hungry for some variety in her diet, the fruit is all gone from the fruit bowl and the milk is running out, Gemma realized that they could no longer put off phoning Bridget and asking her to pick up some salad, fruit, bread, and milk on her way home from work. When Bridget arrived Gemma was so emotional and grateful to see her and for the help that she burst into tears, explaining that she couldn't eat cheese sandwiches anymore and asked if Bridget could please do some shopping if she made a list.

Bridget explained that she had no idea that Mason couldn't manage going around a supermarket and couldn't cook! Gemma changed from someone who had always silently coped, she had to swallow her pride, ask, and accept help for herself, which is a new challenge for her while she's physically disabled, and very appreciative that she reared such a supportive and capable daughter. Gemma hops with the use of a walking frame or crutches with no weight bearing on her left leg for six weeks then she will go into an odd-looking chunky moon boot that only comes in black, she will have to wear that for a further six weeks. The time went painfully slow in many ways as she relied on home help to shower and to have an opportunity of intelligent conversation.

After recuperating within the confines of the house for a couple of weeks she became desperate to get outside, just to hop around the garden and have some fresh air and freedom. The hurdle is having to get down three steps, these steps consume all of her thoughts as she set about planning her escape from what had become a prison, when she was well, she could at least have time at the peaceful pond or a walk with her thoughts, but now she's confined with no escape from listening to repetitive questions.

Realistically it's not safe to ask Mason to assist her to get down the steps so that's not an option besides the fact that he doesn't understand her obsession about going out into the garden. To just check on the chickens, glance over the paddocks to see the sheep are all there would surely help in her recovery even though Bridget has done a quick look at her request.

She plans to get out of the house when Mason goes to bowls on Tuesday that will be her day out. It's both exciting and nerve racking as she doesn't want to have a fall. However, it's so important to her mental wellbeing now, she has to take the risk.

Tuesday arrives and she waves Mason goodbye feeling very motivated and excited that she might be able to get outside the confine of these walls. Dreaming of fresh air, warm sunshine soaking into her skin, flowers to smell and to see how much everything has grown in the garden.

Pushing the walking frame towards the back door she carefully lifted it over the doorstep and onto the landing, thank goodness there was quite a large area for it to sit steady on the floor while reassuring herself that if she fell, she did have a moonboot on for a little support. Shuffling her feet towards the top step she gripped onto the side of the windowsill, which is next to the top step, leaving the walking frame behind so it didn't topple down the stairs.

All of a sudden she found that the steps were quite high if she should happen to fall, it's a bit daunting and wonders if she should abandon the idea, if only there was a handrail down the side of the steps that she could manage to lean on, then this wouldn't be such a mission. No, determined that she could do this she lowered herself to sit on the top step using the windowsill to lean her arm on, she made it to the floor of the landing and sat for a moment to rest.

She hadn't called on this much energy in a long time while recovering from broken bones and was already shattered. After a short rest determination loomed again, she pushed the walking frame over the side of the steps, lowering it to the ground so she could use it once she got there. Edging herself toward the front of the step on her bottom, slowly lowering herself down each step and then reaching for the frame to help her stand up on the cracked path, she made it.

Oh how wonderful, she pushed it around the lawn and looked at the garden, it's beautiful, what a pleasure to see after such a lengthy time. Just to be outside encouraged her that she's on the mend, she looked over the fence and counted the sheep, everything seemed okay, but she would get Mason to open another gate and just let them have two paddocks to nibble on until she could manage to move them down the race to fresh grass. There had been rain lately so everything was green, and they had enough grass for a brief time.

After a pleasant look around the garden and what's growing in the vegetable patch she decided to try getting back into the house before anyone spotted her, afraid that Mason would be angry if he arrived home to find her outside. Then he would demand all sorts of unreasonable chores from her. Maneuvering the walking frame beside the stairs she would be able to pull it up once sitting down on the top step. Swinging her bottom around to sit down on the cold middle step she just about missed the edge and would have landed on the ground instead, once positioned okay she quickly shuffled backwards, then lifted herself backwards up onto the top step, grateful for strong arms from wrestling with lambs and sheep when she docks tails and vaccinates them. Finally she called on all of her strength to lift herself off the floor using the windowsill and both hands while shuffling her feet backwards, this was the hardest part, nevertheless she's determined to make it, tugging the walking frame back up to the landing was also quite difficult.

Adrenaline flowed quickly along with fear, she was able to get herself back into the kitchen because she had to! Feeling content to know that she could get out if she needed to, now satisfied to put her feet up for a rest.

When in the house Gemma finds that the little table on the

walking frame was more useful than using crutches, because she couldn't carry anything. Nothing is perfect though as the walker only has two front wheels and she has to lift and place it every time she hopped, making it impossible to move a liquid without spilling it. Gemma looks forward to being able to weight bear on her broken leg instead of hopping all the time which does take a lot of energy during a day.

"I've made us a cup of tea; can you carry mine to bed for me please?" She called out, while balancing on two crutches.

"Get it yourself."

"I can't on crutches." She replied, feeling tired and desperately wanting to rest and rid the pain from her leg.

"You're useless, you can't even cross the road without falling over." He screamed back.

Well, if that's not hitting her when she's down! The excruciating pain of the broken leg didn't compare to the stabbing in her heart, bones would heal but the attack on her self-esteem, the belittling of her as a person would remain with her. Struggling to convince herself he doesn't understand the abuse he inflicts. Gemma's life was like a prison simply because she is a person who cares for others, cruelly breaking someone's spirit goes deeper and was worse than any physical damage that heals. She decided no matter what was wrong in her brain, demeaning behavior would never exist within her as it would be out of character and unacceptable.

Some counselling for him might help but when suggested by the doctor he refused, he's angry, not at Gemma more at himself for becoming mentally impaired, she is always his scape goat. Mason's family don't see it, no one sees the physical and emotional abuse he inflicts on Gemma, all the time and every day.

Will she become physically ill and die because of the extreme stress and the absence of a positive way out, or perhaps become a victim of Stockholm's disease all because of a duty of care, her heart rules as there is no one else to care for him, protect him and support him.

Gemma is committed to his care, stuck with listening, hurting, and being reduced to tears nearly every day. He forgets what he says and does, and she has to believe that tomorrow will be better because that helps her to keep pushing through the dark days. Being trapped in a sad place, aware of a growing unhappiness and of valuing a memory of things that once were, feelings that once existed but are now fast fleeting because life has changed, her little bit of light is her dog that appreciates her, and he keeps her going.

Gemma's leg pain is worse as she can't rest it, Mason is demanding and wants her to lean at the stove cooking and helping him with everyday needs, she questioned herself how he can be so cruel to take advantage of a cripple after all she had done for him and now he appears to enjoy demoralizing her when she is helpless and in pain.

In similar circumstances she didn't leave his side and did everything she could to help, in contrast to him now taking full advantage of her being incapacitated.

"I didn't ask you to make the tea." He said.

"No doubt you will be taking yours to bed and you have two hands." She retorted back, without speaking he picked both cups up and they went to bed without a thank you, kiss or even a word to each other. That wasn't the end to it, the next day he refused to take the two plates of food to the table for their evening meal together, he's annoyed that she is still struggling between walking frame and crutches. He took his plate of food that she struggled to cook at the stove and rushed off to eat in the lounge.

"Can you take my plate as well please; it will slide off the walker tray." She called out to him.

"No, you're useless you stupid cow." He yelled back from the lounge. She put the plate of food on top of a tea towel in the hope that would stop it from moving, as she lifted up the back of the walking frame to carefully push the front wheels, bang, crash, and splatter as one of her beautiful plates hit the floor and broke.

Casserole was spreading everywhere, he's so selfish! Pain and upset engulfed her and she couldn't reach the floor to clean it up, now she had no food. Instead of him helping he came to see what had happened and swore abuse at Gemma as she made her way to the bedroom humiliated and in tears.

CHAPTER 28

Gemma understands his vulnerability with her being unable to look after him, but she stands at the stove on one leg, now her hip is under strain and has become very painful from hopping for six weeks, making every effort to care for her husband is not enough, they cannot manage.

Days, months, years have passed looking after him and her feelings and disappointments she remains hidden from him, she is slowly disintegrating until she can't feel at all, to just mundanely existing, day after day numb to actual living. Her husband has changed Gemma's perspective on life, even though nothing could ever shake her belief that we are all here for a reason, maybe to save Mason's life.

Sometimes she tried to focus her mind on visions of yellow roses, quiet times, longing for peace and freedom, she can only imagine what that would be like, and without hope and dreaming to take her from the reality of her life she would never reach old age. It is Friday, another chilly day in May and she wonders if it is really the weather or is it just permanently cold in her world, in the very depth of her body and soul lies a chilling loneliness.

"I have a hospital appointment to x-ray my broken leg today, so I'll be home to pick you up at 12.45pm, to come with me." She struggled to explain while getting ready for work. There is too much information in that sentence for him to comprehend as she rushed to get ready for work, so scribbling down a note she left it on the bench for Mason.

Why is everything so incredibly hard and exhausting? Just to communicate with him. Plus she still has pain and struggling on crutches to carry a handbag and things she needed for work today, down the steps and into the car. Some people have a normal life and a husband to help them.

"No, I don't need to come, you can go on your own." He called back after reading the note.

It felt like he had just stabbed her in the chest, and yet at the same time she's relieved that he seemed to understand the instructions and she didn't have to explain again, so she ignored his words and left the little note on the bench telling him to be ready and dressed tidy because she would like him to come with her. Driving down the road her thoughts were racing as she recalled all the times spent giving emotional support to Mason in his many visits to various hospital appointments, he had never had to go on his own and she tried to fight back the grief knowing that he cannot remember any of them, she reprimands herself. He does not have a normal brain that helps him to understand, and she subconsciously makes excuses for his hurtful betrayal.

Knowing all that did not help as despair and disappointment consumed her soul, the tears starting to flow unabated, and they ran cold and wet down her cheeks as her hands clung to the steering wheel. It's a short day because of the appointment, lunch time she drove home anxiously wondering if he would come to the hospital, hobbling through the kitchen door on crutches the dirty dishes are in full view, not done and still scattered around the benches. He appeared from around the corner of the dining room and is dressed in tidy black jeans and a clean shirt, her heart melted filling with pride, swelling with love for him, she was so pleased and any regret of how her life had turned out was replaced with hope that he might still improve one day.

"You found yourself some nice clothes to wear and you look lovely." She praised him as she props herself up against a bench so she can affectionately wrap her arms around him. There is no response, no warmth, and a puzzled look he did not understand what she was talking about.

After a quick visit to the bathroom to freshen up before struggling back into the car, she now takes a moment to be aware of how she feels a little apprehensive about her leg, gosh she hopes it's knitted together okay, and then it hits her that she never has time to think about herself anymore, every day is spent rushing around helping others. The hot tap was left running again, water flowing freely all the time she was at work and the water has run cold.

So, after the usual long wait for an x-ray to be done and a quick talk with the surgeon, they now know that Gemma's leg still hasn't knitted together which would account for the constant ache that she always lives with on top of everything else. Gemma tried to find something positive to think of and be happy about.

"It's nice that I didn't have to travel and wait at the hospital on my own, I'm so lucky I still have you with me darling."

"Oh okay." He replied completely emotionless.

Gemma is shattered, its 3.30pm and she never had any lunch today.

She suggested, "Let's get some fried chicken on our way home." Not waiting for an answer they headed for the drive through, there's not enough energy left in her to struggle into a shop with moonboot and crutches. They sat in the car to look at the menu, Mason couldn't decide, the cars were building up behind them, the girl shuffles indignantly from behind the glass window waiting for the order, the stress was too much, and so Gemma ordered for Mason and the air clears while everyone's tension dissipates. That's right! Arriving home she remembers she must phone the television repair man or Mason will start complaining when he finds out it doesn't work. It's been another hectic day, and she again feels cheated of a normal life, certain that it's being shortened with all the rushing around and not having time to think or do any fun stuff, she hasn't seen a hairdresser for three months now.

After six long weeks on one leg Gemma is finally allowed to put weight on two feet, and now she has empathy for anyone using only one leg and understands how dreadful it is. Returning home from the check-up the first thing she wanted to do was walk her little friend Ombre' to the orchard 100 metres from the house, being able to walk on two feet in long grass is a real pleasure and the following morning her endeavor is to get around her garden again. That is when she noticed that the brass fittings on the hoses have been replaced with cheap plastic ones that spray out water all over the place.

"Where have my brass fittings gone off the hose Mason?" she enquired.

"I've put them away because someone might steal them."

"Well they're no good to me in the shed! And these ones leak everywhere, go, and put them back on the hoses for me." She snapped impatiently.

There seemed to be nothing around here that he didn't cause a problem with. She's not sure why all these things happen but there must be a good reason, believing that her life must change for the better one day and that trauma is sent to teach us to be better people.

Mason trusts that he can always turn to Gemma when there's a problem to face, they have confronted death, financial hardship, and have struggled every day to make sense of his cognitive difficulties and confusion for five years now and Gemma continues to love him so immensely that she can't accept that he won't improve, while he depends on her she can't give up or walk away from her marriage commitment, and the most important thing was to be there to support her husband.

The brain aneurysm damaged not only his brain, but it destroyed their life as they once knew it. His character can never be repaired, the damage spreading like a cancer and it's getting worse. A result of his memory lose, they lost a normal way of living, and yet when they cuddle up together at night he puts his arm around her and it's like old times, just as he learnt to drive again his automatic reactions take over. As his mouth surrounded by his soft beard presses against her pale skin and his hands search out her body, time stands still when the warmth of flesh and soft bedding blend into one they are here together, they have each other and everything that has happened during the day fades into oblivion, until tomorrow.

Wednesday night after finishing tea there's an enormous thunder crash and the stormy night weather takes out the power, the lights go out and Mason began to panic, Gemma called out to him to get the torch from the laundry, he ran madly around the house like a man possessed flicking on light switches to no avail.

"It's a power cut so they won't work darling, but don't worry it will come back on again soon, lets push on the battery light beside the bed for you and we can go to bed early and sleep, so we don't need the power." She explained, trying to calm him down.

He started to yell, "You can't cross a road without falling over." And rambles on talking a lot of nonsense as he loses understanding of what is happening. Gemma removed the moon boot and climbed into bed in the hope he would follow, which he did thank goodness, she gratefully cuddles into him, and they fall asleep. The morning arrives and everything looks better except he's lying in bed with wide empty looking eyes, a terrible time follows where he continues to swear and be nasty the whole day. His inability to make decisions, tackle problems and to reason anything whether its clothes, food, hunger, storms etc. makes Mason vulnerable to upset and angry responses.

Thursday afternoon, and another day has finished at work, and she found that her recovering leg had been more of a struggle than first expected it would be. Through her entire day, the warmth of friendship and kindness embraced her from teaching colleagues and a simple contentment and pleasure she got assisting the students to overcome their individual difficulties. Driving home at the end of the day she looked forward to relaxing with her foot up before having to cope with cooking tea, after parking in the garage, she found that the back door was locked which is unusual. Ombre' greets her with whole body wags but he manages to restrain himself from licking her hands as he often would do, she acknowledges him reaching her arms around his solid body for a hug, he's content with that and she told him how nice it is to see him when she arrives home.

Unlocking the door Gemma wondered if Mason has gone out, looking into the bedroom his car keys are still on the dresser, she began to feel a little anxious as the kitchen still looked exactly the same as when she left it this morning, she was hoping it would be tidied up. The burgundy drapes haven't been opened in the lounge all day! What if something had happened to him and no one was here to help him.

Dumping her handbag down on the floor she quickly kicks off her shoes. Removed her good jumper and slides her feet into the gumboots on the back porch, frantic to find him adrenalin is pumping and the pain in her leg is obscured out of concern for Mason.

Walking around in the orchard she was able to glance over the top paddock as well, so she could see he wasn't in those two places.

She bids Ombre' "Find Mason for me." He ran around sniffing; goodness knows if that was the correct thing to do but he was pleased to be helping.

With a moon boot for protection and walking with some trepidation, not wanting to have another fall her stomach churning like milk turning into butter as she fought back the acid rush of panic and fear. Continuing to look for him she walked the length of the 4 hectares asking herself how could she stand it if something had happened to Mason, and why does she feel this panic to find him?

All of these fears and insecurities have grown over the years because of the unknown nature of his illness, and she is tired of the continuing drama, managing an adult who has a mind of his own and can attempt dangerous things without his being aware of it.

Down at the pond Mason looks up as Ombre' woofs and ran up to him, Mason's first response is, "Oh shit."

He has been burning gorse only a metre away from the dry wooden Gazebo, he knows it's risky and Gemma would be upset. It has been very windy today and she had repeatedly told him that if he must burn fires he should do it safely somewhere else on the property. Last summer she didn't get to enjoy the relaxation of the water and birdlife because he continually had smoke. The stress was too much anyway, as she tried to make it into a park-like setting and Mason kept cutting the trees down. There's little natural cover to sit out of the sun so Gemma had the gazebo built there for all-weather shelter. It was expensive and he continually puts it at risk, so he can sit in it close to where he has lit a fire. It is amazing that he understands what he's doing wrong, that part of brain works, but he still takes risks.

He made his way up to the gate and sulks while passing Gemma, "Why are you burning that rubbish so close to the wooden building when you have four hectares to use?"

"Shut up and piss off." Received for her concerns.

When she returned to the house with Ombre' Mason is in the bedroom looking very guilty while Gemma started to put her clothes away. He went to push her out of the room as she stood in the doorway and she reminded him about her healing leg, he continued yelling for her to shut up and was really close up in her face. Gemma could see he had opened the tiny battery doors on his hearing aids as they're hanging out of his ears, making it impossible for him to hear anything. Then he gave her a hard shove as he pushed past, she grabbed for the door jamb clinging on to support herself, terrified of falling after going through months of pain to get to this stage of her bones healing.

Her tears began to well up yet again, choking her as she couldn't believe how crazy he was, his eyes flaring with anger and all the time yelling in her face, she was scared! Turning her back she made her way to the phone to dial 111 for help in case it escalates. No doubt he had been in the heat of the fire all day and was dehydrated or was she making excuses for him again.

"What service do you need?" Came the response on the other end of the phone.

"Police please." She was desperate, and waited to be put through to the correct office, the well-rehearsed voice is heard,

"What's happening now?"

"My husband is pushing me, and I'm scared because I already have a broken leg." Was her frantic reply. In Gemma's mind she tries to justify ringing for help, she knows feeling scared of your own husband is just not right and she shouldn't have to put up with this anymore, it has been five long years that she has protected him.

Being brain damaged didn't give him the right to threaten anyone, maybe if he doesn't understand what he's doing, but he does, and it really hurts her to know that it's not important to him if she's at risk of amputation. If the metal work gets damaged or bent in a fall, who will cook his tea for him then.

Upon informing him that the police are coming to talk to him he straight away took off the smelly smoke-filled clothes and changed into his best jeans and sweatshirt, grabbed his car keys, and headed out the door. She knows that he'll seek sympathy from his son Peter who will get some far-fetched story about how terrible Gemma was to him.

Three constables turned up and spoke to her about what happened, and she explained to them that Mason is becoming dangerous and that something needed to be done. Being very distraught her voice refused to co-operate as she chokes up and her stomach hurt, she struggled to keep some composure, but the tears kept coming, they had a mind of their own, she felt like a useless human being to have to call the police. Wishing she could have a normal life like other people, the police records show that this is the second time in a few months that police have been called to help her, at least this time it's not as humiliating as when her husband wanted to cut her head off. They talked about a protection order and again she explained that would make him wilder and she would be too scared to do that.

Gemma promised to seek help from the doctor as well as investigating the mental health organization and any services that were available. Before police left, Mason arrived through the kitchen door with a big smile and asked what's going on?

The male officer suggested that the two-woman constables stay and talk with her while he took Mason into the car and spoke with him. The outcome was just to stress on him that violence was never the answer, Mason's memory loss prevented him from remembering anything so he just made up whatever he thought would fit. She put the jug on and offered Mason a cup of tea before the police left. Deciding to watch television in different rooms which they sometimes do these days if they want to see different programs, she doesn't think he remembered anything that happened and they both went to bed to sleep, another day tomorrow and she had to find out what her options were for the future as the police advised her to do.

Waiting and praying for help she continued to show as much love and caring to Mason as she could, reassuring him and telling him the days of the week so they don't all become one long continuous time warp with no beginning or end. Her compassion for his situation was never ending while she now accepts all the caring and love in the world can't fix this!

"I know that it's hard sometimes for you to remember what's happening, but the bowls and your jigsaw puzzles are helping with your co-ordination and thinking skills. Thank goodness you're still here with me." She says to him with a smile.

He looks up from the stool he sits on as he concentrates on the colorful 1000-piece puzzle.

CHAPTER 29

Friday morning and she's thankful that another week is nearing an end, feeling really unwell and struggling to accept the inconvenience of being emotionally and physically tired, she's conscious of his needs and she wants to help, but her everyday year after year is consumed with caring or worrying about him, there is no let up and life is too short. Gemma's skin is dull with dark furrows under her eyes, the lack in vitality a result of being sleep deprived and any lust for life was fast draining from her.

Life has changed and she has become accustomed to living in the face of fear and despair, although she's proud of his personal success in learning some essential skills and grateful for every little success he makes, the disappointment cannot be pulled from deep within her that he never makes any effort to go back to some kind of little job, he is complacent about ever wanting to work again when she suggested helping to find something he would enjoy doing, it pains her to think he doesn't care enough about her or providing for them, and it's hard to watch him accept being a sliver of the man he once was, spending most of the winter sitting at his jigsaw puzzles. All of these factors have an effect on Gemma's body, the pain and disappointment is very real, feeling like her stomach could hemorrhage at any moment with all the churned and pent-up emotions and grieving for her lost husband eats away. Sitting, she forced down another cup of tea and starts to get ready for work, her mind won't think straight as it's full of well-meaning advice and people to ring and things she needs to investigate. Forcing herself to nibble on a slice of toast to prevent stress produced acid from burning her stomach lining, she felt sick.

Retrieving all the phone numbers that she had written down for senior services advice, her doctor and victim support and stuffing them into her handbag ready to head off to work.

Things to investigate in her lunch hour, the main thing is to get to work on time and try to focus and clear her mind. It's too much stress and she needed someone to care as the tears silently ran down her face while she drove her comfortable little white Honda to work, watching people smiling and walking to school, she broods on how strange it is that she no longer understands what happy is any more.

Another day and she is met with a beautiful crisp spring morning, once warmed up it shows promise and the sun is coming out with a glimmer of shiny golden hope for better days, believing that everything will burst into life and things will get better for them as well. They both finish a relaxing breakfast; Mason is happiest when she's at home with him, if only they didn't have bills to pay she would love for them both to go for drives and spend days sitting in the sun watching the birds and enjoying nature stress free like they used to do, that was like a thousand years ago when she didn't need to earn the main income and worry about him.

Just a quick tidy up around the kitchen and then relaxing on the bed enjoying a cuppa with one of their magazines, Gemma budgets for buying one that has short stories for her and puzzles for the man in her life, sometimes he calls out the questions and she gives him the answers, it's a lot of fun working on them together and it seems to work to keep his mind intellectually active. Bang! door slams, looking around to see Mason coming down the hall towards her, his face looks wild, crazy eyes glaring at her. What can she do? Fear rushed through her as adrenalin surged through veins. She sat up ready to ward off any attack, feeling helpless and vulnerable and having no idea what's wrong with him and what has angered him, she knew the look.

"You gave the dog some toast with peanut butter on it!" He shouted.

"I had automatically put the peanut butter on without thinking and only realized after he had eaten it." She explained.

"If you didn't waste stuff you wouldn't have to go to work, you're doing it on purpose to go out and leave me at home." He screamed at her.

Scared, she had to think fast to try to calm him down.

"It's Ombre's birthday today so he's just had a little treat to keep him well, he's quite old now and he's good company for you isn't he."

Mason turned and stomped down the hall while she breaths a little sigh keeping Ombre' safe beside her, what a relief as she just smiled like nothing was wrong as he left the room. This can't go on, she wakes most mornings now in a panic, heart racing stress filled her every moment, and it's huge! She knows she needs help with Mason and can't walk around on eggshells all the time. There must be some help out there besides his Tuesday bowls morning.

This winter was worse than normal with her broken leg, but now spring is here she is motivated things will be more pleasant, waking every day praying and trying to approach it in a positive way.

Later in the day they both enjoy a sit on the top of the paddock looking down at the golden daffodils that have started to flower, lambs will be born soon, and she is resolved to be stronger.

How wonderful sitting with the warmth of the sun soaking in to warm them both, while the light flickers between the branches of tea tree, brisk spring air is still a bit cool but enjoyable after winter. Mason declines her suggestion to go down to the pond, he doesn't want to walk that far, so she set off with Ombre' as Mason happily goes off in another direction.

The sparkles seem to leap off the top of the still pond water, and the cool breeze blew the long grass sideways making a parting for Ombre' and her to sit down and contemplate life and how things are unfolding. Silence is golden when all you hear are the birds and the rustling of firm flaxes, watching the pine tree dust floating down is relaxing.

Whirling around in excited anticipation Ombre' shows his appreciation for the precious time they have together, he's not getting any younger and she'll always be grateful for the constant companionship he has provided her, he was a gift she was meant to have to help her through the tough times. Looking forward to more daffodils to come as they shoot their yellow spires up to the sunshine before opening to face the light above them. They stand on their frail lengths of green, determined like a volcano erupts from the dead ground they have a short life, but they make the best of it.

Recalling a friend's advice Gemma contemplates, as everyone seemed to be giving their opinion on what she should do, sitting here weighing up her options, what are they?

Knowing that she is unhappy, feeling trapped out of devotion, love, commitment, and compassion that he can't help being cognitively impaired makes every day unbearable beyond all understanding. He doesn't comprehend or care what he's doing to her, to them as a couple. Where is his soul in this distant non-existent person like an empty shell, no one seems to be behind those beautiful grey eyes, he's gone.

The inability to handle his own actions or his behavior is unacceptable in this setting and dangerous to any human being, repulsive cruelty and inept beyond reason. Gemma's struggle with right and wrong, duty of a wife to care for her husband and compassion for his situation are all issues to face and question what she can do.

While believing that good things come to those that wait, and that the best things don't come easy. She asks herself how long she must wait or should she accept that no good can ever come from him now. Church and friends have warned her not to stay at the expense of her life but when and how can she give up on her wedding vows and the devotion she has to helping him with his cognitive rehabilitation. There are days when she gets a glimpse of the man he once was and that continues to give her hope he might come back.

Bridget came around for a visit yesterday and asked about everything, was she all right and can she get some help for Mason, Gemma nodded and explained that she had made an appointment with the doctor to have an assessment done.

"Why."

Gemma unexpectedly blurted out. "I'm afraid of him!"

"Oh mum." She gasped.

Surprised to hear herself say those terrible words about her husband only goes to show how desperate she had become. Bridget agreed that it is the right thing to do to get an idea of where he's at.

Saturday morning at 7.30am and she made her way to peep into the lounge where Mason was lying on the comfortable sofa.

"Morning husband." She called to him cheerfully and pushed open the double white doors, he turned upon hearing the familiar squeak that they made.

"Morning wife" He responds sounding a little down, he's watching infomercials, so she goes off to make cups of tea and returns with them.

"You could watch country calendar on the other channel if you want, those are infomercials." He looked angry, arms flinging around he snaps back. "I've been waiting for hours to see the date!"

"It's Saturday today and the breakfast show only comes on during the weekdays, you can have a look at the calendar hanging on the wall if you're not sure."

"No! I always watch channel one and it gives me everything I need to know." He's getting louder.

He's angered quickly, goodness knows how long he had been waiting for something that's not going to happen. Now yelling abuse like it's her fault so she put down his cup of tea and made a hasty retreat, Gemma was not wanting to cope with another grumpy day from him even though she does understand it must be very frustrating not knowing what day it is. After leaving the room he drank his cuppa and decided to switch the television off, coming into the bedroom to get dressed he complained he didn't like his track pants.

"Wear your other pair then!" She replied cheerfully trying to appear unaware of his volatile state, he ignored her as he didn't really want an answer, he just wanted to have a moan and continued to wear the pair he had on, she's not sure what's wrong with them as he didn't seem to know.

"I was thinking we could go down to the shops today and have lunch out at a café." She quickly tried diversion to help him forget the television.

"Yes, let's go." He scampered off to get his shoes on. Well that must be record time to get him into the car, he hadn't had any breakfast, so she just goes with the flow while he's keen.

Mason's mood is anxious as they park at the mall and he opens the car door, Gemma has become finely tuned to his moods after all these years and can feel his tension weighing heavy in the air.

"We don't need to go to the supermarket so you should enjoy just looking around. Before we get out of the car, here is your wallet I grabbed on the way out, I've put $40 in it. You can buy the lunch for us, but it's up to you." Reaching over to the passenger seat to plant a kiss on his lips.

Gemma felt that giving Mason his own money for him to be in charge was important, as it must be humiliating for a man to let the woman pay and perhaps it draws unwanted attention to himself.

"Oh cool, I might have a look at the discount shop." He smiled and seemed to relax.

"Is there something you want to buy?" She asked while slamming the car door shut.

"No, just want to have a look." They laugh and the mood is lightened.

If there are more than three shoppers in a shop they wait outside and then Mason goes in, he found a set of small screw drivers he wants to buy, slowly takes them to the counter and gets out a $20 note. Gemma watches on, proud of how he's coping with the lights, people, and money. The change is handed to him, and a few coins drop to the bare floor making a loud clatter, two people stop talking and look as she bends to quickly gather up the coins.

"Aar thanks." He said as he grabbed the paper bag and wallet rushing for the door.

"Here is your change, let's go and get something to eat and have a rest, my leg is killing me." Gemma quickly grabs his attention to keep him from having a meltdown.

Maybe if they just keep his mind on new things all the time he won't have time to dwell on whatever upsets him. They don't speak, and it's a shame as he struggles to be normal, to fit in without drawing attention to himself and again her heart is torn apart, it's terrible for him. Wanting to cheer him up and probably overcompensating they pretend nothing has happened and walk over to the home bakery for lunch, Gemma knows that he'll love to have a crispy sausage roll and a cream butterfly cake, she buys a nice pink iced pastry to compensate for all her worries.

"We can take it across the road to the park if you want." She suggests.

"Okay." He smiles, and he has been won over with goodies from the bakery.

"The cake is hot." He says. A little weird, but he's obviously still rattled and means the sausage roll, so she treads carefully.

"Is the cream nice
though?"

"Yeah."

"We've had a good morning out." She smiles cheerfully, hopefully his memory loss will kick in soon. Sometimes it's a good thing to have when she needs him to calm down. On arriving home, he starts to pull on the car door handle as soon as they drive up to the front of the garage door.

"Don't open it until the car stops."

Anxiety kicks in again, and there's no reply as he ready's himself to leap out the first minute he can, he then started talking nonstop about the news on the car radio this morning on the way out. Every day events are exceedingly difficult and now she's running on autopilot to keep him on an even keel, his moods are unpredictable with anything able to set him off.

Spring flowers are always a welcome distraction for Gemma, it feels like a new beginning to her every year when the hundreds of daffodils they planted 14 years ago burst through the grass in the paddock with a cheerful yellow promise of happy bright days to come. Even today she has a glimmer of hope that maybe it will be true for them this year, can it please be possible that this spring is the start of something better in her gloomy dark looking future.

It's a fine day and the bunches of flowers she picked yesterday have all sold at the gate, she's managing to walk very carefully with a moonboot and using only one crutch while holding onto a bucket in the other. It is challenging and she is still unstable on a sloping paddock of long grass.

"Mason can you help pick some daffodils today, they're selling faster now." She called out.

He pulled a face and grunts but even with brain damage he knew it's unreasonable of him not to help when she is trying so hard to be back to normal. It's sad and hurtful to look at the flower beds that she tended so lovingly around the front lawn before her leg surgery because they now look unkempt and full of weeds however she consoles herself knowing that she will clean it up once she can kneel again.

Mason has seen his doctor as the police recommended that Gemma have him do and it didn't go well for him, an appointment has been made to visit the mental health unit at the hospital for a better assessment, they have to wait to hear back from them.

Questioning what might happen is nightmarish for Gemma, this is unfamiliar territory, she tried not to worry by staying busy. Once he left for bowls this morning, she could no longer bottle it up as she is overcome by emotion and chokes up, reaching to sit down on the edge of the bed her body gives way to heart wrenching sobbing, releasing all the stress!

Preparing to take him to the doctors yesterday, worried how he might react was incredibly stressful and these days she's so fearful and emotionally exhausted that it took all of her reserves to go through with it. Asking for help was difficult after five years of living in fear of losing him but longing for improvement. Gemma's tears also flow out of disappointment that it will probably be another week before she can start to get much needed respite, she remained positive that it's going to be okay, and she will finally get some help.

CHAPTER 30

One day follows another and when she arrived home from work on Thursday the lawn mowing guy had been and it looked tidy, this little thing brought a little flicker of satisfaction, ignoring Mason's grumpiness as he thinks she should mow them even with her leg mending. Going inside to throw on some old jeans and a gumboot, she finds the heater still going in the bedroom, making Mason aware of it he says it wasn't him that left it running all day while the sun was shining outside. Exasperated with the upcoming expense of it all, she explained that surely he must accept by now that he has memory loss, is the only one here and it had to be him! Finishing by saying that he needs to stop blaming everyone else and check everything is turned off properly. Then she asked that he help her rake up the grass clippings.

Poor timing as he sulked and refuses to rake or put them into a wheelbarrow to use on the garden, so she briskly takes the rake in both hands while walking carefully in the moonboot without any crutches, determined to do it all herself. Returning to the kitchen at dusk, she's very tired so throws some frozen pies and chips into the oven to cook quickly, she is becoming much older than her years but hopefully can get a sleep-in tomorrow morning as she doesn't leave for work until 10.00am on Fridays.

The next morning on opening her eyes, Mason offers a cup of tea in bed before she needs to get up. His attitude has completely changed as he asked if she would like a slice of toast put in the toaster, a delighted smile spread across her face while hiding the sentimental tears wheeling up in her eyes. These are the times that her heart warms to him, as she occupies the shower then heads into the kitchen to see him washing the dishes, this is a first and her insides swell to nearly bursting, she just wants to cry and hug him all at the same time, are her dreams finally coming true, is this really happening?

He says, "You smell nice, what's that called?"

Wow! What's changed, finding it difficult to believe she watched in anticipation to see the glimmer of the person she married and a few seconds of sanity just to keep her feeling that she must stay strong and keep fighting with as much hope in her heart as she can muster, a sense of duty and all of her love still remains with a passion.

The weekend saw them welcome the first new lambs being born even though it's Gemma that has to move mothers and babies to a separate paddock and spray iodine on the lamb's umbilical cord with some difficulty as she maneuvers in the moon boot, but she manages. Walking back up to the house her attention is drawn to Mason's hair getting really long and she wants him to look nice for his appointment when it arrives.

"Shall I trim up your hair tonight, so you look tidy?"

"No leave it!" He screams at her.

"Why? It won't take me long and you have bowls on Tuesday." She offered but didn't pursue it because he's irritable again, so she just kept walking. It's not worth getting him all aggressive and her getting hurt over a haircut. Hopefully, someone in authority will see how bad he looks and understand the problems with taking care of him. It's impossible to take him to a public hairdresser.

The following week the appointment date arrives to go off to see Dr Martin a psychiatrist at the mental health unit and he talks with Mason about trying to help him with any problems he's having. They did a series of tests while Gemma sat in the waiting room.

"You obviously have some memory loss, has something happened to you to cause it?" asked the doctor while reading the notes from the GP.

"No, it just happened." Replied Mason, after five years of being told and shown the horrendous scars on his head following the aneurysm and brain surgery.

"Well, unfortunately you didn't do well with the testing, so I'd like to see you again soon, I'll get the nurse to send you an appointment, are you happy with that?" he asked.

"Yes, my wife will bring me."

Dr Martin spoke quietly with Gemma in the waiting room, his observation was a welcoming surprise when he said he knew Mason had been making things up and couldn't answer simple questions about what he did all day at home.

Oh, there's always plenty to do, was all he could produce for what he does all day every day, as he clearly had no idea.

What a relief to return home, Gemma went and hid in the toilet finding it a peaceful private place to clear her thoughts, it's all good, relief surges through her that someone recognized what she already knew. She just wished she could do more to help her poor confused husband.

The next morning he's very distressed when asked to put his dish into the dishwasher.

"I don't know why we're using that thing." He screams at her after just enjoying a nice breakfast together.

"Because you refuse to help wash the dishes anymore."

"Well, everything was okay until you got up." He snarled because he wanted her to put his plate in the machine. "Do I have to see the doctor today?"

"No, you saw him yesterday that's why we have this form for a blood test." Pointing to the form sitting on the bench. Continuing to reassure him that they don't need to worry about it just yet, no rush. He stormed off, Gemma followed him down to the bedroom to see if he's okay. It's terrible to see him upset and confused as to what's happening, she could see how vulnerable he was, and it hurts her to not be able to stop his tortuous nightmare.

Sitting on the edge of the bed looking out of the old, weathered window she gingerly sat beside him taking his hand in hers, quietly for a moment of togetherness soaking in the warmth and calmness she stroked his hand before gently asking him,

"Don't you remember going to the Doctors yesterday?"

"No." Was the angry reply and she went on to ask if he would like his hair trimmed after she gets home from work, or would he prefer to go to the hairdresser?'

"No! Piss off." So Gemma decided to just leave him to get over things in his own way while she got ready for work. Tears began to sting her face yet again, as she drove and reflected on what had happened this morning, from good to worse.

When she wakes the next morning to find Mason is not beside her it has become usual for her body to instantly panic and her heart starts pounding, fear sets in thinking he might be lighting fires again by the gazebo. She tells herself to stay calm, it's Saturday, just wake up and have some breakfast before facing whatever happens today, it doesn't matter. Taking her cup of tea back to bed and trying to relax, let him manage, try not to worry about fire, taking down fences or falling into the pond, she needed to manage her own health as well. Lying on top of the bed with a lovely hot cup of tea, Ombre's pleading eyes drill into her.

"I'm okay, you want a cuddle, and you know the panic I'm feeling don't you." A front paw plonks on top of her knee, he knows somethings wrong. He must sense the stress in her. Gemma puts her arms around his neck and bent forward to sink her face into his soft, thick fur, soaking in the comfort she cherishes having someone that cares for her while she envisages the first day of two weeks school holidays with Mason.

He appears in the kitchen as she stacked dishes into the dishwasher, he's angry with huge eyes flaring, asking how many lambs they have? And she explained twins were born on Monday and he said he watched one being born yesterday, they will come thick and fast now. Thank goodness she'll be home to help if needed and she's hoping to have some time with Bridget in the two weeks' school holidays.

"Come and look out the bedroom window darling." She called out excitedly. He followed her to view tiny twin lambs under the gum tree beside the house, with mum cleaning them, they all look good, so she had time to take a shower.

"Mason if you go to feed chickens can you have a walk around and see if all is well with the ewes I can't see from the window. I won't be long." She shouts while grabbing old track pants and sweatshirt, a glimpse of weak sunshine already clear at 8.00am but it's a bit windy. Returning from the shower to find Mason had fed the chickens which is fantastic, he continued to put the jug on.

"How many lambs are in the paddocks altogether."

"I don't know until I have a look, didn't you count them?" he asked. He had already forgotten that she asked him to check them while he fed the chickens.

"No, I want to have breakfast first, you were already out there." She explained. "I'll quickly have breakfast then check if everything is okay."

Calling Ombre' to come and check the sheep and walk to the pond with her and on the way she found a ewe and twins in the back yard, how can that be while standing in front of the closed gate? But on investigation she finds the wire is hanging loose at the top and sides. All the end ties have been removed and were sitting on top of the fence post, lying on the ground are twisted ties which couldn't have fallen off, they've been removed.

Now she knows why Mason was missing this morning, unable to stop the feeling of hopelessness and despair. Walking back to the house and forgetting about time at the pond she seeks help from Mason to twist these ties back around the hurricane fence wire, carefully asking him to find a pair of pliers in a non-judgmental way. He goes to have a look at the problem and flew off the handle, exclaiming "I didn't do it!"

"Can you see anyone else here Mason? It doesn't matter, just help me as my arthritic fingers can't do it." She pleaded.

"Shut up and piss off." He stormed off into the bedroom refusing to help and leaving the lambs vulnerable to loss from dogs. Gemma swiped a hand across her eyes impatiently wishing the tears would stop, Bridget and John are coming to visit today so she'll ask them to help, she is ready to walk away from everything absolutely beyond mortified, no words can express how emotionally at her wits end and completely fatigued she is, mentally reminding herself these things don't matter, she would get it fixed somehow.

Those happy days of joy that teachers experience after longing for school holidays to begin, are just a distant memory, these days Gemma longs to be back at school tutoring her students, listening to their happy chatter about things they have done on their weekends. She finds enjoyment by living through others' lives, she loves to watch their expressions, smiles, and discussions of the movies they have seen and the latest teenage bands they enjoy.

Happy laughter in the classroom leads to more open learning, helping each other with their various learning difficulties without any inhibition, all the time unaware of the simple pleasure they're giving her to see them happy. Two weeks to get through before she can go back to work, and she is so thankful that Bridget no longer lives in Christchurch.

She can't do anything until Bridget arrives so decided to sit down on the soft paddock bank with Ombre' and watch over the new lambs with their mothers. In silent contemplation she remembers when her husband was a lovely placid person and how she has had to watch him slowly slip away to this cruel selfish individual who lashes out with hurtful comments in what seems like uncontrolled tantrums. Sometimes she silently questions if he can control it if he wanted to, and wonders if he's mentally incapable or just without feeling. Gemma constantly berates herself for becoming intolerant finding his behavior difficult to endure and yet at the same time understanding that neither of them can help being in this predicament, so it doesn't matter who's at fault, only that she must continue to survive to care for him the best way she can, she still strives to make his every day as pleasant as possible.

Monday evening the psychiatrist Dr Martin phones up while they watch TV, he had heard from their general practitioner that Mason drove himself to bowls on a Tuesday and he expresses his critical concern over.

"Okay, well I can drive him there as I'm home and I'll pick him up at lunch time that's no problem." She promised him.

Tuesday arrives and after dropping Mason at bowls and driving back home, the land line was ringing she answers it as fast as she can with a sore leg, and it's him, Dr Martin!

"Can you bring Mason in today at 12.30pm? To the clinic attached to the local hospital." He questions.

"Yes I can, straight after bowls if you want." She's a little surprised to hear from him.

"I will have another doctor waiting and also a security guard as a precaution as I need to explain to Mason that he should go into Kaitaia hospital for an assessment.

I'm sorry that I'm asking you to come in early for his appointment before the end of the week as we arranged but there's a bed available. If we miss this bed it might take a while before we can get Mason any help."

"That's okay, we should be able to get there straight after his bowls."

It was discussed with Mason that he do a five-week assessment of his needs and ability's to see what can be done to help him, Gemma was really nervous as she didn't want to be without him, at the same time things couldn't go on the way they were. Maybe they can enforce that he must take respite as a regular occurrence to let her have a break and to recharge her batteries. It has all been explained to Mason by his doctor, but he will have forgotten all about it, now a week has passed.

"Do you want to put his toiletries in a bag for him and leave it in the car, that way if he agrees he can go straight from the meeting directly to the hospital? We will arrange to transport him, so you don't have to worry."

"Oh no I'll come home and get his things later and then visit him." It sounded like the doctor was worried that Mason might become aggressive and then later on refuse to see her, she's frantic about how the meeting will go. Help! She was so nervous but there seemed to be no choice but to allow this to happen to make progress, and she must put her trust in these professional people and allow them to do their job by doing what they suggest.

Unable to focus on packing anything she gathers enough self-control to automatically throw a few things on the bed, wondering around the house picking up puzzles he likes to do, pen and paper, hearing aid batteries, and going into the bathroom to collect deodorant, toothbrush and tooth paste while her stomach was churning, nauseous with anticipation that this is what they need to do, self-affirming that she mustn't be selfish thinking about how lonely she'll be for the five weeks without him she forced herself to keep going.

Having not had any time to think since driving Mason to bowls, she decided to start by tying up her hair as its windy outside, she's feeling confused and bewildered about having him assessed.

Entering the community hall at 11.30am fixing a cheerful smile on she wandered over to join his mates having a coffee and chatting small talk all the time with this nightmare at the back of her mind, this is so hard to do. She didn't want it to be a sad time for him, as they talked about how well he played at bowls today she was informed that he had a great time.

The psychiatrist sat quietly facing Mason and then after a

solemn pause before speaking he said. "You do have some problems with your memory, how would you feel about going into hospital to see if we can do some tests and maybe find medication that might help you? Would you be okay to go into hospital today as we do have a bed available?"

"Yes that would be okay." Mason agreed. A silent pause hung over the gathering.

They were both quietly surprised and relieved that he would go willingly. Thank goodness he's not mad with her, she can't help feeling that she has let him down, on the way home she stops the car to buy a small overnight bag for his stuff and sits stunned and disbelieving that the world is about to change again. He was happy to travel with three nurses that are going to the hospital after telling him that she would follow on with things he might need from home.

After finding the invalid parking at the hospital, she leant sideways on one crutch as she made the long arduous journey through corridors holding on to his small bag in her other hand. Finding his ward sent a shudder down her spine when she read he's in a secure unit, that's something that hadn't occurred to her. After frantically looking around she felt upset, then Mason appeared looking at the garden. She commented on the plants and said that everything looked really nice there, her heart melted that he looked pleased to see her. He reached out his arms pulling her close to his chest for a hug and planted a soft kiss on her cheek, causing her to choke up and fight for control of her emotions. Walking back inside they found his room already had his name on the door and they started to unpack his belongings before dubiously looking around the inside of the unit. Looking down, he picked up the important things to him.

"Oh, my puzzle book and pen, that's good." He says with an appreciative smile.

CHAPTER 31

The longer she stayed in the unit the more her heart ached for this childlike human being, he's looking more and more like a lost soul, and her pain is only alleviated by the closer it got to teatime, because she knew he always enjoys food. Mason started to eat, and she planned her goodbye, carefully bending so as not to fall with the moonboot and one crutch, conscience that there are people everywhere, she plants a quick platonic kiss on his warm face with those beautiful grey eyes now looking sad and hollow as she informed him she will be back tomorrow as early as she can.

Arriving home with wary mind and tired body running on autopilot she checks the animals and feeds the dog, her mind, heart, and her soul are with Mason in his muddled state in that place of wondering weird people. Its gut wrenching to think of him not being home with her tonight and she was over-come with a choking fog of compassion and despair for the lost person that is her husband. As she struggled with this uncomfortable lump in her throat, tears threatening to fall, she knew she must be strong and brave to get through these five weeks' assessment. Working with the elderly in the past had unsuspectingly prepared her to be able to support her darling Mason while he has needed her understanding and practical help during these past five years following his brain surgery.

Convincing herself it's one night to get through before seeing him in the morning, the loneliness and empty bed made it difficult for her to sleep, it's so different to what she is used to, and she hoped he would be tired and it easier for him. Morning lights up their bedroom with the strange realization, she's alone! Taking time to look at her reflection in the mirror seeing this pale-tired face looking back, hollow sad eyes that are searching for something, reflecting the silent struggle, the pain, loss of the man she married and the struggle to get him well. How could her clavicle be sticking out like that without her ever noticing? She's so busy just getting through each day and whatever it threw at her that she hadn't noticed her body changing so dramatically.

Now taking time in front of the mirror she can see the results of too many missed meals and times of fearing for her safety when she couldn't wait to leave the kitchen or being too upset at the verbal abuse that she's often too sick to eat. She is horrified to see this person and wonders about her mind, emotions and nervous system, the walking on eggshells and living on edge afraid of her own husband, must have taken its toll in numerous ways.

She wonders how much this alienated life has affected her socially, isolating her, thank goodness she works, even just part-time allows her to keep the wonderful friendship of work colleagues who have supported her with their gregarious laughter at intervals and lunch times in the school staffroom.

Will she be a changed person for better or worse because of what she has endured? After a week of drifting around at home wondering what to do with the extra time, visiting the secure ward after work and phoning Mason every night for a chat before bed, she's relieved that he has settled into hospital. Schoolwork preparation had occupied her mind a little as end of year exams are coming up for the students. She was emotionally wary but thankful that she could now get rest for her painful leg.

Impatient to visit him every day after commitments of looking after the animals and whatever else needed doing, she treks along the corridors length in her moon boot. The next morning she wakes with terrible Arthritis pain and a shocking headache unable to cope with her new responsibilities, unable to do the vacuuming she struggles to just walk around and only do what is essential, thank goodness she washed Mason's clothes for him yesterday and they're ready to take back to hospital, she will tackle that trip this afternoon. The lawns get mowed today so they'll look better, and she just plods along on medication with an appalling pain in her neck, she has been worrying and stressed out too much and it's a lesson to accept that she is not superhuman.

Five weeks of feeling lonely during the day followed by sleepless nights and visits to the hospital while they run tests, the whole team of psychiatrists and various nurses assess Mason, she continually prayed, and the day finally arrived when they hold a round table discussion with the doctor about where to go from here.

The doctor (whose name Gemma instantly forgot because she's was nervous) began to read out the five-week extensive assessment written up with input from the Physiotherapist, Occupational Therapist, nursing staff and Psychiatrists. Her stomach had butterflies, and she could barely concentrate, putting all her focus on the end conclusion, diagnosis, and recommendations.

After reading about his inability to use a cell phone, manage toaster settings, sustain a conversation because of his lack of memory and difficulty with recall he continues to read,

"Mason Brownlie has a diagnosis of Dementia and is a danger to himself and to others, and it is strongly recommended that he go into Long Term Residential Care."

The day thwarted five years ago had come around again, this recommendation left Gemma shocked and speechless as she shrinks into her seat deflated, the doctor looked up sympathetically and reaching across the table passed her a box of tissues, he began to speak again.

"You've done extremely well to have kept Mason home for as long as you have, he's made milestones that could only be put down to his personal home life, but a decision needs to be made now on where he's going to live. I've seen a report from your doctor referring to several police callouts and physical violence against you, we need you to realize that you're of small stature and

Mason could do some serious harm."

Gemma's eyes pooled with tears as she gulped when her throat tightened, unable to release the pain, but pride no longer able to hold back the tears, although it was difficult to speak she had to.

"But he's, my husband!" Is all she could splutter while struggling to keep composure and not break down completely.

"It's a big decision and a lot to take in. You will need to talk about it together, we have explained it to Mason, and he seems to accept that it isn't safe for him to remain at home alone while you're at work, but you'll need to go over it again because of his memory loss."

Gemma pulled tissues from the box as she's still choked up and all she's capable of doing is nod in agreement as she dabs away the tears streaming down her face.

Silently walking back to the ward with just the metallic clip of her crutch being heard on the polished floor, they sat closely on the bed together and she wondered how much he understood.

This is horrible, what do we do? Her first instinct is to take him and run, the thought of living without her husband is abhorrent and people won't understand her letting him live in a rest home, she felt like she had failed him. In her distant memory she recalls the doctor's words *'Dementia'* and he continued to stress the hopelessness of her husband being able to stay at home. The words now resounded in her mind as she went over what he said.

"The CT scan shows the amount of brain damage the frontal lobe sustained in the past, which means he has no control over his feelings. He's unable to control any anger management and if he has to make decisions or is under any stress there is no way of knowing how he will react. We have applied to Land Transport Authority to have his driver's license revoked as he definitely shouldn't be driving anymore, if something happened,

he could easily accelerate instead of braking and would also be a good candidate for road rage."

All this and more, was explained quietly to them both and now that it's just sinking in, she's an absolute mess with Mason just sitting beside her unperturbed like it doesn't matter. He's forgotten!

A family meeting was called by the mental health unit, herself and both his sons with Mason as well, asked if they could help out with keeping him at home and providing their stepmother with some support or if he could live with either of them, they both refused to offer any help or give her any break from caring for Mason, her last hope was taken away.

Peter said looking at the report he felt that his father would be too much trouble for him to manage. In that moment she couldn't express how disgusted she felt that they wouldn't come up with a few hours minding him each week or convince their dad to have a week-end respite at the rest home, which wouldn't put either of them out. In desperation she cried out for them to please offer something to prevent him going away. There is just non-committal silence!

Finally forced to accept the medical professional's explanation for Mason's behaviors that have alienated him from the real world as we all know it, he had his own confused version of what is real and was is not, a very narrow line distinguishes fact from fantasy and unless you have been living with him it's alien for outsiders to notice or understand, but through all the difficulties they have endured together she loves him deeply and doesn't know how she can let him go, to relinquish his care after every moment of every day for years it has been down to her.

The thought is breaking her heart, he will have central heating to ensure he's kept warm, he will be fed when he doesn't know if he's eaten or not, and he will be safe with trained people around him. All his necessities will be supplied, but what about the invisible? How will he know he is loved if she can't show him by caring for him? He understands only what he sees, he'll have visiting hours, sleep alone in his bed and be confused as to why she's not making his coffee for him.

Panic set in as dark fear gripped her heart, the anguishing hunger to show love to her poor lost man who is drawn into his own world. The darkness gnawing away inside her, she looked down at her restrictive crutches and she knew she couldn't stop this happening, the inevitable heart ache as all hope is taken from her. She will do this for him, be brave and convince him he will have a great new life. He can't comprehend the loss of the unseen, the invisible love he can't feel is still here. Gemma loves him enough to let him go, to succumb to the practicalities of life and the acceptance of the appalling pain dwelling within her. Just two ordinary people going through an extraordinary life situation wondering what they need to do next.

Using the large hospital window as a distraction, she stared out of it and watched a couple aimlessly walking about, devastated, and bewildered this is not what she wanted, surely it can't be the only option. The anguish and inability of not being able to help him anymore, that it's really out of her control after five years of staying positive and praying for him to get better, always making excuses for him and one of the most important things that got her through it all, constantly remembering the gentle man he was when she married him. To give up now seemed beyond all endurance, but she must hide her fear from him, the thought of him being away from her alone with strangers who don't love him, is unfathomable.

Sitting on the edge of his bed, she wrapped her arms tightly around his waist and let her face snuggle into his chest hiding the wet eyes and tightness within her trying to sound normal.

"Darling, they think it's time for you to move into a rest home." She says cuddling up to him. "I need to have more surgery on my leg and then I want to bring you home. Just treat it like a motel stay and make friends okay."

"Okay." Came the emotionless reply and who knows if he's just agreeing with everything.

It's a dark abyss for Gemma to be without her man, her vows '*until death do we part*' resounding in her head, she's unavoidably trapped and heartbroken that there is no other way!

Mason will be happy, safe, medicated and have the routine he needs.

She prays to be well enough to one day bring him home to visit the life they once shared, an unknown world, now a blank. Gemma believes God has a plan we don't always understand, she trusts he knows best, and understands that he saved her life many times over.

About the author.

A New Zealand mother of two who loves the rural life, dancing, gardening, reading, teaching, and writing. This book came about by having had a love for writing all of my life and a varied career with a lot of wonderful learning experiences from Healthcare, Real Estate, Secretarial, Retail, and Special Education teaching.

Over the years my voluntary work and faith in God has equipped me with the gift of insight and empathy for those with disabilities and survivors of violence, causing me to question and acknowledge our own powerful beliefs, I hope to not only entertain but to stimulate food for thought and compassion for others as I write overlooking my beautiful garden.

Let me know if you enjoyed the story.

Instagram.com @l.j.bernard

YouTube.com/@LJB2024

Email: authornewsletterljb@gmail.com

www.ingramcontent.com/pod-product-compliance
Lightning Source LLC
Chambersburg PA
CBHW050244110726
47898CB00007B/2276

* 9 7 8 0 4 7 3 6 9 5 4 7 7 *